INSTRUCTOR'S TESTING MANUAL

JAMES J. BALL
Indiana State University

USING AND UNDERSTANDING MATHEMATICS
A QUANTITATIVE REASONING APPROACH
FOURTH EDITION

Jeffrey O. Bennett
University of Colorado at Boulder

William L. Briggs
University of Colorado at Denver

PEARSON

Addison
Wesley

Boston   San Francisco   New York
London Toronto Sydney Tokyo Singapore Madrid
Mexico City Munich Paris Cape Town Hong Kong Montreal

Reproduced by Pearson Addison-Wesley from electronic files supplied by the author.

Copyright © 2008 Pearson Education, Inc.
Publishing as Pearson Addison-Wesley, 75 Arlington Street, Boston, MA 02116.

ISBN-13: 978-0-321-45922-0
ISBN-10: 0-321-45922-9

2 3 4 5 6 OPM 10 09 08

PEARSON
Addison
Wesley

Table of Contents

Unit 1A Test 1

1. Explain what is meant by an appeal to ignorance.

   _____

   _____

   _____

2. Explain what is meant by the fallacy of personal attack.

   _____

   _____

   _____

3. Explain what is meant by a straw man.

   _____

   _____

   _____

4. Give an example of an argument that involves a hasty generalization.

   _____

   _____

   _____

5. Give an example of an argument that involves an appeal to emotion.

   _____

   _____

   _____

6. Give an example of an argument that involves a diversion (red herring).

   _____

   _____

   _____

Unit 1A Test 1 *(continued)*

7. For the following argument, identify one or more of the 10 fallacies described in this unit. Explain how the fallacy is involved.
   Use Sparkle tooth paste – all the Hollywood stars use it!

   _____

   _____

   _____

8. For the following argument, identify one or more of the 10 fallacies described in this unit. Explain how the fallacy is involved.
   You need to clean your room or it will be a mess.

   _____

   _____

   _____

9. For the following argument, identify one or more of the 10 fallacies described in this unit. Explain how the fallacy is involved.
   Every time I park my car under that big shade tree, I get a perfect score on my exams. That tree must give me good luck.

   _____

   _____

   _____

10. For the following argument, identify one or more of the 10 fallacies described in this unit. Explain how the fallacy is involved.
    Two African-American motorists were cited for speeding on Highway 1 in Fairview. Fairview law enforcement must practice racial profiling.

    _____

    _____

    _____

Unit 1A Test 2

1. Explain what is meant by a hasty generalization.

_____

_____

_____

2. Explain what is meant by circular reasoning.

_____

_____

_____

3. Explain what is meant by a diversion (red herring).

_____

_____

_____

4. Give an example of an argument that involves false cause.

_____

_____

_____

5. Give an example of an argument that involves an appeal to emotion.

_____

_____

_____

6. Give an example of an argument that involves a straw man.

_____

_____

_____

Unit 1A Test 2 *(continued)*

7. For the following argument, identify one or more of the 10 fallacies described in this unit. Explain how the fallacy is involved.
Nobody has conclusively proven that there is no intelligent life on the moons of Jupiter. Therefore, there is intelligent life on the moons of Jupiter.

_____

_____

_____

8. For the following argument, identify one or more of the 10 fallacies described in this unit. Explain how the fallacy is involved.
Are you still spending all of your money gambling at the race track?

_____

_____

_____

9. For the following argument, identify one or more of the 10 fallacies described in this unit. Explain how the fallacy is involved.
Sheriff Brad Ellis is unfit to be elected to the U.S. Congress. When his daughter received a speeding ticket, he tried to get it tossed out.

_____

_____

_____

10. For the following argument, identify one or more of the 10 fallacies described in this unit. Explain how the fallacy is involved.
Since Company K sells more computers than any other company in the United States, their computers must have the best quality.

_____

_____

_____

Unit 1A Test 3

Name:_____

Date:_____

Choose the correct answer to each problem.

1. Which of the following describes an argument based on the idea that since one event preceded another event, the first event must have caused the second?

   (a) Hasty generalization **(b)** Limited choice **(c)** False cause **(d)** Appeal to ignorance

2. Which of the following describes an argument based on the idea that since something is associated with attractive or happy people, it must be true or desirable?

   (a) Circular reasoning **(b)** Appeal to ignorance
   (c) Appeal to popularity **(d)** Appeal to emotion

3. Which of the following describes an argument based on the idea that since something has not been proved to be false, it must therefore be true?

   (a) Hasty generalization **(b)** Appeal to Ignorance
   (c) Diversion (red herring) **(d)** Straw man

4. Which argument involves an appeal to popularity?

   (a) Buy this television—it's the most popular brand!
   (b) Three dentists on Main Street recommend SuperWhite Toothpaste. Therefore, all dentists prefer SuperWhite.
   (c) If you didn't have Wheatie O's for breakfast, then you must have had granola.
   (d) A television commercial for a board game features healthy, happy people enjoying the game.

5. Which argument involves limited choice?

   (a) Steve bought a new car, and then he got into a traffic accident. Buying the new car must have caused the accident.
   (b) If Rosie didn't go to the beach, she must be at the mall.
   (c) O.J. Simpson was not found guilty of murdering Nicole Brown Simpson. Thus, he is innocent.
   (d) If you don't let me go to the movie, you'll regret it!

6. Which argument involves circular reasoning?

   (a) You'd better get there on time, since otherwise you'll be late.
   (b) Since the Bill of Rights guarantees freedom of speech, America's Founding Fathers would certainly have
      opposed any ban on pornography.
   (c) Since most people are in favor of the bill, it must certainly be a good law.
   (d) There is no evidence that this product causes heart attacks. Therefore, it is perfectly safe.

7. *Four students have already complained about the new instructor. Therefore, nobody is going to like his classes.*
   This argument is an example of which of the following fallacies?

   (a) Circular reasoning **(b)** False cause
   (c) Straw man **(d)** Hasty generalization

8. *Evolution is false! How could a mouse evolve into an elephant?*
   This argument is an example of which of the following fallacies?

   (a) Straw man
   (c) Appeal to ignorance

   (b) Diversion (red herring)
   (d) Circular reasoning

9. *A senatorial candidate favors eliminating affirmative action programs. His opponent writes that "The other candidate doesn't think there's anything wrong with discriminatory hiring practices."*
   This argument is an example of which of the following fallacies?

   (a) Hasty generalization
   (c) Personal attack (ad hominem)

   (b) Limited choice
   (d) Straw man

10. *When confronted with questions from the press about alleged political scandals, a congress woman replies that the allegations against her should be ignored since her accuser is part of a vast right-wing conspiracy.*
    This argument is an example of which of the following fallacies?

    (a) Appeal to popularity
    (c) Personal attack

    (b) Circular reasoning
    (d) Limited choice

Unit 1A Test 4

Name:_____

Date:_____

Choose the correct answer to each problem.

1. Which of the following describes an argument based on the idea that since many people believe something is true, it must be true?

   (a) Appeal to ignorance
   (c) Straw man
   (b) False cause
   (d) Appeal to popularity

2. Which of the following describes an argument based on the idea that since one thing is false, a second must be true (when, in fact, there are other possibilities that ought to be considered)?

   (a) Limited choice
   (c) Circular reasoning
   (b) Hasty generalization
   (d) False cause

3. Which of the following describes a conclusion which is drawn from an inadequate number of cases or causes that have not been sufficiently analyzed?

   (a) Appeal to ignorance
   (c) Diversion (red herring)
   (b) Hasty generalization
   (d) Circular reasoning

4. Which argument involves an appeal to ignorance?

   (a) Since Paul is not at work, he must be at the hardware store.
   (b) Four eye doctors in town all recommend Krystal Kleer contact lenses. Therefore, all eye doctors recommend Krystal Kleer contact lenses.
   (c) We have never been able to communicate with beings from another planet. Therefore, the earth is the only planet with intelligent life.
   (d) Buy this stereo system—it's the most popular brand!

5. Which argument involves a personal attack (ad hominem)?

   (a) Dad: "If you want to do well in life, you should do well in school."
       Son: "Oh yeah? Well, Mom tells me your grades weren't very good either."
   (b) Roberta washed her car, and then it started to rain. Washing her car must have caused the rain to fall.
   (c) We must raise taxes because of the children. Children are our most important resource, and we must do everything that we can to give them a brighter future.
   (d) If Proposition S is passed, there will be more pollution.

6. Which argument involves a straw man?

   (a) There is no evidence that this medicine causes drowsiness. Therefore, you can drive safely while taking this medicine.
   (b) The last two times I called Mary she wasn't home. Mary is never home.
   (c) Since America's Founding Fathers fought to give us freedom of religious expression, they would not have opposed human sacrifices in religious ceremonies.
   (d) Since Shelfco sells more bookcases than any other company, Shelfco bookcases must be the best available.

Unit 1A Test 4 *(continued)*

7. *All children need ample attention from their parents. Therefore, mothers should stay at home and be a good parent.*
This argument is an example of which of the following fallacies?

   (a) False cause
   (c) Diversion (red herring)

   (b) Hasty generalization
   (d) Circular reasoning

8. *A television commercial shows two senior citizens enjoying rock climbing and scuba diving and then drinking a certain kind of vitamin drink.*
This is an example of which of the following fallacies?

   (a) Hasty generalization   (b) Appeal to ignorance   (c) Limited choice   (d) Appeal to emotion

9. *We must limit immigration to the United States in order to sustain the prosperous economy. A strong economy is vital to the health and wealth of the American people and the future of our children.*
This argument is an example of which of the following fallacies?

   (a) False cause
   (c) Straw man

   (b) Diversion (red herring)
   (d) Appeal to force

10. *Every time I decide to take a vacation, the price of gasoline goes up. I am going to quit taking vacations.*
This argument is an example of which of the following fallacies?

   (a) Hasty generalization
   (c) Personal attack (ad hominem)

   (b) False cause
   (d) Circular reasoning

Unit 1B Test 1

1. Explain what is meant by a proposition.

   _____

   _____

   _____

2. Explain what is meant by logically equivalent.

   _____

   _____

   _____

3. Explain what is meant by a disjunction.

   _____

   _____

   _____

4. Give an example of a negation.

   _____

   _____

   _____

5. Give an example of a conditional statement and its inverse.

   _____

   _____

   _____

6. Give an example of a conjunction.

   _____

   _____

   _____

Name:_____

7. What is the converse of the contrapositive of *if p, then not q.*

_____

_____

_____

8. Make a truth table for the statement *if p, then not q.*

_____

_____

_____

9. Let *p* be true and let *q* be false. What does *r* have to be in order for the proposition
   if p, then q or not r to be true?

_____

_____

_____

10. Make a truth table for *(not p) and q..*

Unit 1B Test 2

Name:_____

Date:_____

1. Explain what is meant by a negation.

   _____

   _____

   _____

2. Explain what is meant by a converse.

   _____

   _____

   _____

3. Explain what is meant by a conjunction.

   _____

   _____

   _____

4. Give an example of a proposition.

   _____

   _____

   _____

5. Give an example of logically equivalent statements.

   _____

   _____

   _____

6. Give an example of a disjunction.

   _____

   _____

   _____

Unit 1B Test 2 *(continued)*

7. What is the inverse of the contrapositive of *if not p, then q?*

_____

_____

_____

8. Make a truth table for the statement *if p, then not q.*

_____

_____

_____

9. Let *p* be false and let *r* be false. What does *q* have to be in order for the proposition *if (not p) and q, then r* to be false?

_____

_____

_____

10. Make a truth table for *(not p) and q.*

Unit 1B Test 3

Name:_____

Date:_____

Choose the correct answer to each problem.

1. Which of the following is **not** a proposition?

   (a) Jeremy has brown eyes.
   (c) Toads can sing opera.

   (b) What is your IQ?
   (d) $15 - 12 = 18$

2. *Susie lives in a green house.*
   Which of the following is the negation of this proposition?

   (a) Billy lives in a green house.
   (b) Susie lives in a blue house.
   (c) Susie does not live in a green house.
   (d) Susie does not live in a house that is not green.

3. *Jane will not vote for a candidate who opposes a ban on hand guns.*
   Assuming this statement is true, which of the following is false?

   (a) Jane supports a ban on hand guns.
   (b) Jane may vote for a candidate who does not own a hand gun.
   (c) Jane might vote for Senator Jones who supports a ban on hand guns.
   (d) If Senator Jones opposes a ban on hand guns, then Jane will vote for her.

4. If p is false, q is false, and r is true, which of the following is true?

   (a) *(p and q) or r*   (b) *p and (q or not r)*   (c) *(p and not q) or not r*   (d) *p and (q or r)*

5. If p is false, q is false, and r is true, which of the following is false?

   (a) *If not p, then (q and r).*
   (c) *If not p, then (q or r).*

   (b) *If p, then q and r.*
   (d) *If p, then (q or r).*

6. Determine the truth values of the hypothesis and the conclusion in the following statements. Which statement is false?

   (a) If dolphins are birds, then dolphins can fly.
   (b) If ostriches are birds, then ostriches can fly.
   (c) If dolphins are fish, then dolphins live in the water.
   (d) If ostriches are birds, then ostriches have feathers.

7. Use truth tables to determine which statement is logically equivalent to *if p, then q.*

   (a) *p and not q*   (b) *(not p) and q*   (c) *(not p) or q*   (d) *p or not q*

8. *If Peter Pan can fly, then Garfield can sing.*
   Which of the following is the inverse of this statement?

   (a) If Garfield can't sing, then Peter Pan can't fly.
   (b) If Peter Pan can't fly, then Garfield can't sing.
   (c) If Garfield can't sing, then Peter Pan can fly.
   (d) If Garfield can sing, then Peter Pan can fly.

Unit 1B Test 3 *(continued)*

9. Which of the following is logically equivalent to any conditional?

   (a) Inverse
   (c) Contrapositive

   (b) Converse
   (d) Negation

10. You are searching for the book *The Old Man and the Sea* by Ernest Hemingway. Which of the following key word search combinations would **not** have your book on its search list?

   (a) (Man or Sea) and Hemingway

   (b) (Man and Sea) or (Hemingway and Steinbeck)

   (c) (Man or Sea) and (Hemingway or Steinbeck)

   (d) Man and (Hemingway and Steinbeck)

Unit 1B Test 4

Name:_____

Date:_____

Choose the correct answer to each problem.

1. Which of the following is **not** a proposition?

   (a) $7 + 3 - 5 = 8$.
   (c) Alison lives here.
   (b) Bring me a glass of tea.
   (d) Louie likes lobster less than Leslie.

2. *Emily has brown eyes.*
   Which of the following is the negation of this proposition?

   (a) Jason has brown eyes.
   (c) Emily does not have brown eyes.
   (b) Emily has green eyes.
   (d) Emily does not have green eyes.

3. *Michael does not like toothpaste unless it has tartar control.*
   Assuming this statement is true, which of the following is false?

   (a) Michael does not like tartar.
   (c) Michael likes toothpaste without tartar control.
   (b) Michael likes tartar control toothpaste.
   (d) Michael does not like some toothpaste.

4. If p is true, q is false, and r is false, which of the following is true?

   (a) (*p and q*) *or r*
   (b) (*not p*) *and* (*q or r*)
   (c) (*p and not q*) *or r*
   (d) *p and* (*q or r*)

5. If p is true, q is false, and r is true, which of the following is false?

   (a) *If not p, then(q and r).*
   (c) *If not p, then (q or r).*
   (b) *If p, then (q and r).*
   (d) *If p, then (q or r).*

6. Determine the truth values of the hypothesis and the conclusion in the following statements. Which statement is false?

   (a) If California is on the west coast, then Colorado is on the east coast.
   (b) If Colorado is on the east coast, then California is on the west coast.
   (c) If Colorado is on the east coast, then New York is on the west coast.
   (d) If California is on the west coast, then New York is on the east coast.

7. Use truth tables to determine which statement is logically equivalent to *if not p, then not q*.

   (a) *p and not q*
   (b) (*not p*) *and q*
   (c) (*not p*) *or q*
   (d) *p or not q*

8. *If Rachel passes her CPA exam, then I will lose my job.*
   Which of the following is the converse of this statement?

   (a) If I don't lose my job, then Rachel will not pass her CPA exam.
   (b) If I don't lose my job, then Rachel will pass her CPA exam.
   (c) If Rachel does not pass her CPA exam, then I won't lose my job.
   (d) If I lose my job, then Rachel will pass her CPA exam.

9. Which of the following is logically equivalent to any conditional?

   (a) Inverse   (b) Contrapositive
   (c) Negation   (d) Converse

10. You are searching for the book *Little Women* by Louisa May Alcott. Which of the following key word search combinations would **not** have your book on its search list?

    (a) (Little and Women) and Alcott   (b) Women and (Alcott and Bronte)
    (c) (Little or Women) and (Alcott or Bronte)   (d) (Little and Women) or (Alcott and Bronte)

Unit 1C Test 1

Name:_____

Date:_____

1. Explain what is meant by a subset.

   _____

   _____

   _____

2. Explain what is meant by a categorical proposition.

   _____

   _____

   _____

3. Explain what is meant by overlapping sets.

   _____

   _____

   _____

4. Give an example of a categorical proposition.

   _____

   _____

   _____

5. Give an example of disjoint sets.

   _____

   _____

6. Give an example of a set of integers, which is not a set of whole numbers.

   _____

   _____

   _____

Unit 1C Test 1 *(continued)*

Use the information below to answer questions 7 and 8.

Pop's Pizza Parlor offers pizza with three choices of topping: pepperoni (P), onions (O), and mushrooms (M). The table shows how many pizzas with the choices of toppings they sold one day.

Topping	Number	Topping	Number
P only	15	P and M only	3
O only	5	O and M only	6
M only	2	All 3	8
P and O only	12	None	19

7. How many pizzas had mushrooms but no onions?

8. How many pizzas had pepperoni or onions, but no mushrooms?

9. In a survey of 40 musicians, it was found that 20 people played the piano, 25 played the guitar, and 7 played both instruments. Draw a Venn diagram to represent this situation.

10. In a class of 30 students, 18 were history majors, 12 were science majors, and 7 were dual majors. Draw a Venn Diagram to represent this situation.

Unit 1C Test 2

Name:_____

Date:_____

1. Explain what is meant by a set.

_____

_____

_____

2. Explain what is meant by a Venn diagram.

_____

_____

_____

3. Explain what is meant by disjoint.

_____

_____

_____

4. Give an example of overlapping sets.

_____

_____

_____

5. Give an example of a subset of the natural numbers.

_____

_____

_____

6. For the categorical proposition, *All roses are fragrant*, write the subject and predicate sets.

_____

_____

_____

Unit 1C Test 2 *(continued)*

Use the information below to answer questions 7 and 8.

An ice cream shop sells sundaes with 3 types of toppings: fudge (F), strawberries (S), and nuts (N).

The table shows how many sundaes with the choices of toppings they sold in one day.

Classes	Number	Classes	Number
F only	24	F and N only	15
S only	8	N and S only	3
N only	7	All 3	18
F and S only	2	None	3

7. How many sundaes had strawberries but no nuts?

8. How many sundaes had fudge or strawberries, but no nuts?

9. In a veterinary waiting room, there were a total of 16 individuals, 8 of whom brought dogs, 5 brought cats, and three brought both dogs and cats.
    Draw a Venn diagram to represent this situation.

10. In a freshman class of 50 students, 30 students are taking math, 24 students are taking history, and 15 students are taking both math and history.
    Draw a Venn diagram to represent this situation.

Unit 1C Test 3

1. Which of the following sets of numbers does **not** include 0 as a member?

   (a) Rational numbers   (b) Whole numbers
   (c) Natural numbers   (d) Real numbers

2. Which of the following sets are **not** disjoint?

   (a) Poets and playwrights   (b) Cats and dogs
   (c) Men and women   (d) Democrats and Republicans

3. Which of the following sets are **not** disjoint?

   (a) Mothers and sons   (b) Mothers and fathers
   (c) Fathers and daughters   (d) Mothers and daughters

Use the following information about classes students are taking to answer questions 4 and 5.

An art studio offers 3 types of classes: sculpting (S), drawing (D), and oil painting (O).

The table below shows how many classes students registered at the studio are taking.

Classes	Number	Classes	Number
S only	14	S and O only	12
D only	9	D and O only	2
O only	3	All 3	6
S and D only	10	None	7

4. How many students are taking sculpting or drawing, but not oil painting?

   (a) 16   (b) 23
   (c) 33   (d) 63

5. How many students are taking sculpting, but not drawing?

   (a) 17   (b) 29
   (c) 26   (d) 32

6. In a Venn diagram, overlapping circles indicate

   (a) Sets that potentially share common members   (b) Disjoint sets
   (c) Sets of numbers   (d) Subsets

Unit 1C Test 3 *(continued)*

Use this Venn diagram, which describes the desserts people ordered at a party, to answer questions 7 and 8.

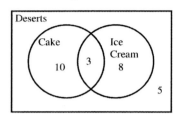

7. How many people ordered cake?

   (a) 26   **(b)** 10   **(c)** 21   **(d)** 13

8. How many people ordered ice cream but not cake?

   (a) 8   **(b)** 21   **(c)** 16   **(d)** 3

Use this Venn diagram, which describes the cars on a used car lot, to answer questions 9 and 10.

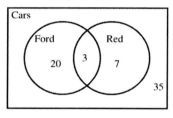

9. How many Fords are on the lot?

   (a) 20   **(b)** 23   **(c)** 17   **(d)** 30

10. How many cars on the lot are not red?

   (a) 35   **(b)** 58   **(c)** 55   **(d)** 38

Unit 1C Test 4

1. Which of the following sets are overlapping?

   (a) Fathers and daughters   (b) Fathers and sons
   (c) Mothers and fathers   (d) Mothers and sons

2. Which of the following sets of numbers does **not** include negative numbers?

   (a) Integers   (b) Real numbers
   (c) Whole numbers   (d) Rational numbers

3. Which of the following sets are **not** disjoint?

   (a) Cloudy days and holidays   (b) Brothers and sisters
   (c) Fords and Chevrolets   (d) Democrats and Republicans

Use the information below to answer questions 4 and 5.

Students living off-campus were asked about the electronic products they own: VCRs, DVD and MP-3 players.

The table below shows the number of students and the types of products they own.

Player	Number	Player	Number
VCR only	4	VCR and MP-3 only	2
DVD only	16	DVD and MP-3 only	10
MP-3 only	8	All 3	15
VCR and DVD only	9	None	6

4. How many own a VCR or DVD player, but not an MP-3 player?

   (a) 29   (b) 9
   (c) 20   (d) 56

5. How many own an MP-3 player but not a DVD player?

   (a) 20   (b) 8
   (c) 14   (d) 10

6. In a Venn diagram, a circle drawn inside another circle represents

   (a) Sets of numbers   (b) A subset
   (c) Overlapping sets   (d) Disjoint sets

Unit 1C Test 4 *(continued)*

Use this Venn diagram, which describes the optional features ordered by new telephone customers in one day, to answer questions 7 and 8.

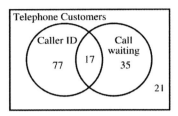

7. How many customers ordered call waiting?

   (a) 77   (b) 35   (c) 52   (d) 17

8. How many customers did not order caller ID?

   (a) 56   (b) 77   (c) 73   (d) 52

Use this Venn diagram, which describes the types of cookies in a bakery, to answer questions 9 and 10.

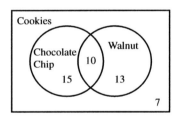

9. How many chocolate chip cookies do not also have walnuts?

   (a) 25   (b) 32   (c) 10   (d) 15

10. How many cookies have neither chocolate chips nor walnuts?

   (a) 10   (b) 7   (c) 17   (d) 3

Unit 1D Test 1

1. Explain what is meant by a valid argument.

_____

_____

_____

2. Explain what is meant by a sound argument.

_____

_____

_____

3. Explain what is meant by the strength of an inductive argument.

_____

_____

_____

4. Give an example of an invalid conditional argument. Explain why it is invalid.

_____

_____

_____

5. Give an example of a valid conditional argument. Explain why it is valid.

_____

_____

_____

6. Give an example of a chain of conditionals argument.

_____

_____

_____

Unit 1D Test 1 *(continued)*

7. *All professors are rich.*
   All rich people buy expensive cars.
   All professors buy expensive cars.
   Is this argument valid? Is it sound? Why or why not?

   _____

   _____

   _____

8. Give an example that invalidates the following mathematical rule:
   The difference of two positive numbers is always positive.

   _____

   _____

   _____

9. *If I work hard, I will get a promotion.*
   If I get a promotion, I can buy a new house.
   What can you deduce from these propositions?

   _____

   _____

   _____

10. *All heavy cars are comfortable to ride in..*
    No car that is comfortable to ride in is cheap.
    No heavy car is cheap.
    Use a Venn diagram to determine the validity of this argument.

Unit 1D Test 2

Name:_____

Date:_____

1. Explain what it means to affirm the hypothesis (modus ponens).

    _____

    _____

    _____

2. Explain what is meant by a deductive argument.

    _____

    _____

    _____

3. Explain what is meant by a proof.

    _____

    _____

    _____

4. Give an example of a valid argument that is not sound. Explain why it is not sound.

    _____

    _____

    _____

5. Give an example of an invalid argument. Explain why it is invalid.

    _____

    _____

    _____

6. Give an example of an inductive argument.

    _____

    _____

    _____

Unit 1D Test 2 *(continued)*

7. *All birds have wings.*
   All turkeys are birds.
   All turkeys have wings.
   Is this argument valid? Is it sound? Why or why not?

   _____

   _____

   _____

8. Give an example that invalidates the following mathematical rule:
   $$(a+b)\times c = a+(b\times c)$$

   _____

   _____

   _____

9. *If gasoline prices go up, then I will have to walk to work.*
   If I walk to work, then I will have better health.
   What can you deduce from these propositions?

   _____

   _____

   _____

10. *All pediatricians are doctors.*
    Some pediatricians have partners.
    Some doctors have partners.
    Use a Venn diagram to determine the validity of this argument.

Unit 1D Test 3

Name:_____

Date:_____

Choose the correct answer to each problem.

1. Which of the following is a valid argument?

   (a) All cars have engines.
   Mustangs are cars.
   Mustangs have engines.

   (b) All airplanes have engines.
   747s have engines.
   747s are airplanes.

   (c) All Mustangs have engines.
   All Corvettes have engines.
   All Ferraris have engines.
   All cars have engines.

   (d) Some cars have sun roofs.
   Liza's Honda does not have a sunroof.
   Liza's Honda is not a car.

2. Which of the following is a sound argument?

   (a) All birds can fly.
   Eagles are birds.
   Eagles can fly.

   (b) All birds have wings.
   Ducks are birds.
   Ducks have wings.

   (c) Eagles have feathers.
   Sparrows have feathers.
   Ducks have feathers.
   All birds have feathers.

   (d) Some birds have feathers.
   Sparrows are birds.
   Sparrows have feathers.

3. *If the congressman is lying, then no one will vote for him.*
   If no one votes for the congressman, then he will not win the election.
   What can be deduced from these premises?

   (a) The congressman is lying.
   (b) The congressman will not win the election.
   (c) If the congressman does not win the election, then he was lying.
   (d) If the congressman is lying, then he will not win the election.

4. *If bats can sing, then elephants can dance.*
   Elephants can dance.
   Bats can sing.
   This invalid argument is an example of which of the following?

   (a) Affirming the hypothesis
   (c) Affirming the conclusion

   (b) Denying the hypothesis
   (d) Denying the conclusion

5. *Some lakes always freeze in the winter.*
   Tahoe does not always freeze in the winter.
   What can be deduced from these premises? Use a Venn diagram to test your answer.

   (a) Tahoe is not a lake.
   (c) Nothing can be deduced.

   (b) Tahoe sometimes freezes in the winter.
   (d) Some lakes do not always freeze in the winter.

Unit 1D Test 3 *(continued)*

6. *Some monsters live under my bed.*
   Cookie Monster lives on Sesame Street.
   Some monsters do not live under my bed.
   Which of the following describes this argument?

   (a) Valid and sound
   (c) Not valid and sound

   (b) Valid and not sound
   (d) Not valid and not sound

7. *All cats have four legs.*
   Some cats are black.
   Some four-legged animals are black.
   Which of the following describes this argument?

   (a) Valid and sound
   (c) Not valid and sound

   (b) Valid and not sound
   (d) Not valid and not sound

8. Use inductive reasoning to test the following mathematical rules.
   Which statement do you think is true?

   (a) $-1 \times a < 0$
   (b) $-1 \times a = -a$
   (c) $-1 \times a < a$
   (d) $-1 \times a > a$

9. Use inductive reasoning to test the following mathematical rules.
   Which statement do you think is false?

   (a) $a \times 1 = a$
   (b) $1 \times a = a$
   (c) $\dfrac{a}{1} = a$
   (d) $\dfrac{1}{a} = a$

10. Which of the following is an example of inductive logic?

   (a) If I got an A in my last four math classes then I will get an A in this math class.
   (b) If I get an A on every test, then I will get an A in the class.
   (c) If I study very hard then I will get an A.
   (d) If I get an A in my math class then I will take another math class next year.

Unit 1D Test 4

Choose the correct answer to each problem.

1. Which of the following is a valid argument?

   (a) Bank robbers are in jail.
   Burglars are in jail.
   Extortionists are in jail.
   All criminals are in jail.

   (b) Some criminals go to jail.
   Burglars go to jail.
   Burglars are criminals.

   (c) All burglars are in jail.
   Ernie is a burglar.
   Ernie is in jail.

   (d) Some bank robbers are in jail.
   Burt is a bank robber.
   Burt is in jail.

2. Which of the following is a sound argument?

   (a) All fruit grow on trees.
   Money doesn't grow on trees.
   Money is not a fruit.

   (b) Some trees have fruit.
   Peaches are fruit.
   Peaches grow on trees.

   (c) Peach trees have fruit.
   Apple trees have fruit.
   Cherry trees have fruit.
   All trees have fruit.

   (d) Apples grow on trees.
   Apples are fruit.
   Some fruit grow on trees.

3. *If Lori is sick then Tony will drive.*
   If Tony drives then Susan will not go.
   What can be deduced from these premises?

   (a) Susan will not go.

   (b) Lori is sick.

   (c) If Lori is sick then Susan will not go.

   (d) If Susan does not go, then Lori is sick.

4. *If dinosaurs live in trees, then dinosaurs eat berries.*
   Dinosaurs do not live in trees.
   Dinosaurs do not eat berries.
   This invalid argument is an example of which of the following?

   (a) Affirming the hypothesis

   (b) Denying the hypothesis

   (c) Affirming the conclusion

   (d) Denying the conclusion

5. *Some dogs bite.*
   Chihuahuas are dogs.
   What can be deduced from these premises? Use a Venn diagram to test your answer.

   (a) Some dogs do not bite.

   (b) Some Chihuahuas bite.

   (c) Nothing can be deduced.

   (d) Some dogs are Chihuahuas.

6. *Every musician owns a guitar.*
   Johnny Bravo owns a guitar.
   Johnny Bravo is a musician.
   Which of the following describes this argument?

   (a) Valid and sound

   (b) Valid and not sound

   (c) Not valid and sound

   (d) Not valid and not sound

Unit 1D Test 4 *(continued)*

Name:_____

7. *If you were born after 1900, you were not in the Civil War.*
   <u>*U.S. Grant was in the Civil War.*</u>
   U.S. Grant was not born after 1900.
   Which of the following describes this argument?

   (a) Valid and sound   **(b)** Valid and not sound
   (c) Not valid and sound   **(d)** Not valid and not sound

8. Use inductive reasoning to test the following mathematical rules.
   Which statement do you think is true?

   (a) $0 - a = a$ **(b)** $0 - (-a) = a$ **(c)** $a - 0 = -a$ **(d)** $-a - 0 = a$

9. Use inductive reasoning to test the following mathematical rules.
   Which statement do you think is false?

   (a) $-b + a = -(b - a)$ **(b)** $a - b = -b + a$ **(c)** $a - b = -(b - a)$ **(d)** $a - b = b - a$

10. Which of the following is an example of inductive logic?

   (a) If there is an accident on the freeway then we will be late for the play.
   (b) If you lost the last two tennis matches, you will likely lose the next one too.
   (c) I have to leave work earlier if the bank closes at 5:00 today.
   (d) If I get a raise next week then I can buy a new car.

Unit 1E Test 1

1. Give an example of a sales argument in which the consumer needs to be aware of missing information.

   _____

   _____

   _____

2. Explain what is meant by a hidden assumption.

   _____

   _____

   _____

3. *I want to find the best airfare to Phoenix because my sister is getting married there next month and I want to fly to the wedding.*
   State the conclusion of this argument.

   _____

   _____

   _____

4. Give an example of an argument with an intermediate conclusion that is not sound. Explain why it is not sound.

   _____

   _____

   _____

5. A basic yearly cellular telephone service contract is advertised as costing only $20 per month. However, there is a $10 per month penalty if you cancel the contract before the end of the year. Calculate the total cost of the service if you cancel at the end of one month.

   _____

   _____

   _____

Unit 1E Test 1 *(continued)*

6. *All bills should be paid on time because a bad credit report will make it difficult to get a loan.*
Identify any hidden assumptions or intermediate conclusions in this argument.

_____

_____

_____

7. *It is important to have a vaccination every year to avoid getting the flu.*
Identify any hidden assumptions or intermediate conclusions in this argument.

_____

_____

_____

8. The costs per day of driving to work are $6 for gas, $12 for parking, and $1 of wear and tear on the car. Taking the train to work costs $8.50 each way, plus $1.50 per day to park at the train station. What are the total costs per day of each option?

_____

_____

_____

9. The cost to rent a car for 4 days is $20 per day plus $0.25 per mile. The weekly rate is $100 including mileage. If you plan to drive approximately 100 miles during a 4-day period, which is the better option?

_____

_____

_____

10. *I should buy a new car. Interest rates are low and I just received a 3% raise. Also, my car is very old and will soon need expensive repairs.*
Identify the premises, any hidden assumptions or intermediate conclusions, and the conclusion for this argument. Discuss its strength.

_____

_____

_____

Unit 1E Test 2

1. Consider the following ballot question:
   Shall there be an amendment to the state constitution to prohibit the state legislature from adopting any law which inhibits the freedom of religious expression?
   Explain the meaning of a *no* vote.

   _____

   _____

   _____

2. *The dictator of a foreign country has enacted a ban on all firearms, citing accidental deaths among children as his main concern.*
   Identify other issues that might be involved in his decision to ban firearms.

   _____

   _____

   _____

3. *The stores at the mall should stay open later this month. After all, it is the holiday season and there are more shoppers.*
   State the conclusion of this argument.

   _____

   _____

   _____

4. Give an example of a sound argument with a hidden assumption. Explain your answer.

   _____

   _____

   _____

5. An Internet service provider advertises a year's worth of service for only $15 per month. However, there is a $10 per month penalty if you cancel the contract before the end of the year. Calculate the total cost of the service if you cancel at the end of one month.

   _____

   _____

   _____

Unit 1E Test 2 *(continued)*

6. *The campfire should be extinguished before we go fishing because the ranger can cite us for illegal activities.*
Identify any hidden assumptions or intermediate conclusions in this argument.

_____

_____

_____

7. *Swimming is healthy because it improves your cardiovascular system.*
Identify any hidden assumptions or intermediate conclusions in this argument.

_____

_____

_____

8. If we drive to the airport we will pay $6 for gas each way and $30 to park in the long term parking lot. If we take a taxi to the airport it will cost $22 each way. What is the total cost for each option?

_____

_____

_____

9. You want a new car, but plan to use it for only 2 years. If you lease the car, you will pay $2,000 up front and $275 per month for two years. If you buy the car for $20,000 you can expect to sell it in two years for approximately $12,000. Which is the better option?

_____

_____

_____

10. *Jeremy needs a new bike. He rides his bike to school every day and he is getting too large for it. Also, the new models have a safer braking system.*
Identify the premises, any hidden assumptions or intermediate conclusions, and the conclusion for this argument. Discuss its strength.

_____

_____

_____

Unit 1E Test 3

Choose the correct answer to each problem.

1. Which of the following are stated explicitly in an argument?

   (a) Hidden assumptions
   (c) Valid premises

   (b) Missing information
   (d) Other possible conclusions

2. *Since Jerry's birthday is coming up, I should buy him a basketball as a gift.*
   Which of the following intermediate conclusions can be deduced from this argument?

   (a) Jerry plays basketball every Saturday.
   (c) Jerry's birthday is next week.

   (b) Jerry doesn't have a basketball.
   (d) Jerry bought me a birthday present last year.

3. *Neptunes are the most comfortable car on the road because they have the most elaborate suspension system.*
   Which of the following hidden assumptions is being used in this argument?

   (a) Other cars on the road are not comfortable.
   (b) If you are going to buy a new car, then you should buy a Neptune.
   (c) The suspension system is the most important factor in determining car comfort.
   (d) The suspension system on the Neptune is better than on any other car.

4. You are leasing a summer home for twelve weeks and need to cut the grass every week. If you do it yourself you can buy a new power mower for $340 and sell it at the end of the summer for $100. Or you can rent a power mower for $20 each day. The neighbor's son will charge you $9 per hour for 2 hours and has his own equipment. Which is the least expensive option?

   (a) Buy a new mower.
   (c) Hire the neighbor's son.

   (b) Rent a mower.
   (d) They all cost the same.

5. *We get two weeks of vacation this year. We are going camping for one week and skiing for one week, so we will have to visit Aunt Martha next year.*
   Which of the following propositions is the conclusion of this argument?

   (a) We get two weeks of vacation this year.
   (b) We are going camping for one week and skiing for one week this year.
   (c) We will have to visit Aunt Martha next year.
   (d) We need more vacation time this year.

6. We should all drink 8 glasses of water a day because being properly hydrated will improve our health.
   Which of the following propositions is the conclusion of this argument?

   (a) Drinking 8 glasses of water per day will keep us properly hydrated.
   (b) We should all be properly hydrated.
   (c) We should all drink 8 glasses of water per day.
   (d) Drinking 8 glasses of water per day will improve our health.

7. To help make a complex argument clear, visual aids may include all **except** which of the following?

   (a) Written descriptions
   (c) Graphs

   (b) Venn diagrams
   (d) Flow charts

Unit 1E Test 3 *(continued)*

8. A box of 20 Crunchy Munchy cookies costs $2.50 and a box of 40 Crunchy Munchy cookies costs $4.00. One quart of milk costs $1.50. Which of the following is a better bargain?

   (a) A box of 20 cookies that comes with a free quart of milk
   (b) A box of 40 cookies with a quart of milk that costs $1.50
   (c) The cost of each option is the same

9. Betty has to go to New Orleans for business. If she flies there and back on the same day her round trip airfare will cost $800. If she stays overnight, her roundtrip airfare will cost $500, her hotel will cost $175, and three extra meals will cost $50.
   Which is the better option?

   (a) Staying overnight in New Orleans   (b) Flying there and back on the same day
   (c) The cost of each option is the same.

10. Two friends are planning a vacation. It will cost $350 each way for each of them to fly to San Francisco or $450 round trip for each of them to fly to New York. If they fly to San Francisco, they can stay with friends for free. If they fly to New York they will pay $100 a night for a hotel. Which of the following situations would make flying to San Francisco the better option?

   (a) They want to stay for 5 days   (b) They want to stay for 7 days
   (c) It will cost more to eat in San Francisco (d) It will cost less to rent a car in New York

Unit 1E Test 4

Choose the correct answer to each problem.

1. Alice needs to compute the average of her exam scores. She has already received scores of 60, 70, and 80 and has one more exam to take. Which of the following is not missing information?

   (a) Grading scale
   (c) Weight of each exam

   (b) Number of exams to be averaged
   (d) Score on the last exam

2. *Edith is taking her cat, Pico, to the vet next week because Pico is due for a vaccination. Cats should be vaccinated every year.*
   Which of the following intermediate conclusions can be deduced from this argument?

   (a) Pico is due for a vaccination.
   (b) Pico wants to be vaccinated.
   (c) Edith could not get an appointment with the veterinarian until next week.
   (d) It has been at least one year since Pico was last vaccinated.

3. *We should not vote for the incumbent because he has already been in office for three consecutive terms.*
   Which of the following hidden assumptions is being used in this argument?

   (a) We should never vote for an incumbent.
   (b) The incumbent has already been elected three times.
   (c) Four consecutive terms is too many.
   (d) We should vote for the underdog.

4. You are leasing a summer home for twelve weeks and need to cut the grass every week. The neighbor's son will charge you $10 per hour for 2 hours and has his own equipment. If you do it yourself, you can buy a new power mower for $350 and sell it at the end of the summer for $100. Or you can rent a power mower for $18 each day. Which is the least expensive option?

   (a) Hire the neighbor's son.
   (c) Rent a mower.

   (b) Buy a new mower.
   (d) They all cost the same.

5. *We are all out of gasoline. Since I want to finish cutting the lawn before it rains, I need to go to town.*
   Which of the following propositions is the conclusion of this argument?

   (a) We are out of gasoline.
   (c) I need to go to town.

   (b) I need gasoline to mow the lawn.
   (d) The grass needs to be cut.

6. *Jenny must have found a new job because I haven't seen her in the career center for weeks.*
   Which of the following propositions is the conclusion of this argument?

   (a) Jenny hasn't been to the career center for weeks.
   (b) I haven't seen Jenny in the career center for weeks.
   (c) Jenny needs a job.
   (d) Jenny must have found a new job.

Unit 1E Test 4 *(continued)*

7. Which of the following is not a hidden danger with a calling plan that offers all calls of up to 20 minutes for just 99¢?

   (a) The cost of reaching a friend's answering machine
   (b) The cost per minute after the first 20 minutes
   (c) The cost of a 20-minute call
   (d) Monthly service fees

8. Carrots cost $0.11 each or $0.99 for a one pound bag. There are about 7 to 10 carrots in a pound. Which is the better option?

   (a) A one pound bag of large carrots   (b) 10 large carrots
   (c) The cost of each option is the same.

9. Larry has to decide whether to drive from San Francisco to Santa Barbara or fly. If he drives it will take 5 hours. If he flies it will take 45 minutes to drive to the airport, one hour to check-in, one and a half hours in the air, and one hour to rent a car and drive from the airport to his destination. Which is the faster option?

   (a) Driving to Santa Barbara   (b) Flying to Santa Barbara
   (c) Each option takes the same amount of time.

10. Mr. Burns is going to Miami and wants to rent a car there. The price per day to rent a car is $25 and the first 100 miles are included. After 100 miles the price per mile is $0.50. The weekly rate to rent a car is $100 plus $0.20 per mile. The weekly rate is for seven days. Which of the following situations would make the weekly rate more economical?

    (a) Mr. Burns is staying in Miami for 3 days and plans to drive 50 miles.
    (b) Mr. Burns is staying in Miami for 6 days and plans to drive 200 miles.
    (c) Mr. Burns is staying in Miami for 4 days and plans to drive 125 miles.
    (d) Mr. Burns is staying in Miami for 2 days and plans to drive 250 miles.

Unit 2A Test 1

1. Identify the units you would expect for speed of a toy rocket found by dividing a distance measured in feet by a time measured in seconds.

   _____

   _____

   _____

2. Given that 1 yard = 36 inches, explain how you would find the number of cubic inches in a cubic yard.

   _____

   _____

   _____

3. Suppose your car gets 36 miles per gallon of gasoline, and you are driving at 50 miles per hour. Using unit analysis only, explain how you would find the number of hours it takes to use one gallon of gas.

   _____

   _____

   _____

4. If a Norwegian kroner is worth $0.149, what is the value of $1.00 in kroners?

   _____

   _____

   _____

5. An acre is equal to 43,560 square feet, and there are 5280 feet in a mile. If a farm has the shape of a rectangle measuring 0.6 mile by 0.9 mile, what is the area of the farm in acres? You must show the use of units.

   _____

   _____

   _____

Unit 2A Test 1 *(continued)*

6. You need to put carpet in a rectangular room that measures 15 feet by 13 feet at a cost of $23.50 per square yard. Assuming that you can buy precisely the amount of carpet you need, how much will the carpet for the room cost? You must show the use of units.

_____

_____

_____

7. Suppose you drive a distance of 495 miles at a speed of 55 miles per hour. How many hours does it take?

_____

_____

_____

8. Suppose that two current exchange rates are $1 = 0.5 pounds and 1 rupee = $0.022. What is the value of 1 rupee in pounds? You must show the use of units.

_____

_____

_____

9. Suppose water flows from a shower at a rate of 0.35 cubic feet per minute. Do you use more water by taking a 15-minute shower or by filling a bathtub with 0.5 cubic yards of water? You must show the use of units.

_____

_____

_____

10. Assuming that you breathe once every 10 seconds, how many breaths do you take in 3 weeks? You must show the use of units.

_____

_____

_____

Unit 2A Test 2

1. Identify the units you would expect for the price of gravel found by dividing its total cost in dollars by its total weight in tons.

   _____

   _____

   _____

2. Given that 1 foot = 12 inches, explain how you would find the number of cubic inches in a cubic foot.

   _____

   _____

   _____

3. Suppose your car gets 25 miles per gallon of gasoline, and you are driving at 60 miles per hour. Using unit analysis only, explain how you would find the number of gallons of gas you use every hour.

   _____

   _____

   _____

4. If a New Zealand dollar is worth $0.725, what is the value of U.S. $1.00 in New Zealand dollars?

   _____

   _____

   _____

5. An acre is equal to 43,560 square feet, and there are 5280 feet in a mile. If a farm has the shape of a rectangle measuring 0.6 miles by 1.2 miles, what is the area of the farm in acres? You must show the use of units.

   _____

   _____

   _____

Unit 2A Test 2 *(continued)*

Name:_____

6. You need to put carpet in a rectangular room that measures 14 feet by 18 feet at a cost of $24.50 per square yard. Assuming that you can buy precisely the amount of carpet you need, how much will the carpet for the room cost? You must show the use of units.

_____

_____

_____

7. Suppose you drive a distance of 630 miles at a speed of 45 miles per hour. How many hours does it take?

_____

_____

_____

8. Suppose that two current exchange rates are $1 = 10.6045 pesos and 1 euro = $1.169. What is the value of 1 euro in pesos? You must show the use of units.

_____

_____

_____

9. Suppose water flows from a shower at a rate of 0.38 cubic feet per minute. Do you use more water by taking a 14-minute shower or by filling a bathtub with 0.6 cubic yards of water? You must show the use of units.

_____

_____

_____

10. Assuming that you breathe once every 4 seconds, how many breaths do you take in 4 weeks? You must show the use of units.

_____

_____

_____

Unit 2A Test 3

Name:_____

Date:_____

Choose the correct answer to each problem.

1. Which of the following is a conversion factor?

    (a) $A = lw$ **(b)** 240 miles   **(c)** feet per second   **(d)** $1 \text{ yd}^2 = 9 \text{ ft}^2$

2. Given that 1 meter = 100 centimeters, find the number of cubic centimeters in a cubic meter.

    (a) 100   **(b)** 10,000   **(c)** 1,000,000   **(d)** 100,000,000

3. Suppose your car gets 28 miles per gallon of gasoline, and you are driving at 55 miles per hour. Using unit analysis, find the amount of gas you use every hour.

    (a) 1.45 gallons   **(b)** 1.96 gallons   **(c)** 0.75 gallons   **(d)** 0.51 gallons

4. If a Norwegian kroner is worth $0.149, what is the value of $1.00 in kroners?

    (a) 6.71 kroners   **(b)** 14.9 kroners   **(c)** 5.43 kroners   **(d)** 0.149 kroners

5. An acre is equal to 43,560 square feet, and there are 5280 feet in a mile. If a farm has the shape of a rectangle measuring 0.9 miles by 1.5 miles, what is the area of the farm in acres?

    (a) 0.164 acre   **(b)** 11.14 acres   **(c)** 864 acres   **(d)** 1050 acres

6. You need to put carpet in a rectangular room that measures 12 feet by 17 feet at a cost of $27.50 per square yard. Assuming that you can buy precisely the amount of carpet you need, how much will the carpet for the room cost?

    (a) $204.00   **(b)** $623.33   **(c)** $741.82   **(d)** $1870.00

7. Suppose you drive a distance of 210 miles at a speed of 50 miles per hour. How many hours does it take?

    (a) 4.2 hours   **(b)** 3.5 hours   **(c)** 2.7 hours   **(d)** 0.238 hour

8. Suppose that two current exchange rates are US $1 = 7.7631 Hong Kong dollars and 1 euro = US $1.169. What is the value of 1 Hong Kong dollar in euros?

    (a) 0.151 euros   **(b)** 6.641 euros   **(c)** 0.110 euros   **(d)** 9.075 euros

9. Suppose water flows from a shower at a rate of 0.44 cubic feet per minute. Do you use more water by taking an 8-minute shower or by filling a bathtub with 0.45 cubic yards of water, and by how much?

    (a) Bath uses an additional 0.53 cubic feet of water
    (b) Bath uses an additional 8.63 cubic feet of water
    (c) Shower uses an additional 2.17 cubic feet of water
    (d) Shower uses an additional 3.07 cubic feet of water

10. Assuming that your heart beats 70 times per minute, how many times does your heart beat in 6 days?

    (a) 25,200   **(b)** 201,600   **(c)** 604,800   **(d)** 36,288,000

Unit 2A Test 4

Choose the correct answer to each problem.

1. Which of the following is a conversion factor?

   (a) miles per hour
   (b) $\dfrac{24 \text{ hours}}{1 \text{ day}} = 1$
   (c) 3 seconds
   (d) $V = lwh$

2. Given that 1 mile = 8 furlongs, find the number of cubic furlongs in a cubic mile.

   (a) 8 cubic furlongs
   (b) 64 cubic furlongs
   (c) 512 cubic furlongs
   (d) 4096 cubic furlongs

3. Suppose your car gets 36 miles per gallon of gasoline, and you are driving at 45 miles per hour. Using unit analysis, find the number of hours it takes to use 1 gallon of gas.

   (a) 0.62 hour
   (b) 0.8 hour
   (c) 1.25 hours
   (d) 1.62 hours

4. If a dollar is worth 0.0279 Indian rupee, what is the value of 1 rupee in dollars?

   (a) 0.0279 dollar
   (b) 2.79 dollars
   (c) 27.90 dollars
   (d) 35.84 dollars

5. An acre is equal to 43,560 square feet, and there are 5280 feet in a mile. If a farm has the shape of a rectangle measuring 0.8 mile by 1.1 miles, what is the area of the farm in acres?

   (a) 684.3 acres
   (b) 563.2 acres
   (c) 106.7 acres
   (d) 13.75 acres

6. You need to put carpet in a rectangular room that measures 13 feet by 22 feet at a cost of $19.50 per square yard. Assuming that you can buy precisely the amount of carpet you need, how much will the carpet for the room cost?

   (a) $619.67
   (b) $681.82
   (c) $1466.67
   (d) $1859.01

7. Suppose you drive a distance of 338 miles at a speed of 52 miles per hour. How many hours does it take?

   (a) 0.15 hour
   (b) 1.76 hours
   (c) 4.8 hours
   (d) 6.5 hours

8. Suppose that two current exchange rates are US $1 = 117.9 Japanese yen and 1 Cuban peso = $0.0476. What is the value of 1 peso in Japanese yen?

   (a) 5.612 Japanese yen
   (b) 2476.89 Japanese yen
   (c) 23,485.29 Japanese yen
   (d) 89.37 Japanese yen

9. Suppose water flows from a shower at a rate of 0.32 cubic feet per minute. Do you use more water by taking a 12-minute shower or by filling a bathtub with 0.4 cubic yards of water, and by how much?

   (a) Bath uses an additional 6.96 cubic feet of water
   (b) Bath uses an additional 0.24 cubic feet of water
   (c) Shower uses an additional 3.44 cubic feet of water
   (d) Shower uses an additional 2.64 cubic feet of water

10. Assuming that your heart beats 68 times per minute, how many times does your heart beat in 5 days?

   (a) 32,400,000
   (b) 540,000
   (c) 489,600
   (d) 22,500

Unit 2B Test 1

Name:_____

Date:_____

1. Determine whether the following statement is sensible or ridiculous. Explain why.
   Ken ran a distance of 2000 meters in 35 seconds.

   _____

   _____

   _____

2. Keith is 6.2 feet tall. What is his height in centimeters? State your answer to the nearest tenth.

   _____

   _____

   _____

3. A pond contains 8.3 cubic yards of water. Find the volume of the water in cubic meters. State your answer to the nearest tenth.

   _____

   _____

   _____

4. Two cities are 582 kilometers apart. Convert this distance to miles. State your answer to the nearest tenth of a mile.

   _____

   _____

   _____

5. A field of grass has an area of 523,000,000 square millimeters. Convert this area to square hectometers.

   _____

   _____

   _____

6. Suppose onions at a store in Switzerland are priced at 0.60 francs per kilogram, where one dollar is worth 1.252 francs. What is the price of the onions in dollars per pound? State your answer to the nearest $0.01 per pound.

   _____

   _____

   _____

Unit 2B Test 1 *(continued)*

7. Convert $92° F$ to degrees Celsius. State your answer to the nearest tenth of a degree.

_____

_____

_____

8. Suppose your utility company charges 8¢ per kilowatt-hour of electricity. How much does it cost to operate a chandelier with five 60-watt light bulbs for 75 minutes?

_____

_____

_____

9. A 2-pound object has a volume of 8 cubic inches. Find its density.

_____

_____

_____

10. Suppose a necklace is made from 16-karat gold and weighs 66 grams. Find the weight, in carats, of the pure gold in the necklace.

_____

_____

_____

Unit 2B Test 2

Name:_____

Date:_____

1. Determine whether the following statement is sensible or ridiculous. Explain why.
   Barbara drove a distance of 6.9 liters to get to the store.

   _____

   _____

   _____

2. Betty is 5.2 feet tall. What is her height in meters? State your answer to the nearest tenth of a meter.

   _____

   _____

   _____

3. A pond contains 7.6 cubic yards of water. Find the volume of the water in cubic centimeters. State your answer to the nearest tenth.

   _____

   _____

   _____

4. Two cities are 614 kilometers apart. Convert this distance to miles. State your answer to the nearest tenth of a mile.

   _____

   _____

   _____

5. A field of grass has an area of 4,230,000 square centimeters. Convert this area to square decameters.

   _____

   _____

   _____

6. Suppose asparagus at a store in Portugal is priced at 135 escudos per kilogram, where one dollar is worth 171 escudos. What is the price of the asparagus in dollars per pound? State your answer to the nearest $0.01 per pound.

   _____

   _____

   _____

Unit 2B Test 2 *(continued)*

7. State how much larger or smaller a square kilometer is than a square meter.

_____

_____

_____

8. Convert $40°\,F$ to degrees Celsius. State your answer to the nearest tenth of a degree.

_____

_____

_____

9. Suppose your utility company charges 8¢ per kilowatt-hour of electricity. How much does it cost to keep a 100-watt light bulb lit for one day?

_____

_____

_____

10. Suppose a necklace is made from 21-karat gold and weighs 72 grams. Find the weight, in carats, of the pure gold in the necklace.

_____

_____

_____

Unit 2B Test 3

Choose the correct answer to each problem.

1. Three of the four statements below are reasonable, while one is ridiculous. Which one is ridiculous?

   (a) The fish weighed 1.6 pounds.

   (b) Jimmy held his breath for 18,000 milliseconds.

   (c) Rebecca ate 3 meters of fudge.

   (d) The bananas cost 45 cents per kilogram.

2. Richard is 6.1 feet tall. Find his height in meters to the nearest tenth.

   (a) 20.7 meters   (b) 5.8 meters   (c) 6.9 meters   (d) 1.9 meters

3. A pond contains 9.4 cubic yards of water. What is the volume of the water in cubic meters to the nearest tenth?

   (a) 12.3 cubic meters   (b) 8.6 cubic meters   (c) 10.3 cubic meters   (d) 7.2 cubic meters

4. Two cities are 379 kilometers apart. Convert this distance to miles to the nearest tenth.

   (a) 346.6 miles   (b) 609.9 miles

   (c) 235.5 miles   (d) 146.3 miles

5. A field of grass has an area of 618,000,000 square millimeters. Convert this area to square hectometers.

   (a) 0.0618 square hectometers   (b) 6.18 square hectometers

   (c) 61.8 square hectometers   (d) 6180 square hectometers

6. Suppose the potatoes at a store in the Netherlands are priced at 0.42 guilders per kilogram, where one dollar is worth 1.91 guilders. What is the price of the potatoes in dollars per pound?

   (a) $0.10 per pound   (b) $0.36 per pound   (c) $0.48 per pound   (d) $1.77 per pound

7. State how much larger a square meter is than a square centimeter.

   (a) Larger by a factor of 100   (b) Larger by a factor of 1000

   (c) Larger by a factor of 10,000   (d) Larger by a factor of 1,000,000

8. Convert $33°C$ to degrees Fahrenheit.

   (a) $0.6°F$ (b) $83.2°F$ (c) $91.4°F$ (d) $117.0°F$

9. Wally ran 5 miles in 34.7 minutes. Find his speed in meters per second.

   (a) 3.7 meters per second   (b) 3.9 meters per second   (c) 4.7 meters per second   (d) 6.1 meters per second

10. A 16-gram object has a volume of 40 cubic centimeters. Find its density.

    (a) $0.4 \dfrac{g}{cm^3}$ (b) $2.5 \dfrac{cm^3}{g}$ (c) $490 \; g \cdot cm^3$ (d) $21 \; cm^3$

Unit 2B Test 4

Choose the correct answer to each problem.

1. Three of the four statements below are reasonable, while one is ridiculous. Which one is ridiculous?

   (a) The table is 2 meters long.
   (b) The broccoli costs 89 cents per minute.
   (c) Sandra went to a concert that lasted 5400 seconds.
   (d) Jonathan weighs 142 pounds.

2. Estelle is 5.6 feet tall. Find her height in centimeters to the nearest tenth.

   (a) 1.8 cm   (b) 148.9 cm   (c) 170.7 cm   (d) 27.9 cm

3. A pond contains 7.2 cubic yards of water. What is the volume of the water in cubic meters to the nearest tenth?

   (a) 21.6 cubic feet   (b) 64.8 cubic feet   (c) 5.5 cubic meters   (d) 253.8 cubic
   feet

4. Two cities are 512 kilometers apart. Convert this distance to miles to the nearest tenth.

   (a) 468.2 miles   (b) 824.0 miles
   (c) 197.7 miles   (d) 318.2 miles

5. A field of grass has an area of 6,420,000 square centimeters. Convert this area to square decameters.

   (a) 0.0642 square decameters   (b) 6.42 square decameters
   (c) 64.2 square decameters   (d) 6420 square decameters

6. Suppose the eggplants at a store in Thailand are priced at 1.24 baht per kilogram, where one dollar is worth 1.37 baht. What is the price of the eggplants in dollars per pound?

   (a) $3.75 per pound   (b) $2.00 per pound   (c) $0.77 per pound   (d) $0.41 per
   pound

7. Convert $21°C$ to degrees Fahrenheit.

   (a) $6.1°F$ (b) $61.8°F$ (c) $69.8°F$ (d) $95.4°F$

8. Jennifer ran 6 miles in 43.7 minutes. Find her speed in meters per second.

   (a) 3.7 meters per second   (b) 3.9 meters per second   (c) 5.2 meters per second   (d) 7.0 meters per
   second

9. What is the cost of lighting a 500-watt outdoor light for 8 hours, if electricity costs 7.5¢ per kilowatt-hour?

   (a) 45 cents   (b) 67 cents   (c) 60 cents   (d) 30 cents

10. Suppose a necklace is made from 20-karat gold and weighs 60 grams. Find the weight, in carats, of the pure gold in the necklace.

    (a) 13   (b) 250   (c) 270   (d) 324

Unit 2C Test 1

1. A traffic counter consists of a thin black tube stretched across a street or highway and connected to a "brain box" at the side of the road. The device registers one "count" each time a set of wheels (that is, wheels on a single axle) rolls over the tube. A normal automobile (two axles) registers two counts, and a light truck (three axles) registers three counts. Suppose that, during a one-hour period, a particular counter registers 41 counts on a residential street on which only two-axle vehicles (cars) and three-axle vehicles (light trucks) are allowed. Give a possible answer for the number of cars and the number of light trucks that passed over the traffic counter.

_____

_____

_____

2. Paul and Saul ran a 50-meter race. When Paul crossed the finish line, Saul had run only 48 meters. Then they ran a second race, with Paul starting 2 meters behind the starting line. Assuming that both runners ran at the same pace as in the first race, who won the second race?

_____

_____

_____

3. Suppose you have 12 white socks and 5 black socks in a drawer. How many socks must you take from the drawer to be certain of having a pair of *white* socks?

_____

_____

_____

4. Two bicyclists, 48 miles apart, begin riding toward each other on a long straight avenue. One cyclist travels 15 miles per hour and the other 25 miles per hour. At the same time, Spot (a greyhound), starting at one cyclist, runs back and forth between the two cyclists as they approach each other. If Spot runs 35 miles per hour and turns around instantly at each cyclist, how far has he run when the cyclists meet?

_____

_____

_____

Unit 2C Test 1 *(continued)*

5. Suppose that you begin with a red bucket containing 12 red marbles and a yellow bucket containing 12 yellow marbles. You move *three* marbles from the red bucket to the yellow bucket, and then you move any *four* marbles from the yellow bucket to the red bucket. Which is greater, the number of yellow marbles in the red bucket or the number of red marbles in the yellow bucket?

_____

_____

_____

6. Suppose that 8 turns of a wire are wrapped around a pipe with a length of 60 inches and a circumference of 4 inches. What is the length of the wire?

_____

_____

_____

7. You are considering buying 15 silver coins that look alike, but you have been told that one of the coins is a lightweight counterfeit. How can you determine the lightweight coin in a maximum of three weighings on a balance scale?

_____

_____

_____

8. Suppose that China's population policy is modified so that every family could have children until either a boy is born or two children are born, whichever comes first. Assuming that every family chooses to have as many children as possible under this policy, and that boys and girls are equally likely, what fraction of the children would be girls and what fraction would be boys?

_____

_____

_____

Unit 2C Test 2

1. A traffic counter consists of a thin black tube stretched across a street or highway and connected to a "brain box" at the side of the road. The device registers one "count" each time a set of wheels (that is, wheels on a single axle) rolls over the tube. A normal automobile (two axles) registers two counts, and a light truck (three axles) registers three counts. Suppose that, during a one-hour period, a particular counter registers 43 counts on a residential street on which only two-axle vehicles (cars) and three-axle vehicles (light trucks) are allowed. Give a possible answer for the number of cars and the number of light trucks that passed over the traffic counter.

_____

_____

_____

2. Pat and Dan ran a 75-meter race. When Dan crossed the finish line, Pat had run only 70 meters. Then they ran a second race, with Dan starting 8 meters behind the starting line. Assuming that both runners ran at the same pace as in the first race, who won the second race?

_____

_____

_____

3. Suppose you have 10 white socks and 6 black socks in a drawer. How many socks must you take from the drawer to be certain of having a pair of *black* socks?

_____

_____

_____

4. Two bicyclists, 48 miles apart, begin riding toward each other on a long straight avenue. One cyclist travels 18 miles per hour and the other 12 miles per hour. At the same time, Spot (a greyhound), starting at one cyclist, runs back and forth between the two cyclists as they approach each other. If Spot runs 36 miles per hour and turns around instantly at each cyclist, how far has he run when the cyclists meet?

_____

_____

_____

Unit 2C Test 2 *(continued)*

5. Suppose that you begin with a green bucket containing 14 green marbles and a black bucket containing 14 black marbles. You move *four* marbles from the green bucket to the black bucket, and then you move any *three* marbles from the black bucket to the green bucket. Which is greater, the number of black marbles in the green bucket or the number of green marbles in the black bucket?

_____

_____

_____

6. Suppose that 12 turns of a wire are wrapped around a pipe with a length of 42 inches and a circumference of 12 inches. What is the length of the wire?

_____

_____

_____

7. You are considering buying 18 silver coins that look alike, but you have been told that one of the coins is a lightweight counterfeit. How can you determine the lightweight coin in a maximum of three weighings on a balance scale?

_____

_____

_____

8. Suppose that China's population policy is modified so that every family could have children until either a boy is born or three children are born, whichever comes first. Assuming that every family chooses to have as many children as possible under this policy, and that boys and girls are equally likely, what fraction of the children would be girls and what fraction would be boys?

_____

_____

_____

Unit 2C Test 3

Choose the correct answer to each problem.

1. A traffic counter consists of a thin black tube stretched across a street or highway and connected to a "brain box" at the side of the road. The device registers one "count" each time a set of wheels (that is, wheels on a single axle) rolls over the tube. A normal automobile (two axles) registers two counts, and a light truck (three axles) registers three counts. Suppose that, during a one-hour period, a particular counter registers 47 counts on a residential street on which only two-axle vehicles (cars) and three-axle vehicles (light trucks) are allowed. Which of the following is a possible answer for the number of cars and the number of light trucks that passed over the traffic counter?

   (a) 7 cars and 11 light trucks
   (c) 13 cars and 6 light trucks

   (b) 9 cars and 10 light trucks
   (d) 23 cars and 24 light trucks

2. Candi and Sandi ran an 80-meter race. When Candi crossed the finish line, Sandi had run only 72 meters. Then they ran a second race, with Candi starting 8 meters behind the starting line. Assuming that both runners ran at the same pace as in the first race, who won the second race?

   (a) Candi
   (c) They tied.

   (b) Sandi
   (d) More information is needed.

3. Suppose you have 7 striped socks and 3 red socks in a drawer. How many socks must you take from the drawer to be certain of having a pair of *striped* socks?

   (a) 2   (b) 4   (c) 5   (d) 6

4. Two bicyclists, 44 miles apart, begin riding toward each other on a long straight avenue. One cyclist travels 16 miles per hour and the other 17 miles per hour. At the same time, Spot (a greyhound), starting at one cyclist, runs back and forth between the two cyclists as they approach each other. If Spot runs 39 miles per hour and turns around instantly at each cyclist, how far has he run when the cyclists meet?

   (a) 48 mi   (b) 52 mi   (c) 57 mi   (d) 64 mi

5. Suppose that you begin with a red bucket containing 16 red marbles and a yellow bucket containing 16 yellow marbles. You move *five* marbles from the red bucket to the yellow bucket, and then you move any *four* marbles from the yellow bucket to the red bucket. Compare the number of yellow marbles in the red bucket to the number of red marbles in the yellow bucket.

   (a) The number of red marbles in the yellow bucket is greater.
   (b) The number of yellow marbles in the red bucket is greater.
   (c) They are the same.
   (d) More information is needed.

6. Suppose that 7 turns of a wire are wrapped around a pipe with a length of 35 inches and a circumference of 12 inches. What is the length of the wire?

   (a) 35 inches   (b) 84 inches   (c) 91 inches   (d) 70 inches

7. You are considering buying 27 silver coins that look alike, but you have been told that one of the coins is a lightweight counterfeit. Find the least number of weighings on a balance scale that you can use to be certain you have found the counterfeit coin.

   (a) 2   (b) 3   (c) 4   (d) 5

Unit 2C Test 3 *(continued)*

8. Suppose that China's population policy is modified so that every family could have children until either a boy is born or two children are born, whichever comes first. Assuming that every family chooses to have as many children as possible under this policy, and that boys and girls are equally likely, how many children would be born in a typical group of 1000 families?

   (a) 1500   **(b)** 1750   **(c)** 1875   **(d)** 2000

Unit 2C Test 4

Name:_____

Date:_____

Choose the correct answer to each problem.

1. A traffic counter consists of a thin black tube stretched across a street or highway and connected to a "brain box" at the side of the road. The device registers one "count" each time a set of wheels (that is, wheels on a single axle) rolls over the tube. A normal automobile (two axles) registers two counts, and a light truck (three axles) registers three counts. Suppose that, during a one-hour period, a particular counter registers 53 counts on a residential street on which only two-axle vehicles (cars) and three-axle vehicles (light trucks) are allowed. Which of the following is a possible answer for the number of cars and the number of light trucks that passed over the traffic counter?

   (a) 7 cars and 16 light trucks
   (c) 13 cars and 9 light trucks
   (b) 12 cars and 10 light trucks
   (d) 42 cars and 11 light trucks

2. Perry and Barry ran an 120-meter race. When Barry crossed the finish line, Perry had run only 105 meters. Then they ran a second race, with Barry starting 15 meters behind the starting line. Assuming that both runners ran at the same pace as in the first race, who won the second race?

   (a) Perry
   (c) They tied.
   (b) Barry
   (d) More information is needed.

3. Suppose you have 10 striped socks and 6 red socks in a drawer. How many socks must you take from the drawer to be certain of having a pair of *red* socks?

   (a) 4   (b) 7   (c) 11   (d) 12

4. Two bicyclists, 52 miles apart, begin riding toward each other on a long straight avenue. One cyclist travels 16 miles per hour and the other 10 miles per hour. At the same time, Spot (a greyhound), starting at one cyclist, runs back and forth between the two cyclists as they approach each other. If Spot runs 32 miles per hour and turns around instantly at each cyclist, how far has he run when the cyclists meet?

   (a) 48 mi   (b) 52 mi   (c) 57 mi   (d) 64 mi

5. Suppose that you begin with a green bucket containing 18 green marbles and a black bucket containing 18 black marbles. You move *four* marbles from the green bucket to the black bucket, and then you move any *five* marbles from the black bucket to the green bucket. Compare the number of black marbles in the green bucket to the number of green marbles in the black bucket.

   (a) The number of green marbles in the black bucket is greater.
   (b) The number of black marbles in the green bucket is greater.
   (c) They are the same.
   (d) More information is needed.

6. Suppose that 8 turns of a wire are wrapped around a pipe with a length of 48 inches and a circumference of 3 inches. What is the length of the wire?

   (a) 24.1 inches   (b) 64.5 inches   (c) 48.2 inches   (d) 53.7 inches

7. You are considering buying 45 silver coins that look alike, but you have been told that one of the coins is a lightweight counterfeit. Find the least number of weighings on a balance scale that you can use to be certain you have found the counterfeit coin.

   (a) 2   (b) 3   (c) 4   (d) 5

8. Suppose that China's population policy is modified so that every family could have children until either a boy is born or three children are born, whichever comes first. Assuming that every family chooses to have as many children as possible under this policy, and that boys and girls are equally likely, how many children would be born in a typical group of 5000 families?

   (a) 7500   **(b)** 8750   **(c)** 9375   **(d)** 2500

Unit 3A Test 1

Name:_____

Date:_____

1. Determine whether the percentage in the following statement is used to express a fraction, to describe a change, or to make a comparison.
   In the 2004 presidential election, approximately 90% of African-American voters cast their votes for Democratic candidate John Kerry.

   _____

   _____

   _____

2. The price for a gallon of regular gasoline rose from $2.70 on Monday to $2.84 on Friday. Find the absolute change and the relative change in the price.

   _____

   _____

   _____

3. If Kenny earns 142% of Benny's salary, how much more does Kenny earn than Benny (in percentage terms)?

   _____

   _____

   _____

4. If the balance in your bank account increases by 1% during the first half of the year and 2% during the second half of the year, does it follow that the balance has increased by 3% over the entire year? Explain.

   _____

   _____

   _____

5. If 50% of the students in your class are men and 20% of the men have blond hair, does it follow that (50%)(20%) = 10% of the students in your class are men with blond hair? Explain.

   _____

   _____

   _____

Unit 3A Test 1 *(continued)*

6. A political candidate knows that 45% of the voters are Democrats and 40% of the voters are union members. If all of the Democrats and union members vote for the candidate, does it follow that she will get at least 50% of the vote? Explain.

_____

_____

_____

7. If 462 women at a conference comprise 55% of all people at the conference, how many people are at the conference?

_____

_____

_____

8. The after-tax price of a chair is $186.88. If a 6% sales tax was charged, what was the pre-tax price of the chair?

_____

_____

_____

9. Given that a dollar is worth 1.91 Dutch guilders, how much larger is a dollar than a guilder? Answer in percentage terms.

_____

_____

_____

10. The population of a town increased from 50,210 to 196,450 in one decade. What was the percent change of the population?

_____

_____

_____

Unit 3A Test 2

1. Determine whether the percentage in the following statement is used to express a fraction, to describe a change, or to make a comparison.
   Gasoline prices rose 7% last week, to $1.69 per gallon.

   _____

   _____

   _____

2. Define absolute and relative differences.

   _____

   _____

   _____

3. If Jill earns 210% of Jack's salary, how much more does Jill earn than Jack (in percentage terms)?

   _____

   _____

   _____

4. If the population of a city increases by 4% one year and by 6% the next, does it follow that the population has increased by 10% over the two-year period? Explain.

   _____

   _____

   _____

5. If 60% of the students in your class are women and 50% of the students have brown hair, does it follow that (60%)(50%) = 30% of the students in your class are women with brown hair? Explain.

   _____

   _____

   _____

Unit 3A Test 2 *(continued)*

6. A political candidate knows that 40% of the voters are Republicans and 25% of the remaining voters support budget cuts. If all of the Republicans and budget cut supporters vote for the candidate, does it follow that he will get at least 50% of the vote? Explain.

_____

_____

_____

7. If 473 men at a conference comprise 55% of all people at the conference, how many people are at the conference?

_____

_____

_____

8. The after-tax price of a bookcase is $85.20. If an 8% sales tax was charged, what was the pre-tax price of the bookcase?

_____

_____

_____

9. Given that a S. Irish punt is worth $1.53, how much larger is a punt than a dollar? Answer in percentage terms.

_____

_____

_____

10. The population of a town increased from 24,730 to 72,210 in one decade. What was the percent change of the population?

_____

_____

_____

Unit 3A Test 3

Name:_____

Date:_____

Choose the correct answer to each problem.

1. Which of the following statements illustrates the use of a percentage to compare two quantities?

   (a) So far, we have collected only 12% of the money we need.
   (b) This year, the number of students increased by 23%.
   (c) Crunchy O's have 35% more fiber than the leading brand.
   (d) The price of scanners has decreased by 28% over the last year.

2. The new CD burner costs 12% less at the new electronics store. This statement shows the use of which of the following concepts?

   (a) Absolute change   (b) Absolute difference
   (c) Relative change   (d) Relative difference

3. If Romeo earns 108% of Juliet's salary, how much more does Romeo earn than Juliet (in percentage terms)?

   (a) 8%   (b) 64%   (c) 80%   (d) 108%

4. Suppose your bank account was worth $5000 at the beginning of last year. If your balance increased by 2% during the first half of the year and by 3% during the second half, what was your balance at the end of the year?

   (a) $5250.00   (b) $5253.00   (c) $5125.75   (d) $7500.00

5. If 50% of the students in your class are men and 20% of the students have blond hair, which of the following describes the percentage of students in your class who are men with blond hair?

   (a) 50% + 20% = 70%
   (b) (50%)(20%) = 10%
   (c) 50% − 20% = 30%
   (d) The percentage cannot be determined from the given information.

6. A political candidate knows that 40% of the voters are Democrats and 25% of the remaining voters are union members. If all of the Democrats and union members vote for the candidate, what is the minimum possible percentage of voters who will vote for him?

   (a) 40%   (b) 50%   (c) 55%   (d) 65%

7. If 462 artists at a conference comprise 55% of all people at the conference, how many people are at the conference?

   (a) 254   (b) 820   (c) 840   (d) 1190

8. The after-tax price of a bicycle is $237.42. If a 7% sales tax was charged, what was the pre-tax price of the bicycle?

   (a) $220.80   (b) $221.89   (c) $226.95   (d) $254.04

Unit 3A Test 3 *(continued)*

9. Given that an English pound is worth $1.64, how much larger is a pound than a dollar? Answer in percentage terms.

    (a) 56%   **(b)** 61%   **(c)** 64%   **(d)** 164%

10. The population of a town increased 60,450 to 195,610 in one decade. What was the percent change of the population?

    (a) 69%   **(b)** 24%   **(c)** 224%   **(d)** 324%

Unit 3A Test 4

Name:_____

Date:_____

Choose the correct answer to each problem.

1. Which of the following statements illustrates the use of a percentage to describe a fraction?

   (a) So far, we have collected only 12% of the money we need.
   (b) This year, the number of students increased by 23%.
   (c) Crunchy O's have 35% more fiber than the leading brand.
   (d) The price of scanners has decreased by 28% over the last year.

2. This year, the price of a Gizmo Supreme increased by $6.35. This statement shows the use of which of the following concepts?

   (a) Absolute change   (b) Absolute difference   (c) Relative change   (d) Relative difference

3. If Alice earns 156% of Wally's salary, how much more does Alice earn than Wally (in percentage terms)?

   (a) 6%   (b) 50%   (c) 56%   (d) 156%

4. Suppose that the population of a city was 1000 at the beginning of one year. If the population increased by 10% that year and by 7% the following year, what was the population at the end of the two years?

   (a) 1017   (b) 1170   (c) 1177   (d) 1287

5. If 40% of the students in your class are women and 50% of the women have brown hair, which of the following describes the percentage of the students in your class who are women with brown hair?

   (a) (40%)(50%) = 20%
   (b) 50% − 40% = 10%
   (c) 40% + 50% = 90%
   (d) The percentage women cannot be determined from the given information.

6. A political candidate knows that 51% of the voters are Republicans and 39% of the voters support budget cuts. If all of the Republicans and budget cut supporters vote for the candidate, what is the minimum possible percentage of voters who will vote for her?

   (a) 51%   (b) 39%   (c) 45%   (d) 90%

7. If 578 scientists at a conference comprise 85% of all people at the conference, how many people are at the conference?

   (a) 491   (b) 630   (c) 650   (d) 680

8. The after-tax price of a guitar is $340.03. If a 4% sales tax was charged, what was the pre-tax price of the guitar?

   (a) $318.96   (b) $326.43   (c) $326.95   (d) $353.63

Name:_____

9. Given that a U.S. dollar is worth 1.36 Canadian dollars, how much larger is a U.S. dollar than a Canadian dollar? Answer in percentage terms.

   (a) 36%   **(b)** 43%   **(c)** 74%   **(d)** 136%

10. The population of a town increased from 35,320 to 82,650 in one decade. What was the percent change of the population?

    (a) 57%   **(b)** 134%   **(c)** 234%   **(d)** 334%

Unit 3B Test 1

Name:_____

Date:_____

1. Convert 2×10^9 from scientific notation to ordinary notation and write its name.

_____

_____

_____

2. Convert 0.00059 to scientific notation.

_____

_____

_____

3. Suppose that you add $10^{67} + 10^{37}$. What, approximately, is the answer. Explain.

_____

_____

_____

4. Calculate $(2.5 \times 10^6) \times (7.2 \times 10^9)$. Show your work clearly. Express the final answer in scientific notation.

_____

_____

_____

5. Calculate $(5.11 \times 10^{12}) \div (1.4 \times 10^5)$ without using a calculator. Show your work clearly. Express the final answer in scientific notation.

_____

_____

_____

6. The distance from the Earth to the Sun is about 1.5×10^8 km, while the distance from the Earth to the moon is about 3.8×10^5 km. If a scale model of the solar system is constructed so that the distance from the Earth to the Sun is 100 meters, what will be the distance from the Earth to the moon?

_____

_____

_____

7. Assuming you can count 1 dollar bill per second, how many days would it take to count 400,000 dollar bills?

_____

_____

_____

8. If one inch on a map represents 50 miles, what is the scale ratio?

_____

_____

_____

9. If a stack of $5 bills is worth $75 billion, what is the height of the stack in kilometers? Assume each bill is 0.2 millimeters thick.

_____

_____

_____

10. Bryan is 63 years old. Find his age in seconds. State your answer in scientific notation. You may round your answer by writing only two digits (as in 3.2×10^5).

_____

_____

_____

Unit 3B Test 2

1. Convert 8×10^9 from scientific notation to ordinary notation and write its name.

   _____

   _____

   _____

2. Convert 0.0000034 to scientific notation.

   _____

   _____

   _____

3. Suppose that you subtract $10^{34} - 10^{22}$. What, approximately, is the answer? Explain.

   _____

   _____

   _____

4. Calculate $(5.5 \times 10^7) \times (4.2 \times 10^4)$. Show your work clearly. Express the final answer in scientific notation.

   _____

   _____

   _____

5. Calculate $(7.15 \times 10^{11}) \div (2.6 \times 10^4)$ without using a calculator. Show your work clearly. Express the final answer in scientific notation.

   _____

   _____

   _____

6. How many years would it take a worker making $12.00 per hour to earn $48,000,000? Assume she works 260 8-hour days per year.

   _____

   _____

   _____

Unit 3B Test 2 *(continued)*

7. The diameter of the moon is about 1.1×10^7 feet and the diameter of Uranus is about 1.7×10^8 feet. If a scale model of the solar system is constructed so that the diameter of the moon is 3.5 feet, what will be the diameter of Uranus?

_____

_____

_____

8. If one inch on a map represents 120 miles, what is the scale ratio?

_____

_____

_____

9. If a stack of $20 bills is worth $120 billion, what is the height of the stack in kilometers? Assume each bill is 0.2 millimeters thick.

_____

_____

_____

10. Susan is 38 years old. Find her age in seconds. State your answer in scientific notation. You may round your answer by writing only two digits (as in 3.2×10^5).

_____

_____

_____

Unit 3B Test 3

Name:_____

Date:_____

Choose the correct answer to each problem.

1. Which of the following is equal to 5×10^{-4}?

   (a) five thousandths
   (c) five hundred-thousandths

   (b) five ten-thousandths
   (d) five millionths

2. Convert 78,000,000 to scientific notation.

   (a) 78×10^6
   (b) 7.8×10^6
   (c) 7.8×10^7
   (d) 7.8×10^8

3. Suppose that you add $10^{62} + 10^{19}$. What, approximately, is the answer?

   (a) 10^{19}
   (b) 10^{62}
   (c) 10^{81}
   (d) 10^{1178}

4. Which of the following is equal to $(9.4 \times 10^9) \times (2.5 \times 10^4)$?

   (a) 2.35×10^{13}
   (b) 2.35×10^{14}
   (c) 2.35×10^{15}
   (d) 2.35×10^{36}

5. Calculate $(9.87 \times 10^{12}) \div (4.2 \times 10^4)$.

   (a) 2.35×10^3
   (b) 2.35×10^6
   (c) 2.35×10^7
   (d) 2.35×10^8

6. Which is the largest number?

   (a) 1.5 billion
   (b) 1650 million
   (c) 2.3×10^9
   (d) 2.7×10^{-11}

7. How many years would it take a worker making $16.00 per hour to earn $8,000,000, assuming she works 260 8-hour days per year?

   (a) 57 years
   (b) 240 years
   (c) 80 years
   (d) 2740 years

8. If one centimeter on a map represents 280 kilometers, what is the scale ratio?

   (a) 1 to 2.8×10^4
   (b) 1 to 2.8×10^5
   (c) 1 to 2.8×10^6
   (d) 1 to 2.8×10^7

9. If a stack of $10 bills is worth $90 billion, what is the height of the stack in kilometers? Assume each bill is 0.2 millimeters thick.

   (a) 1800 km
   (b) 4500 km
   (c) 18,000 km
   (d) 45,000 km

10. Monique is 43 years old. Which of the following gives her approximate age in seconds?

    (a) 2.7×10^7 seconds
    (c) 1.4×10^9 seconds

    (b) 1.6×10^8 seconds
    (d) 2.7×10^{10} seconds

Unit 3B Test 4

Choose the correct answer to each problem.

1. Which of the following is equal to 3×10^{-6}?

   (a) three thousandths
   (c) three hundred-thousandths

   (b) three ten-thousandths
   (d) three millionths

2. Convert 42,000,000 to scientific notation.

   (a) 4.2×10^6
   (b) 4.2×10^7
   (c) 4.2×10^8
   (d) 42×10^6

3. Suppose that you subtract $10^{43} - 10^{31}$. What, approximately, is the answer?

   (a) -10^{31}
   (b) 10^{12}
   (c) 10^{31}
   (d) 10^{43}

4. Which of the following is equal to $(7.5 \times 10^3) \times (8.2 \times 10^6)$?

   (a) 6.15×10^8
   (b) 6.15×10^9
   (c) 6.15×10^{10}
   (d) 6.15×10^{27}

5. Calculate $(6.3 \times 10^9) \div (3.6 \times 10^3)$.

   (a) 1.75×10^3
   (b) 1.75×10^6
   (c) 1.75×10^7
   (d) 1.75×10^8

6. Which is the largest number?

   (a) 2.9 billion
   (b) 3021 million
   (c) 3.1×10^9
   (d) 8.2×10^{-11}

7. In 2005, Bill Gates donated \$3,300,000,000 to charity. Assuming you could give \$10.00 per day, 365 days per year, how many years would it take you to donate this amount?

   (a) 1.3×10^5 years
   (b) 3.8×10^4 years
   (c) 9.0×10^5 years
   (d) 2.5×10^3 years

8. If one centimeter on a map represents 67 kilometers, what is the scale ratio?

   (a) 1 to 6.7×10^4
   (b) 1 to 6.7×10^5
   (c) 1 to 6.7×10^6
   (d) 1 to 6.7×10^7

9. If a stack of \$5 bills is worth \$175 billion, what is the height of the stack in kilometers? Assume each bill is 0.2 millimeters thick.

   (a) 1750 km
   (b) 7000 km
   (c) 17,500 km
   (d) 35,000 km

10. Herb is 56 years old. Which of the following gives his approximate age in seconds?

   (a) 3.0×10^7 seconds
   (c) 3.0×10^9 seconds

   (b) 1.8×10^8 seconds
   (d) 1.8×10^9 seconds

Unit 3C Test 1

1. Give the meaning of accuracy, and give an example in which a number is very accurate but not very precise.

   _____

   _____

   _____

2. Give the meaning of systematic error, and give an example of a systematic error.

   _____

   _____

   _____

3. The actual age of a tree is known to be 105 years old. Using scientific methods, a biologist estimates the age of the tree to be 98 years old. Find the absolute error and the relative error of the biologist's measurement.

   _____

   _____

   _____

4. Two students measured the width of a swimming pool whose actual width is 18.500 meters. Bobby reported the width as 18.329 meters, while Carolyn reported the width as 18.6 meters. Which student reported the width more accurately? Which student reported the width more precisely?

   _____

   _____

   _____

5. Round the number 65,152.07926 to the nearest thousandth, tenth, ten, and hundred.

   _____

   _____

   _____

Unit 3C Test 1 (continued)

Name:_____

6. The capacity of a bottle is given as 4.5690 liters. State the number of significant digits and the implied precision in this number.

_____

_____

_____

7. Write the number 78,000,000 in scientific notation with four significant digits.

_____

_____

_____

8. Find the sum: 83.73652 + 341.02. Assume that each given number is measured to the indicated precision, and use the rounding rule for addition and subtraction.

_____

_____

_____

9. Find the product: $(4.361 \times 10^5) \times (6.5 \times 10^4)$. Assume that each given number is measured to the indicated precision, and use the rounding rule for multiplication and division.

_____

_____

_____

10. Divide the area 342.478 square meters by the length 12.7 meters. Assume that each given number is measured to the indicated precision, and use the rounding rule for multiplication and division.

_____

_____

_____

Unit 3C Test 2

1. Give the meaning of precision, and give an example in which a number is very precise but not very accurate.

   _____

   _____

   _____

2. Give the meaning of random error, and give an example of a random error.

   _____

   _____

   _____

3. A painting is known to be 525 years old. Using carbon dating, a scientist estimates that the painting is 610 years old. Find the absolute error and the relative error of the scientist's measurement of the age of the painting.

   _____

   _____

   _____

4. Two students measured the height of a building whose actual height is 21.500 meters. Evelyn reported the height as 21.4 meters, while Priscilla reported the height as 22.375 meters. Which student reported the height more accurately? Which student reported the height more precisely?

   _____

   _____

   _____

5. Round the number 32,837.75134 to the nearest thousandth, tenth, ten, and hundred.

   _____

   _____

   _____

Unit 3C Test 2 *(continued)*

6. The capacity of an aquarium is given as 24.75 gallons. State the number of significant digits and the implied precision in this number.

_____

_____

_____

7. Write the number 3,200,000 in scientific notation with five significant digits.

_____

_____

_____

8. Find the sum: 16.47943 + 2335.3. Assume that each given number is measured to the indicated precision, and use the rounding rule for addition and subtraction.

_____

_____

_____

9. Find the product: $(8.02 \times 10^3) \times (6.3153 \times 10^7)$. Assume that each given number is measured to the indicated precision, and use the rounding rule for multiplication and division.

_____

_____

_____

10. Divide the area 8.7 square meters by the length 3.174 meters. Assume that each given number is measured to the indicated precision, and use the rounding rule for multiplication and division.

_____

_____

_____

Unit 3C Test 3

Choose the correct answer to each problem.

1. On a job application, Doris gave her age as 32 years. Her actual age at the time was about 27. How would you describe the way she reported her age?

    (a) Accurate, but not precise
    (c) Both accurate and precise

    (b) Precise, but not accurate
    (d) Neither accurate nor precise

2. Which of the following is an example of a random error?

    (a) In a written survey, people sometimes make errors in filling out the form.
    (b) A telephone survey will not accurately reflect the opinions of people who do not have telephones.
    (c) Measurements are taken using an inaccurate scale that always reports a smaller weight than the correct weight.
    (d) At a clinic, people are wearing shoes when their heights are measured.

3. The actual height of a building is 441 feet. A student reports the height to be 398 feet. Find the relative error of the student's measurement.

    (a) –22%   (b) –1000%   (c) –11.1%   (d) –10.0%

4. Two students measured the width of a table whose actual width is 4.500 feet. Arnie reported the width as 4.7 feet, while Bernie reported the width as 4.932 feet. Which student reported the width more accurately? Which student reported the width more precisely?

    (a) Arnie was more accurate and more precise.
    (b) Bernie was more accurate and more precise.
    (c) Arnie was more accurate, and Bernie was more precise.
    (d) Bernie was more accurate, and Arnie was more precise.

5. Round the number 73,162.47 to the nearest hundred.

    (a) 73,100   (b) 73,160   (c) 73,200   (d) 73,000

6. The height of a mountain is given as 4800 feet. State the number of significant digits and the implied precision in this number.

    (a) 4 significant digits; nearest 100 feet
    (c) 2 significant digits; nearest 100 feet

    (b) 4 significant digits; nearest 1 foot
    (d) 2 significant digits; nearest 1 foot

7. Write the number 57,000,000 in scientific notation with three significant digits.

    (a) 5.70×10^{7} (b) 5.700×10^{5} (c) 45.70×10^{6} (d) 5.700×10^{6}

8. Find the sum: 67.4321 + 67,843.8. Assume that each given number is measured to the indicated precision, and use the rounding rule for addition and subtraction.

    (a) 67,911   (b) 67,911.2   (c) 67,911.23   (d) 67,911.232

9. Find the product: $(3.4 \times 10^7) \times (9.321 \times 10^2)$. Assume that each given number is measured to the indicated precision, and use the rounding rule for multiplication and division.

   (a) 3.2×10^{10} **(b)** 3.17×10^{10} **(c)** 3.169×10^{10} **(d)** 3.1691×10^{10}

10. Divide the area 16 square meters by the length 6.481 meters. Assume that each given number is measured to the indicated precision, and use the rounding rule for multiplication and division.

   (a) 2 meters   **(b)** 2.5 meters   **(c)** 2.47 meters   **(d)** 2.469 meters

Unit 3C Test 4

Name:_____

Date:_____

Choose the correct answer to each problem.

1. A problem in a math book stated "1 mile = 1.6 km," while the actual conversion (to 4 decimal places) is 1 mile = 1.6093 km. How would you describe the way the conversion was given in the problem in the math book?

    (a) Accurate, but not precise
    (c) Both accurate and precise
    (b) Precise, but not accurate
    (d) Neither accurate nor precise

2. Which of the following is an example of a systematic error?

    (a) In a written survey, people sometimes make errors in filling out the form.
    (b) A man is measuring times with a stopwatch, but he occasionally stops the watch at the wrong instant.
    (c) A telephone survey will not accurately reflect the opinions of people who do not have telephones.
    (d) Because people may move or have multiple residences, the census may accidentally count some people twice (or not at all).

3. The actual age of a manuscript is known to be 950 years old. Using scientific methods, an expert estimates that the manuscript is 1000 years old. Find the relative error of his measurement.

    (a) 5.3%   **(b)** 5.0%   **(c)** −5.3%   **(d)** −5.0%

4. Two students measured the height of a statue whose actual height is 11.600 feet. Joyce reported the height as 11.843 feet, while Peter reported the height as 11.7 feet. Which student reported the height more accurately? Which student reported the height more precisely?

    (a) Joyce was more accurate and more precise.
    (b) Peter was more accurate and more precise.
    (c) Joyce was more accurate, and Peter was more precise.
    (d) Peter was more accurate, and Joyce was more precise.

5. Round the number 560,459.76 to the nearest hundred.

    (a) 600,000   **(b)** 560,000   **(c)** 560,460   **(d)** 560,500

6. The distance between two flagpoles is given as 1710.0 meters. State the number of significant digits and the implied precision in this number.

    (a) 3 significant digits; nearest 0.1 meter
    (c) 5 significant digits; nearest 0.1 meter
    (b) 3 significant digits; nearest 10 meters
    (d) 5 significant digits; nearest 10 meters

7. Write the number 63,000,000 in scientific notation with five significant digits.

    (a) 6.30000×10^{6} **(b)** $6.3\,000 \times 10^{6}$ **(c)** 6.30000×10^{7} **(d)** 6.3000×10^{7}

8. Find the sum: 5278.31232 + 26.12. Assume that each given number is measured to the indicated precision, and use the rounding rule for addition and subtraction.

    (a) 5304   **(b)** 5304.4   **(c)** 5304.43   **(d)** 5304.432

9. Find the product: $(4.06 \times 10^6) \times (2.333 \times 10^7)$. Assume that each given number is measured to the indicated precision, and use the rounding rule for multiplication and division.

    (a) 9.5×10^{13} (b) 9.47×10^{13} (c) 9.472×10^{13} (d) 9.4720×10^{13}

10. Divide the area 25.39 square meters by the length 8.26 meters. Assume that each given number is measured to the indicated precision, and use the rounding rule for multiplication and division.

    (a) 3 meters   (b) 3.1 meters   (c) 3.07 meters   (d) 3.074 meters

Unit 3D Test 1

1. Define *deflation*.

   _____

   _____

   _____

2. What is the purpose of the Consumer Price Index?

   _____

   _____

   _____

3. How often is the Consumer Price Index computed and reported?

   _____

   _____

   _____

The following table provides information about median incomes in four states for 2005-2006. Use this information to answer Questions 4–6.

2005–2006 Median Income

State	Income	Index
Alabama	$36,640	97.7
Alaska	$51,661	137.7
Arizona	$37,514	100.0
Arkansas	$29,019	77.4

Source: U.S. Census Bureau

4. Identify the reference value.

   _____

   _____

   _____

Unit 3D Test 1 *(continued)*

5. Given that the 2005–2006 median income for California was $42,791, find the income index for California using the reference value from Question 4.

_____

_____

_____

6. Calculate the income index for each state in the table using the median income from California as the reference value.

_____

_____

_____

7. Given that the Consumer Price Index was 148.2 in 2001 and 152.4 in 2002, find the inflation rate from 2001 to 2002.

_____

_____

_____

In Questions 8–10, use 40.5 as the Consumer Price Index in 1978 and 166.6 as its value in 2006.

8. What would be the price in 2006 of an item that cost $1.00 in 1978 ?

_____

_____

_____

9. What would be the equivalent price in 1978 of a pair of shoes that cost $119 in 2006?

_____

_____

_____

10. If a person earned $15,000 in 1978, how much did that person need to earn in 2006 to maintain the same standard of living?

_____

_____

_____

Unit 3D Test 2

Name:_____

Date:_____

1. What is the benefit of an index number?

   _____

   _____

   _____

2. What government agency computes and reports the Consumer Price Index?

   _____

   _____

   _____

3. What does the Consumer Price Index represent?

   _____

   _____

   _____

4. Define the *rate of inflation*.

   _____

   _____

   _____

5. The following table provides information about diesel fuel prices along the Gulf Coast for four consecutive weeks. Using the price of diesel for the week of 1/29/06 as the reference value, complete the table by calculating the price index for each week.

   Gulf Coast Retail Diesel Prices

Date	Price	Price Index
1/29/06	$1.500	
2/02/06	$1.472	
2/12/06	$1.472	
2/19/06	$1.428	

   Source: Energy Information Administration

Unit 3D Test 2 *(continued)*

6. Given that the Consumer Price Index was 156.9 in 2003 and 160.5 in 2004, find the inflation rate from 2003 to 2004.

_____

_____

_____

In Questions 7–10, use 82.4 as the Consumer Price Index in 1987 and 172.8 as its value in 2007.

7. What would be the price in 2007 of an item that cost $1.00 in 1987?

_____

_____

_____

8. If a certain car cost $9000 in 1987, what would a similar car have cost in 2007?

_____

_____

_____

9. What would be the equivalent price in 1987 of a pair of shoes that cost $129 in 2007?

_____

_____

_____

10. If a person earned $22,000 in 1987, how much did that person need to earn in 2007 to maintain the same standard of living?

_____

_____

_____

Unit 3D Test 3

Choose the correct answer to each problem.

1. In a study of how college education costs have changed since 1980, each year's average cost of tuition is expressed as a percentage of the 1980 cost. Which term refers to the 1980 cost?

    (a) Reference value (b) Index number (c) Rate of inflation (d) Price index

2. What is the primary purpose of index numbers?

    (a) To predict future prices (b) To determine interest rates
    (c) To measure the strength of the economy (d) To facilitate comparisons

3. How often is the Consumer Price Index computed and reported?

    (a) Daily (b) Weekly (c) Monthly (d) Quarterly

4. Which quantity refers to the relative change in the Consumer Price Index from one year to the next?

    (a) Reference value (b) Index number (c) Rate of inflation (d) Price index

5. Which price index measures the price that manufacturers pay for the goods they purchase?

    (a) Consumer Price Index (b) Producer Price Index
    (c) Consumer Confidence Index (d) Health Care Quality Index

The following table provides information about diesel fuel prices in the U.S. by region. Use this information to answer Questions 6 and 7.

Retail Diesel Prices (per gallon, week of 2/19/06)

Region	Price	Price Index
East Coast	$1.499	100.0
Midwest	$1.460	97.4
Gulf Coast	$1.428	
Rocky Mountain	$1.517	101.2

Source: U.S. Census Bureau

6. Calculate the price index for the Gulf Coast to complete the table.

    (a) 95.3 (b) 97.8 (c) 100.0 (d) 105.0

7. Given that the retail diesel price for the West Coast during the same week is $1.567, calculate the price index for the Gulf Coast using the West Coast price as the reference value.

    (a) 91.1 (b) 95.7 (c) 104.5 (d) 109.7

Unit 3D Test 3 *(continued)*

8. Given that the Consumer Price Index was 40.5 in 1978 and 172.8 in 2007, find the price in 2007 dollars of an item that cost $100 in 1978.

    (a) $23   (b) $327   (c) $427   (d) $13,320

9. Given that the Consumer Price Index was 152.4 in 2002 and 156.9 in 2003, find the inflation rate from 2002 to 2003.

    (a) 2.87%   (b) 2.95%   (c) 3.13%   (d) 4.50%

10. The Consumer Price Index was 152.4 in 2002 and 172.8 in 2007. If a person earned $31,500 in 2002, how much did he need to earn in 2007 to maintain the same standard of living?

    (a) $27,781   (b) $35,717   (c) $37,103   (d) $39,798

Unit 3D Test 4

Choose the correct answer to each problem.

1. Which quantity provides a simple way to compare measurements made at different times or in different places?

   (a) Reference value
   (c) Rate of inflation
   (b) Index number
   (d) Price of gasoline

2. Which term refers to the rise of prices and wages over time?

   (a) Consumer Price Index
   (c) Rate of inflation
   (b) Inflation
   (d) Adjusted value

3. Who computes and reports the Consumer Price Index?

   (a) U.S. Bureau of the Economic Analysis
   (c) Wall Street Journal
   (b) New York Stock Exchange
   (d) U.S. Bureau of Labor Statistics

4. Which price index measures consumer attitudes so that businesses can gauge whether people are likely to be spending or saving?

   (a) Consumer Price Index
   (c) Consumer Confidence Index
   (b) Producer Price Index
   (d) Health Care Quality Index

5. Which price index represents an average of prices in a sample of more than 60,000 goods, services, and housing costs?

   (a) Consumer Price Index
   (c) Consumer Confidence Index
   (b) Producer Price Index
   (d) Health Care Quality Index

The following table provides information about median incomes in four states for 2005-2006. Use this information to answer Questions 6-8.

2005–2006 Median Income

State	Income	Index
Alabama	$36,640	117.6
Arkansas	$29,019	93.2
Louisiana	$32,566	104.5
Mississippi	$31,152	100.0

Source: U.S. Census Bureau

6. Identify the reference value.

   (a) $36,640   **(b)** $29,019   **(c)** $32,566   **(d)** $31,152

Unit 3D Test 4 (continued)

Name:_____

7. Given that the 2005–2006 median income for Tennessee was $35,690, find the income index for Tennessee using the reference value from Question 6.

   (a) 87.3   (b) 97.4   (c) 114.6   (d) 123.0

8. Calculate the income index for Louisiana using the median income from Tennessee as the reference value.

   (a) 81.3   (b) 91.2   (c) 97.4   (d) 109.6

9. Given that the Consumer Price Index was 144.5 in 2000 and 148.2 in 2001, find the inflation rate from 2000 to 2001.

   (a) 1.89%   (b) 2.49%   (c) 2.56%   (d) 3.70%

10. The Consumer Price Index was 130.7 in 1997 and 172.8 in 2007. If a person earned $20,500 in 1997, how much did he need to earn in 2000 to maintain the same standard of living?

   (a) $15,505   (b) $18,909   (c) $27,103   (d) $33,053

Unit 3E Test 1

Use the information below for the two questions which follow.

A research scientist is testing his theory that drinking coffee increases a person's likelihood to be violent. He collects the information in the table.

		Violent Yes	Violent No
Coffee Drinker	Yes	156	94
	No	17	90

1. What percentage of the 250 coffee drinkers are violent? What percentage of the 107 people who do not drink coffee are violent?

_____

_____

_____

2. Based on the results of the study, the scientist reports that people who drink coffee are much more likely to be violent than people who do not drink coffee. Does the data support this claim? Explain.

_____

_____

_____

Use the information below for the four questions which follow.

The 366 people in the study about the correlation between coffee and violence can be split into two groups, convicted felons and non-felons. The results break down as indicated in the following table.

		Violent Felon Yes	Violent Felon No	Violent Non-felon Yes	Violent Non-felon No
Coffee Drinker	Yes	139	11	5	95
	No	15	1	6	94

3. For felons, what percentage of the 250 felon coffee drinkers are non-violent, and what percentage of the 16 felon non-coffee drinkers are non-violent?

_____

_____

_____

4. For non-felons, what percentage of the 100 coffee drinkers are violent, and what percentage of the 100 non-coffee drinkers are violent?

_____

_____

_____

5. Do coffee drinkers or non-coffee drinkers have the higher rate of violence within each category? Do you think that this is sufficient evidence to make a conclusion about a correlation between coffee and violence? Explain.

_____

_____

_____

6. Consider the results from each category, felon and non-felon, as well as the results when the categories are combined. What design flaw in the study caused Simpson's paradox to occur?

_____

_____

_____

Use the information below for the three questions which follow.

Suppose that a sobriety test is 95% accurate (it will correctly detect 95% of the people who are legally intoxicated and it will correctly identify 95% of the people who are within the legal blood alcohol limit). Each of 1000 drivers pulled over by law enforcement officers for dangerous driving last month was required to take the sobriety test. The test identified 100 drivers as being legally intoxicated, when, in fact, only 75 were legally intoxicated. When this sobriety test indicates that a driver is legally intoxicated, the officers administer other tests to be more certain of intoxication before arresting the driver, but if this sobriety test indicates that the driver's blood alcohol is within the legal limit, no further tests are given. The data are given in the table.

	Legally intoxicated	Within the limit	Total
Test identifies driver as legally intoxicated	74	26	100
Test identifies driver as within the legal limit	1	899	900
Total	75	925	1000

7. What percentage of legally intoxicated drivers were **not** identified by the sobriety test?

_____

_____

_____

8. What percentage of drivers who were **not** legally intoxicated were falsely identified as being legally intoxicated?

_____

_____

_____

9. What percentage of drivers identified as legally intoxicated by the test were actually within the legal blood alcohol limit?

_____

_____

_____

10. Two candidates for mayor of a large city differ in their accounts of the incumbent's record on reducing crime. The incumbent claims that during his term violent crime has decreased, citing average annual homicide rates of 2.9 per 10,000 during the previous mayor's administration and 2.5 per 10,000 during his own administration. The challenger claims that violent crimes have actually increased, citing an average of 161 homicides per year during the previous mayor's administration and 175 homicides per year during the present administration. Explain how both candidates can be right.

_____

_____

_____

Unit 3E Test 2

Use the information below for the two questions which follow.

Some research scientists have gathered data that suggests having an abortion increases a woman's risk of breast cancer. A doctor conducts her own study of 430 women. The following table shows the results of her survey.

		Breast Cancer	
		Yes	No
Abortion	Yes	11	219
	No	11	189

1. What percentage of the 230 women who have had an abortion have breast cancer? What percentage of the 200 women who have **not** had an abortion do **not** have breast cancer?

_____

_____

_____

2. Based on the results of the study, the doctor reports that having an abortion does not increase the risk of breast cancer and may actually reduce the risk of breast cancer. Do these data support this claim? Explain.

_____

_____

_____

Use the information below for the four questions which follow.

The 425 women in the study about the correlation between abortion and breast cancer were split into two groups according to age, those under 40 and those 40 or older. The results break down as indicated in the following table.

		Breast Cancer			
		Under 40		40 or older	
		Yes	No	Yes	No
Abortion	Yes	2	173	2	48
	No	1	99	3	97

Unit 3E Test 2 *(continued)*

3. For women under 40, what percentage of the 175 women who have had an abortion do **not** have breast cancer, and what percentage of the 100 women who have **not** had an abortion have breast cancer?

_____

_____

_____

4. For women 40 or older, what percentage of the 50 women who have had an abortion have breast cancer, and what percentage of the 100 women who have **not** had an abortion have breast cancer?

_____

_____

_____

5. Which group has the higher rate of breast cancer within each age category? Do you think that this is sufficient evidence to make a conclusion about the alleged correlation? Explain.

_____

_____

_____

6. Consider the results from each age group as well as the results when the age groups are combined. What design flaw in the study caused Simpson's paradox to occur?

_____

_____

_____

Use the information below for the three questions which follow.

Suppose that a pregnancy test is 89% accurate (it will correctly detect 89% of the women who are pregnant and it will correctly identify 89% of the women who are not pregnant). Of 1200 women who used the test, 250 were identified as pregnant while only 200 were actually pregnant. The data is given in the table.

	Pregnant	Not pregnant	Total
Test indicates pregnant	182	68	250
Test indicates not pregnant	18	932	950
Total	200	1000	1200

Unit 3E Test 2 *(continued)*

7. What percentage of pregnant women were **not** identified as pregnant by the test?

_____

_____

_____

8. What percentage of women who were **not** pregnant was falsely identified as being pregnant?

_____

_____

_____

9. What percentage of women **not** identified as pregnant by the test was **not** pregnant?

_____

_____

_____

10. Two candidates for mayor of a large city differ in their accounts of the incumbent's record on job growth. The incumbent claims that during his term the job market has improved, citing a drop in the city's unemployment rate from 2.8% to 1.7%. The challenger claims that the job situation has actually deteriorated, citing that over 50,000 jobs were lost and not replaced during the incumbent's administration. Explain how both candidates can be right.

_____

_____

_____

Unit 3E Test 3

Choose the correct answer to each problem.

Use the information below for the two questions which follow.

A television producer tested her theory that watching her new television program improves a child's reading ability. She designed a reading test and gave it to 500 children. She collected the information in the table.

		Test	
		Passed	Failed
Watches the program	Yes	163	87
	No	46	204

1. What percentage of the 250 children who watch the program failed the test, and what percentage of the 250 children who do not watch the program passed the test?

   (a) 34.8% and 34.8%, respectively
   (c) 34.8% and 81.6%, respectively
   (b) 34.8% and 18.4%, respectively
   (d) 81.6 % and 34.8%, respectively

2. Which of the following claims is best supported by the data in the table?

   (a) The program has no effect on a child's reading ability.
   (b) The program improves a child's reading ability.
   (c) The program hinders a child's reading ability.
   (d) The program develops a child's sense of community.

Use the information below for the four questions which follow.

The 500 children in the study about the correlation between watching a television program and reading ability can be split into two groups according to age. The results break down as indicated in the following table.

		Test			
		Age 5		Age 7	
		Passed	Failed	Passed	Failed
Watches the program	Yes	1	49	162	38
	No	5	195	41	9

3. For 5-year olds, what percentage of the 50 children who watch the program passed the test, and what percentage of the 200 children who do not watch the program passed the test?

   (a) 2% and 2.5%, respectively
   (c) 2.5% and 97.5%, respectively
   (b) 2% and 98%, respectively
   (d) 98% and 97.5%, respectively

4. For 7-year olds, what percentage of the 200 children who watch the program passed the test, and what percentage of the 50 children who do not watch the program passed the test?

   (a) 81% and 19%, respectively
   (c) 81% and 82%, respectively

   (b) 19% and 18%, respectively
   (d) 82% and 18%, respectively

5. Which of the following best describes the results?

   (a) Within each age group, children who watch the program read much better than children who do not watch the program.
   (b) Within each age group, children who do not watch the program read much better than children who watch the program.
   (c) Within each age group, children who watch the program do better on the test, but the difference is minor.
   (d) Within each age group, children who do not watch the program do better on the test, but the difference is minor.

6. Consider the results from each age group as well as the results with the age groups combined. Which of the following most likely caused Simpson's paradox to occur?

   (a) The children who watch the program do better on the reading test when 5-year olds and 7-year olds take the test in the same room, but the children who do not watch the program do better when the age groups are tested separately.
   (b) A different television program is actually responsible for the improved reading skills, but the reading test was not designed to distinguish between the effects of the two programs.
   (c) The children who watch the program are mostly 7-year olds, whose reading skills would be expected to be further developed, while the children who do not watch the program are mostly 5-year olds, whose reading skills would be less developed.
   (d) Test scores will vary for a child each time he takes a test. The results showing that children who watch the program did better in a mixed age group than when separated by age are due to the randomness in the variation of scores.

Use the information below for the three questions which follow.

Suppose that a colon cancer test is 97% accurate (it will correctly detect 97% of the patients who have colon cancer and it will correctly identify 97% of the patients who do not have colon cancer). Of 1500 patients who took the test, 79 tested positive for colon cancer while only 50 actually have colon cancer. The data is given in the table.

	Has cancer	Does not have cancer	Total
Test result is positive	49	30	79
Test result is negative	1	1420	1421
Total	50	1450	1500

7. What percentage of patients with colon cancer tested positive?

   (a) About 2%   (b) About 3%   (c) About 97%   (d) About 98%

8. What percentage of patients who do not have colon cancer tested positive?

    (a) About 2%   **(b)** About 3%   **(c)** About 38%   **(d)** About 97%

9. What percentage of patients who tested positive do not have colon cancer?

    (a) About 3%   **(b)** About 38%   **(c)** About 62%   **(d)** About 97%

10. Two candidates for governor of a state differ in their accounts of the state's economy during the incumbent's term. The incumbent claims that during his four-year term the economy has improved, citing a rise in the median household income from $33,000 to $34,500. The challenger claims that the economy has declined, citing that the buying power of families in the state has declined during the four years. Which of the following best explains how both candidates can be right?

    (a) Candidates always tell the truth by nature, so anything either candidate says is automatically true.
    (b) Though the median household income increased, prices increased by a greater percent, meaning that the greater income buys less goods and services.
    (c) The incumbent is referring to the economy within the state, while the challenger is referring to the national economy.
    (d) It is not possible for both candidates to be right; one of them is obviously lying.

Unit 3E Test 4

Choose the correct answer to each problem.

Use the information below for the two questions which follow.

An education specialist tested her theory that home schoolers do not learn mathematics as well as students taught in the traditional classroom setting. She designed a mathematics test and gave it to 800 children. She collected the information in the table.

	Test	
	Passed	Failed
Home school	176	224
Traditional	275	125

1. What percentage of the 400 home schoolers failed the test, and what percentage of the 400 traditional students passed the test?

   (a) About 56.0% and 68.8%, respectively
   (c) About 78.6% and 64.0%, respectively

   (b) About 39.0% and 61.0%, respectively
   (d) About 56.0% and 31.2%, respectively

2. Which of the following claims is best supported by the data in the table?

   (a) Home schoolers do better on mathematics tests than traditional students.
   (b) Home schoolers and traditional students do about the same on mathematics tests.
   (c) Traditional students do better on mathematics tests than home schoolers.
   (d) All students have a perfect understanding of mathematics.

Use the information below for the four questions which follow.

The 800 children in the study about the correlation between home schooling and learning mathematics can be split into two groups according to grade level. The results break down as indicated in the following table.

	Test			
	8th grade		12th grade	
	Passed	Failed	Passed	Failed
Home school	78	222	98	2
Traditional	25	75	287	13

3. For 8th graders, what percentage of the 300 home schoolers failed the test, and what percentage of the 100 traditional students passed the test?

   (a) About 75.7% and 24.3%, respectively
   (c) About 74.0 % and 25.0%, respectively

   (b) About 35.1% and 33.3%, respectively
   (d) About 19.5% and 6.3%, respectively

Unit 3E Test 4 (continued)

Name:_____

4. For 12th graders, what percentage of the 100 home schoolers passed the test, and what percentage of the 300 traditional students passed the test?

   (a) About 25.4% and 74.6%, respectively
   (b) About 98.0% and 95.7%, respectively
   (c) About 24.5% and 71.2%, respectively
   (d) About 34.1% and 65.9%, respectively

5. Which of the following best describes the results?

   (a) Within each grade level, home schoolers do much better in mathematics than traditional students.
   (b) Within each grade level, traditional students do much better in mathematics than home schoolers.
   (c) Within each grade level, home schoolers do better on the test, but the difference is minor.
   (d) Within each grade level, traditional students do better on the test, but the difference is minor.

6. Consider the results from each grade level as well as the results with the grades combined. Which of the following most likely caused Simpson's paradox to occur?

   (a) Home schoolers do better on math tests when 8th graders and 12th graders take the tests in separate rooms, but traditional students do better when they are in a room with both 8th graders and 12th graders.
   (b) A new mathematics curriculum is responsible for the dramatically higher test scores among traditional students. If home schoolers used this curriculum, they would learn mathematics just as well.
   (c) Test scores will vary for a child each time he takes a test. The results showing that home schoolers did better when separated by grade level are due to the randomness in the variation of scores.
   (d) The group of home schoolers is comprised of mostly 8th graders, while the group of traditional students is mostly 12th graders, who would be expected to do better on the test than 8th graders.

Use the information below for the three questions which follow.

Suppose that a pregnancy test is 95% accurate (it will correctly detect 95% of the women who are pregnant and it will correctly identify 95% of the women who are not pregnant). Of 750 women who took the test, 129 tested positive for pregnancy while only 115 are actually pregnant. The data are given in the table.

	Pregnant	Not pregnant	Total
Test result is positive	111	18	129
Test result is negative	4	617	621
Total	115	635	750

7. What percentage of non-pregnant women tested negative?

   (a) About 0.6%   (b) About 97%   (c) About 14.0%   (d) About 95%

8. What percentage of women who are not pregnant tested positive?

   (a) About 2.8%   (b) About 5.0%   (c) About 14.0%   (d) About 95%

Unit 3E Test 4 *(continued)*

9. What percentage of women who tested positive are not pregnant?

    (a) About 2.8%   **(b)** About 5.0%   **(c)** About 14.0%   **(d)** About 95%

10. Two candidates for governor of a state differ in their claims on the quality of education over the incumbent's term. The incumbent claims that per capita spending on education has increased during his term, so the quality of education has improved. The challenger claims that the per student spending on education has decreased during the incumbent's term. Which of the following best explains their claims?

    (a) Both candidates have made up their claims in order to win the election, because all politicians are liars.

    (b) Only the incumbent's claim is correct. If spending increases per capita, it must increase per student.

    (c) Both claims may be correct. While the per capita spending has increased, the number of students may have increased much more than the overall population. Thus, per student spending would have decreased.

    (d) Only one of the claims can be correct. One of the candidates must be lying.

Unit 4A Test 1

Name:_____

Date:_____

1. State an advantage of evaluating your monthly budget.

   _____

   _____

   _____

2. Jason is addicted to video games. With tax, he usually spends $26 every month to buy games. He also subscribes to a video game magazine which costs him $40, twice per year. How much is Jason spending on video games and magazines annually?

   _____

   _____

   _____

3. Elise maintains an average monthly balance on her credit card of about $980. Her credit card company charges 24% annual interest rate, which it bills at a rate of 2% per month. How much is she spending on credit card interest per year?

   _____

   _____

   _____

4. What does it mean to prorate an expense monthly?

   _____

   _____

   _____

Unit 4A Test 1 (continued)

Name:_____

5. The following table shows Brad's bills for electricity for an entire year. Compute a monthly amount for his budget.

January	February	March	April	May	June
$230	$310	$210	$160	$120	$130
July	August	September	October	November	December
$140	$110	$100	$180	$200	$220

_____

_____

_____

6. You drive an average of 500 miles per week in a car that gets 16 miles per gallon. With gasoline priced at $3 per gallon, how much would you save if you had a car that got 32 miles per gallon?

_____

_____

_____

7. Nicole buys 2 CDs every week, and each CD costs $5. She also spends $135 per month for food. On an annual basis, the first set of expenses is _____ % of the second expense.

_____

_____

_____

8. Fred pays $7500 for each of two semesters to attend a local college. He also pays an additional $350 for books each semester. Prorate the given expenses to find the monthly cost.

_____

_____

_____

Unit 4A Test 2

1. List the four basic steps in making a budget.

_____

_____

_____

2. Valerie is addicted to country-western music and buys one CD every week. With tax, each CD costs her about $9. She also attends two concerts each year, the admission charge for each concert amounting to $40. How much is Valerie spending per year on music entertainment?

_____

_____

_____

3. Debbie maintains an average monthly balance on her credit card of about $1300. Her credit card company charges 24% annual interest rate, which it bills at a rate of 2% per month. How much is she spending on credit card interest per year?

_____

_____

_____

4. What is positive cash flow?

_____

_____

_____

Unit 4A Test 2 *(continued)*

5. The following table shows Stan's bills for electricity for an entire year. Compute a monthly amount for his budget.

January	February	March	April	May	June
$300	$310	$210	$160	$120	$130

July	August	September	October	November	December
$140	$90	$100	$180	$200	$220

_____

_____

_____

6. You drive an average of 600 miles per month in a car that gets 18 miles per gallon. With gasoline priced at $2.60 per gallon, how much would you save per month if you had a car that got 30 miles per gallon?

_____

_____

_____

7. Dale spends $48 every week for gasoline and spends $1200 per month on rent. On an annual basis, the first set of expenses is _____ % of the second set.

_____

_____

_____

8. Jeff pays $600 per month for rent, a semi-annual car insurance premium of $900 and an annual membership at his local golf course of $250. Prorate these expenses to find the monthly cost.

_____

_____

_____

Unit 4A Test 3

Name:_____

Date:_____

Choose the correct answer to each problem.

1. For the average person, which category of expense is the greatest?

   (a) Health care   (b) Housing   (c) Food   (d) Entertainment

2. Marshall is addicted to smoking. He smokes about two packages of cigarettes per week. With tax, each package costs him about $6. Twice each year, he purchases a box of cigars costing $50 per box, including tax. How much is Marshall spending on tobacco products per year?

   (a) $362   (b) $724   (c) $412   (d) $700

3. Rob maintains an average monthly balance on his credit card of about $1500. His credit card company charges 21% annul interest, which it bills at 1.75% per month. How much is Rob spending on credit card interest per year?

   (a) $3150   (b) $26.26   (c) $218.75   (d) $315.00

4. What is negative cash flow?

   (a) Negative cash flow occurs when income exceeds expenses over some fixed period of time.
   (b) Negative cash flow occurs when expenses exceed income over some fixed period of time.
   (c) Negative cash flow occurs when you have more sources of expense than sources of income.
   (d) Negative cash flow occurs when your largest bill exceeds your largest source of income.

5. The following table shows Michael's bills for electricity for an entire year. Compute a monthly amount for his budget.

January	February	March	April	May	June
$230	$340	$210	$160	$150	$130
July	August	September	October	November	December
$140	$110	$100	$180	$200	$220

   (a) $180.83   (b) $165.42   (c) $181.52   (d) $225.00

6. You drive an average of 750 miles per week in a car that gets 28 miles per gallon. With gasoline priced at $2.40 per gallon, what would be the difference in total weekly cost for gasoline if you start driving an SUV that gets 20 miles per gallon?

   (a) $25.71 less   (b) $9.82 more   (c) $360.00 more   (d) $25.71 more

7. Every day, Antonio buys 2 cans of soda, each costing $0.75 and spends $860 every six months for car insurance. On an annual basis, the first set of expenses is _____ % of the second set of expenses.

   (a) 3.8%   (b) 31.8%   (c) 15.9%   (d) 12.9%

8. Jim spends $35 per week for gasoline and has an oil change, which costs $27 every three months. Prorate these expenses to find the monthly cost.

   (a) $160.67   (b) $153.92   (c) $175.60   (d) $158.42

Unit 4A Test 4

Name:_____

Date:_____

Choose the correct answer to each problem.

1. For a person under 35, which category of expense would likely be the least?

   (a) Housing   **(b)** Food   **(c)** Donations to charity   **(d)** Transportation

2. Emily loves potato chips and buys a bag every 5 days. Each bag costs $2.50, including tax. Once each month, she also treats herself to dip, which costs $6, including tax. How much is Emily spending on these snacks per year?.

   (a) $254.50   **(b)** $252.00   **(c)** $202.00   **(d)** $620.50

3. John maintains an average monthly balance on his credit card of about $1800. His credit card company charges 18% annual interest, which it bills at 1.5% per month. How much is he spending on credit card interest per year?.

   (a) $226.38   **(b)** $3240.00   **(c)** $324.00   **(d)** $225.00

4. If your cash flow is negative, you should:

   (a) Earn more money and spend more money   **(b)** Spend more money
   (c) Decrease expenses   **(d)** Increase expenses and increase spending

5. The following table shows Rodger's bills for electricity for an entire year. Compute a monthly amount for his budget.

January	February	March	April	May	June
$320	$310	$210	$160	$120	$130
July	August	September	October	November	December
$140	$110	$100	$180	$200	$300

   (a) $183.50   **(b)** $190.00   **(c)** $270.00   **(d)** $195.74

6. You drive an average of 460 miles per week in a car that gets 28 miles per gallon. With gasoline priced at $2.18 per gallon, what would be the difference in total weekly cost for gasoline if you started riding a motorcycle that gets 84 miles per gallon?

   (a) $16.35 less   **(b)** $3.76 less   **(c)** $23.87 less   **(d)** $17.45 more

7. A salesman eats breakfast 5 days per week and spends about $6 for each meal. His phone bill averages $175 per month. On an annual basis, the first set of expenses is _____ % of the second set.

   (a) 59.5%   **(b)** 38.2%   **(c)** 74.3%   **(d)** 25.7%

Unit 4A Test 4 *(continued)*

8. Samantha makes a monthly contribution to the local animal shelter in the amount of $50 and pays a life insurance premium of $600 twice per year. Prorate these expenses to find the monthly cost.

   (a) $54.17   **(b)** $100.00   **(c)** $140.50   **(d)** $150.00

Unit 4B Test 1

1. Suppose that you invest $1800 in an account that earns simple interest at an APR of 6.3%. Determine the accumulated balance after 5 years.

_____

_____

_____

2. Suppose that you invest $25,000 in an account that earns interest at an APR of 3.4%, compounded annually. Determine the accumulated balance after 7 years.

_____

_____

_____

3. Suppose that you invest $175 in an account that earns interest at an APR of 5.6%, compounded quarterly. Determine the accumulated balance after 19 years?

_____

_____

_____

4. Suppose that you invest $5178 in an account that earns interest at an APR of 4.1%, compounded monthly. Determine the accumulated balance after 8 years.

_____

_____

_____

5. Suppose that your savings account earns interest at an APR of 2.8%, compounded quarterly. Determine the annual percentage yield (APY). State your answer to the nearest hundredth of a percent.

_____

_____

_____

Unit 4B Test 1 *(continued)*

6. Suppose that you invest $1384 in an account that earns interest at an APR of 6.7%, compounded continuously. Determine the accumulated balance after 5 years.

_____

_____

_____

7. Suppose that you invest $10,000 in an account with an APR of 3.9%, compounded continuously. Determine the annual percentage yield (APY). State your answer to the nearest hundredth of a percent.

_____

_____

_____

8. Bill invests $7100 in a savings account that compounds interest monthly at an APR of 4.7%. Ted invests $7300 in a savings account that compounds interest annually at an APR of 4.5%. Who will have the higher accumulated balance after 5 years and after 20 years?

_____

_____

_____

9. Suppose that you want to have a $100,000 retirement fund after 40 years. How much will you need to deposit now if you can obtain an APR of 6.4%, compounded daily? Assume that no additional deposits are to be made to the account.

_____

_____

_____

10. Suppose that you want to have $35,000 in a college fund for your daughter after 18 years. How much will you need to invest now if you can obtain an APR of 7.8%, compounded continuously? Assume that no additional deposits are to be made.

_____

_____

_____

Unit 4B Test 2

1. Suppose that you invest $2300 in an account that earns simple interest at an APR of 6.3%. Determine the accumulated balance after 11 years.

2. Suppose that you invest $21,000 in an account that earns interest at an APR of 4.1%, compounded annually. Determine the accumulated balance after 6 years.

3. Suppose that you invest $324 in an account that earns interest at an APR of 5.9%, compounded quarterly. Determine the accumulated balance after 22 years.

4. Suppose that you invest $5649 in an account that earns interest at an APR of 4.2%, compounded monthly. Determine the accumulated balance after 10 years.

5. Suppose that your savings account earns interest at an APR of 4.8%, compounded quarterly. Determine the annual percentage yield (APY). State your answer to the nearest hundredth of a percent.

Unit 4B Test 2 *(continued)*

6. Suppose that you invest $1637 in an account that earns interest at an APR of 6.2%, compounded continuously. Determine the accumulated balance after 7 years.

   _____

   _____

   _____

7. Suppose that you invest $15,000 in an account with an APR of 6.9%, compounded continuously. Determine the annual percentage yield (APY). State your answer to the nearest hundredth of a percent.

   _____

   _____

   _____

8. Tweedledee invests $6200 in a savings account that compounds interest monthly at an APR of 4.9%. Tweedledum invests $6700 in a savings account that compounds interest annually at an APR of 4.8%. Who will have the higher accumulated balance after 5 years and after 20 years?

   _____

   _____

   _____

9. Suppose that you want to have a $90,000 retirement fund after 30 years. How much will you need to deposit now if you can obtain an APR of 9.6%, compounded daily? Assume that no additional deposits are to be made to the account.

   _____

   _____

   _____

10. Suppose that you want to have $45,000 in a college fund for your son after 18 years. How much will you need to invest now if you can obtain an APR of 6.89%, compounded continuously? Assume that no additional deposits are to be made.

   _____

   _____

   _____

Unit 4B Test 3

Choose the correct answer to each problem.

1. Suppose that you invest $4200 in an account that earns simple interest at an APR of 5.2%. Determine the accumulated balance after 5 years.

    (a) $218.40   (b) $5292.00   (c) $5411.62   (d) $1092.00

2. Suppose that you invest $23,000 in an account that earns interest at an APR of 3.2%, compounded annually. Determine the accumulated balance after 8 years.

    (a) $29,591.39   (b) $29,680.07   (c) $29,700.19   (d) $29,709.98

3. Suppose that you invest $217 in an account that earns interest at an APR of 6%, compounded quarterly. Determine the accumulated balance after 16 years.

    (a) $566.74   (b) $565.38   (c) $562.71   (d) $551.26

4. Suppose that you invest $5873 in an account that earns interest at an APR of 4.4%, compounded monthly. Determine the accumulated balance after 7 years.

    (a) $7986.90   (b) $8145.35   (c) $8155.75   (d) $8160.99

5. Suppose that your savings account earns interest at an APR of 7.4%, compounded quarterly. Determine the annual percentage yield (APY), to the nearest hundredth of a percent.

    (a) 7.68%   (b) 7.66%   (c) 7.61%   (d) 7.40%

6. Suppose that you invest $1583 in an account that earns interest at an APR of 6.7%, compounded continuously. Determine the accumulated balance after 6 years.

    (a) $2363.64   (b) $2366.20   (c) $2366.29   (d) $2366.42

7. Suppose that you invest in an account with an APR of 6.1%, compounded continuously. Determine the annual percentage yield (APY), to the nearest hundredth of a percent.

    (a) 4.95%   (b) 6.29%   (c) 6.05%   (d) 5.20%

8. Louise invests $3100 in a savings account that compounds interest monthly at an APR of 5.3%. Thelma invests $2900 in a savings account that compounds interest annually at an APR of 5.6%. Who will have the higher accumulated balance after 5 years and after 20 years?

    (a) 5 years: Louise; 20 years: Louise   (b) 5 years: Thelma; 20 years: Thelma
    (c) 5 years: Louise; 20 years: Thelma   (d) 5 years: Thelma; 20 years: Louise

9. Suppose that you want to have a $90,000 retirement fund after 35 years. How much will you need to deposit now if you can obtain an APR of 12%, compounded daily? Assume that no additional deposits are to be made to the account.

    (a) $1284.29   (b) $1349.60   (c) $1350.53   (d) $1435.59

10. A savings account earns 4.3%, compounded continuously. How much would you need to deposit now in order to have a balance of $12,000 after 3 years? Assume that no additional deposits are to be made.

    (a) $10,115.05   (b) $10,550.12   (c) $10,547.69   (d) $10,513.18

Unit 4B Test 4

Choose the correct answer to each problem.

1. Suppose that you invest $1900 in an account that earns simple interest at an APR of 6.8%. Determine the accumulated balance after 5 years.

   (a) $646.00   (b) $2532.60   (c) $2546.00   (d) $2640.04

2. Suppose that you invest $18,000 in an account that earns interest at an APR of 3.7%, compounded annually. Determine the accumulated balance after 6 years.

   (a) $22,474.03   (b) $22,466.61   (c) $22,451.36   (d) $22,384.38

3. Suppose that you invest $442 in an account that earns interest at an APR of 2.75%, compounded quarterly. Determine the accumulated balance after 19 years.

   (a) $743.99   (b) $745.32   (c) $812.62   (d) $825.40

4. Suppose that you invest $8645 in an account that earns interest at an APR of 5.4%, compounded monthly. Determine the accumulated balance after 9 years.

   (a) $14,038.42   (b) $14,039.73   (c) $13,651.29   (d) $12,846.47

5. Suppose that your savings account earns interest at an APR of 8.2%, compounded quarterly. Determine the annual percentage yield (APY), to the nearest hundredth of a percent.

   (a) 8.20%   (b) 8.46%   (c) 8.52%   (d) 8.55%

6. Suppose that you invest $1429 in an account that earns interest at an APR of 7.2%, compounded continuously. Determine the accumulated balance after 8 years.

   (a) $2542.24   (b) $2542.06   (c) $2541.92   (d) $2537.69

7. Suppose that you invest $7000 in an account with an APR of 7.4%, compounded continuously. Determine the annual percentage yield (APY), to the nearest hundredth of a percent.

   (a) 7.68%   (b) 7.63%   (c) 6.34%   (d) 7.90%

8. Wilbur invests $4800 in a savings account that compounds interest monthly at an APR of 3.7%. Orville invests $5300 in a savings account that compounds interest annually at an APR of 3.4%. Who will have the higher accumulated balance after 5 years and after 20 years?

   (a) 5 years: Wilbur; 20 years: Wilbur   (b) 5 years: Orville; 20 years: Orville
   (c) 5 years: Wilbur; 20 years: Orville   (d) 5 years: Orville; 20 years: Wilbur

9. Suppose that you want to have a $85,000 retirement fund after 40 years. How much will you need to deposit now if you can obtain an APR of 11.2%, compounded daily? Assume that no additional deposits are to be made to the account.

   (a) $878.42   (b) $889.55   (c) $924.39   (d) $964.00

10. A savings account earns 5.2%, compounded continuously. How much would you need to deposit now in order to have a balance of $8000 after 2 years? Assume that no additional deposits are to be made.

    (a) $7209.80   (b) $7209.10   (c) $7200.15   (d) $7354.20

Unit 4C Test 1

Name:_____

Date:_____

1. Your savings account pays an APR of 5.6%, compounded annually. If you deposit $1200 at the end of each year for 8 years, what will be the accumulated balance in the account?

2. Suppose you set up a new IRA (individual retirement account) that pays an APR of 7%, compounded monthly. If you contribute $160 per month for 17 years, how much will the IRA contain at the end of that time?

3. Brandi deposits $75 at the end of each month in an account with an APR of 7%, while Stephen deposits $225 at the end of each quarter in an account with an APR of 7.1%. After 10 years, whose account has a higher balance? (Assume that, for each account, the payment period is the same as the compounding period.)

4. Suppose you want your son's college fund to contain $250,000 after 15 years. If you can get an APR of 8.6%, compounded monthly, how much should you deposit at the end of each month?

5. Suppose you have 18 months in which to save $3100 for a vacation cruise. If you can earn an APR of 4.3%, compounded monthly, how much should you deposit at the end of each month?

Unit 4C Test 1 *(continued)*

Name:_____

6. Suppose that you are 27 years old now, and you would like to retire at the age of 55. Furthermore, you would like to have a retirement fund from which you can draw an income of $72,000 per year—forever! You plan to reach this goal by making monthly deposits into an investment plan. How much do you need to deposit each month? Assume an APR of 4.5%, both as you pay into the retirement fund and when you collect from it later.

_____

_____

_____

7. Explain two different ways that stocks can produce income.

_____

_____

_____

8. Six years after paying $6000 for some shares of a risky stock, you sell the shares for $2500 (at a loss). Use the annual return formula to compute your annual return (to the nearest hundredth of a percent).

_____

_____

_____

9. Suppose that you own 320 shares of a certain stock. If the newspaper lists a dividend of 1.58 for this stock, what total dividend payment should you expect this year?

_____

_____

_____

10. Calculate the yield on a $10,000 Treasury bond with a coupon rate of 8% that has a market value of $9200.

_____

_____

_____

Unit 4C Test 2

1. Your savings account pays an APR of 4.8%, compounded annually. If you deposit $400 at the end of each year for 8 years, what will be the accumulated balance in the account?

_____

_____

_____

2. Suppose you set up a new IRA (individual retirement account) that pays an APR of 8%, compounded monthly. If you contribute $180 per month for 15 years, how much will the IRA contain at the end of that time?

_____

_____

_____

3. Suppose you want your daughter's college fund to contain $160,000 after 16 years. If you can get an APR of 8.2%, compounded monthly, how much should you deposit at the end of each month?

_____

_____

_____

4. Suppose you have 29 months in which to save $3200 for a vacation cruise. If you can earn an APR of 4.8%, compounded monthly, how much should you deposit at the end of each month?

_____

_____

_____

5. Suppose that you are 32 years old now, and you would like to retire at the age of 59. Furthermore, you would like to have a retirement fund from which you can draw an income of $77,000 per year—forever! You plan to reach this goal by making monthly deposits into an investment plan. How much do you need to deposit each month? Assume an APR of 5.5%, both as you pay into the retirement fund and when you collect from it later.

_____

_____

_____

Unit 4C Test 2 *(continued)*

6. Five years after buying 300 shares of a certain stock for $12 per share, you sell the stock for $6800. Use the annual return formula to compute your annual return (to the nearest hundredth of a percent).

_____

_____

_____

7. Four years after paying $7500 for some shares of a risky stock, you sell the shares for $5500 (at a loss). Use the total return formula to compute your total return (to the nearest hundredth percent).

_____

_____

_____

8. Suppose you own 850 shares of a certain stock. If the newspaper lists a dividend of 0.17 for this stock, what total dividend payment should you expect this year?

_____

_____

_____

9. Name three investment considerations.

_____

_____

_____

10. Calculate the yield on a $10,000 Treasury bond with a coupon rate of 9% that has a market value of $10,400.

_____

_____

_____

Unit 4C Test 3

Name:_____

Date:_____

Choose the correct answer to each problem.

1. Your savings account pays an APR of 5.2%, compounded annually. If you deposit $600 at the end of each year for 8 years, what will be the accumulated balance in the account?

   (a) $5700.07   (b) $5760.23   (c) $5770.61   (d) $5023.75

2. Suppose you set up a new IRA (individual retirement account) that pays an APR of 8.2%, compounded monthly. If you contribute $130 per month for 11 years, how much will the IRA contain at the end of that time?

   (a) $27,718.12   (b) $29,833.18   (c) $32,836.83   (d) $34,830.65

3. Suppose you want your daughter's college fund to contain $125,000 after 14 years. If you can get an APR of 7.8%, compounded monthly, how much should you deposit at the end of each month?

   (a) $398.54   (b) $406.64   (c) $412.50   (d) $476.83

4. Suppose you have 15 months in which to save $1800 for a vacation cruise. If you can earn an APR of 3.7%, compounded monthly, how much should you deposit at the end of each month?

   (a) $117.43   (b) $121.78   (c) $124.84   (d) $132.47

5. Suppose that you are 26 years old now, and you would like to retire at the age of 63. Furthermore, you would like to have a retirement fund from which you can draw an income of $65,000 per year—forever! You plan to reach this goal by making monthly deposits into an investment plan. How much do you need to deposit each month? Assume an APR of 5%, both as you pay into the retirement fund and when you collect from it later.

   (a) $1015.23   (b) $1059.82   (c) $1198.45   (d) $1365.40

6. In general, which of the following types of investments carries the most risk?

   (a) Small company stocks   (b) Large company stocks
   (c) Long-term corporate bonds   (d) U.S. Treasury bills

7. Three years after buying 500 shares of a certain stock for $23 per share, you sell the stock for $17,000. Use the annual return formula to compute your annual return (to the nearest whole percent).

   (a) 10%   (b) 14%   (c) 16%   (d) 22%

8. Five years after paying $11,000 for some shares of a risky stock, you sell the shares for $6500 (at a loss). Use the annual return formula to compute your annual return (to the nearest whole percent).

   (a) −9%   (b) −10%   (c) −13%   (d) −18%

9. Suppose you own 650 shares of a certain stock. If the newspaper lists a dividend of 0.24 for this stock, what total dividend payment should you expect this year?

   (a) $156   (b) $172   (c) $195   (d) $226

10. Calculate the yield on a $1000 Treasury bond with a coupon rate of 6% that has a market value of $860.

    (a) 6.42%   (b) 6.73%   (c) 6.98%   (d) 7.04%

Unit 4C Test 4

Name:_____

Date:_____

Choose the correct answer to each problem.

1. Your savings account pays an APR of 5.6%, compounded annually. If you deposit $600 at the end of each year for 8 years, what will be the accumulated balance in the account?

   (a) $5853.89   (b) $5972.62   (c) $6219.74   (d) $6743.85

2. Suppose you set up a new IRA (individual retirement account) that pays an APR of 7.2%, compounded monthly. If you contribute $160 per month for 15 years, how much will the IRA contain at the end of that time?

   (a) $51,600.17   (b) $52,100.19   (c) $52,817.56   (d) $51,605.12

3. Suppose you want your son's college fund to contain $135,000 after 13 years. If you can get an APR of 8.7%, compounded monthly, how much should you deposit at the end of each month?

   (a) $469.17   (b) $482.76   (c) $493.37   (d) $512.58

4. Suppose you have 9 months in which to save $2700 for a vacation cruise. If you can earn an APR of 4.8%, compounded monthly, how much should you deposit at the end of each month?

   (a) $274.79   (b) $295.23   (c) $332.39   (d) $356.32

5. Suppose that you are 38 years old now, and you would like to retire at the age of 65. Furthermore, you would like to have a retirement fund from which you can draw an income of $54,000 per year—forever! You plan to reach this goal by making monthly deposits into an investment plan. How much do you need to deposit each month? Assume an APR of 6%, both as you pay into the retirement fund and when you collect from it later.

   (a) $982.64   (b) $993.45   (c) $1047.45   (d) $1115.87

6. Six years after buying 250 shares of a certain stock for $38 per share, you sell the stock for $15,000. Use the annual return formula to compute your annual return (to the nearest whole percent).

   (a) 8%   (b) 10%   (c) 15%   (d) 18%

7. Three years after paying $11,500 for some shares of a risky stock, you sell the shares for $7000 (at a loss). Use the total return formula to compute your total return (to the nearest whole percent).

   (a) −11%   (b) −16%   (c) −21%   (d) −39%

8. Suppose you own 450 shares of a certain stock. If the newspaper lists a dividend of 0.86 for this stock, what total dividend payment should you expect this year?

   (a) $284   (b) $348   (c) $387   (d) $428

9. In general, which of the following types of investments carries the least risk?

   (a) Small company stocks   (b) Large company stocks
   (c) Long-term corporate bonds   (d) U.S. Treasury bills

10. Calculate the yield on a $1000 Treasury bond with a coupon rate of 8% that has a market value of $1110.

    (a) 7.21%   (b) 7.05%   (c) 7.34%   (d) 8.10%

Unit 4D Test 1

1. Consider a typical 30-year fixed-rate mortgage. During the first few years of the loan, are payments applied primarily toward interest or primarily toward principal? Explain.

_____

_____

_____

2. Suppose you apply for a 5-year loan in the amount of $15,000 with an APR of 9%. Your monthly payment is $311.38. Determine the principal of the loan and the total amount of interest paid over the five years.

_____

_____

_____

3. Calculate the monthly payments for a home mortgage of $265,000 with a fixed APR of 6.8% for 15 years.

_____

_____

_____

4. Suppose you take out an auto loan for $9400 over a period of 6 years at an APR of 8%. Determine your monthly payments, your total payments over the term of the loan, and the amount of interest paid over the loan term.

_____

_____

_____

5. Suppose you have just obtained a 30-year home mortgage in the amount of $74,000 at an APR of 7.3%. Find the required monthly payment and also the monthly payment that you would need to make in order to pay off the loan in 20 years. How much would you save in interest charges by paying off the loan in 20 years?

_____

_____

_____

Unit 4D Test 1 *(continued)*

6. Suppose you have a balance of $5000 on your credit card, which charges an APR of 21%. If you want to pay off the balance in 2 years, how much should you pay each month? Assume that you charge no additional expenses to the card.

_____

_____

_____

7. Suppose you require a $153,000 loan to finance the purchase of your home. You are given a choice of an ARM with a first-year rate of 4.8% or a 30-year fixed-rate loan with an APR of 6.5%. By neglecting changes in principal, estimate your monthly savings during the first year if you select the ARM.

_____

_____

_____

8. The following table shows the expenses and payments on a credit card for 3 months, starting with an initial balance of $630. Fill out the last two columns that show the interest and the balance on the account. Assume that the APR for the credit card is 22%, and that the interest for a given month is based on the balance for the previous month.

Month	Payment	Expenses	Interest	Balance
0	-	-	-	$630.00
1	$420	$530		
2	$360	$105		
3	$420	$160		

_____

_____

_____

Unit 4D Test 2

Name:_____

Date:_____

1. Consider a typical 30-year fixed-rate mortgage. During the last few years of the loan, are payments applied primarily toward interest or primarily toward principal? Explain.

_____

_____

_____

2. Suppose you apply for a 8-year loan in the amount of $12,000 with an APR of 9%. Your monthly payment is $175.80. Determine the principal of the loan and the total amount of interest paid over the six years.

_____

_____

_____

3. Calculate the monthly payments for a home mortgage of $74,000 with a fixed APR of 9.5% for 20 years.

_____

_____

_____

4. Suppose you take out an auto loan for $8300 over a period of 4 years at an APR of 7%. Determine your monthly payments, your total payments over the term of the loan, and the amount of interest paid over the loan term.

_____

_____

_____

5. Suppose you have just obtained a 30-year home mortgage in the amount of $216,000 at an APR of 6.5%. Find the required monthly payment and also the monthly payment that you would need to make in order to pay off the loan in 20 years. How much would you save in interest charges by paying off the loan in 20 years?

_____

_____

_____

Unit 4D Test 2 *(continued)*

6. Suppose you have a balance of $3800 on your credit card, which charges an APR of 21%. If you want to pay off the balance in 1 year, how much should you pay each month? Assume that you charge no additional expenses to the card.

_____

_____

_____

7. Suppose you require a $184,000 loan to finance the purchase of your home. You are given a choice of an ARM with a first-year rate of 5.6% or a 30-year fixed-rate loan with an APR of 7.0%. By neglecting changes in principal, estimate your monthly savings during the first year if you select the ARM.

_____

_____

_____

8. The following table shows the expenses and payments on a credit card for 3 months, starting with an initial balance of $480. Fill out the last two columns that show the interest and the balance on the account. Assume that the APR for the credit card is 16%, and that the interest for a given month is based on the balance for the previous month.

Month	Payment	Expenses	Interest	Balance
0	-	-	-	$480.00
1	$240	$410		
2	$160	$305		
3	$210	$260		

_____

_____

_____

Unit 4D Test 3

Name:_____

Date:_____

Choose the correct answer to each problem.

1. Consider a typical 30-year fixed-rate mortgage. During which of the following years is the highest portion of each payment applied toward principal?

    (a) First year   (b) Tenth year   (c) Twentieth year   (d) Thirtieth year

2. Suppose you apply for a 7-year loan in the amount of $17,000 with an APR of 10%. Your monthly payment is $282.22. Determine the total amount of interest paid over the seven years.

    (a) $6706.48   (b) $9706.48   (c) $11,900.00   (d) $23,706.48

3. Calculate the monthly payments for a home mortgage of $137,000 with a fixed APR of 9.4% for 30 years.

    (a) $998.23   (b) $1465.14   (c) $1032.46   (d) $1141.99

4. Suppose you take out an auto loan for $8800 over a period of 3 years at an APR of 5%. To the nearest $100, determine the total amount of your payments over the term of the loan.

    (a) $9200   (b) $9300   (c) $9400   (d) $9500

5. Suppose you have just obtained a 30-year home mortgage in the amount of $196,000 at an APR of 8.2%. By finding the required monthly payment and also the monthly payment that you would need to make in order to pay off the loan in 20 years, determine the amount you would save in interest charges by paying off the loan in 20 years.

    (a) $123,834.40   (b) $128,280.00   (c) $152,683.60   (d) $174,786.50

6. Suppose you have a balance of $2600 on your credit card, which charges an APR of 20%. If you want to pay off the balance in 15 months, how much should you pay each month? Assume that you charge no additional expenses to the card.

    (a) $102.51   (b) $164.79   (c) $197.33   (d) $143.92

7. Suppose you require a $109,000 loan to finance the purchase of your home. You are given a choice of an ARM with a first-year rate of 6.3% or a 30-year fixed-rate loan with an APR of 8.5%. By neglecting changes in principal, estimate your monthly savings during the first year if you select the ARM.

    (a) $158.47   (b) $174.68   (c) $199.83   (d) $207.43

8. The following table shows the expenses and payments on a credit card for 3 months, starting with an initial balance of $630. Use the table as a guide to help you find the balance at the end of the three months, to the nearest $10. Assume that the APR for the credit card is 14%, and that the interest for a given month is based on the balance for the previous month.

Month	Payment	Expenses	Interest	Balance
0	-	-	-	$630.00
1	$410	$180		
2	$60	$680		
3	$620	$340		

    (a) $750   (b) $760   (c) $770   (d) $780

Unit 4D Test 4

Choose the correct answer to each problem.

1. Consider a typical 30-year fixed-rate mortgage. During which of the following years is the highest portion of each payment applied toward interest?

   (a) First year   (b) Tenth year   (c) Twentieth year   (d) Thirtieth year

2. Suppose you apply for an 12-year loan in the amount of $32,000 with an APR of 6%. Your monthly payment is $312.27. Determine the total amount of interest paid over the twelve years.

   (a) $5385.76   (b) $12,966.88   (c) $13,440.00   (d) $27,485.76

3. Calculate the monthly payments for a home mortgage of $189,000 with a fixed APR of 6.8% for 15 years.

   (a) $1583.42   (b) $1677.72   (c) $1703.59   (d) $1748.34

4. Suppose you take out an auto loan for $15,700 over a period of 5 years at an APR of 9%. To the nearest $100, determine the total amount of your payments over the term of the loan.

   (a) $19,600   (b) $19,700   (c) $19,800   (d) $19,900

5. Suppose you have just obtained a 30-year home mortgage in the amount of $84,000 at an APR of 7.9%. By finding the required monthly payment and also the monthly payment that you would need to make in order to pay off the loan in 20 years, determine the amount you would save in interest charges by paying off the loan in 20 years.

   (a) $43,834.40   (b) $48,280.00   (c) $52,413.60   (d) $74,786.50

6. Suppose you have a balance of $8600 on your credit card, which charges an APR of 17%. If you want to pay off the balance in 30 months, how much should you pay each month? Assume that you charge no additional expenses to the card.

   (a) $353.88   (b) $367.21   (c) $381.17   (d) $409.89

7. Suppose you require a $193,000 loan to finance the purchase of your home. You are given a choice of an ARM with a first-year rate of 6.8% or a 30-year fixed-rate loan with an APR of 9.0%. By neglecting changes in principal, estimate your monthly savings during the first year if you select the ARM.

   (a) $338.84   (b) $353.83   (c) $372.98   (d) $402.57

8. The following table shows the expenses and payments on a credit card for 3 months, starting with an initial balance of $820. Use the table as a guide to help you find the balance at the end of the three months, to the nearest $10. Assume that the APR for the credit card is 19%, and that the interest for a given month is based on the balance for the previous month.

Month	Payment	Expenses	Interest	Balance
0	-	-	-	$820.00
1	$340	$740		
2	$180	$270		
3	$75	$530		

   (a) $1790   (b) $1800   (c) $1810   (d) $1820

Unit 4E Test 1

In the following problems, assume 2006 values for the personal exemption ($3050) and standard deductions ($4750 single, $9500 married filing jointly, $4750 married filing separately, and $7000 head of a household). When necessary, use the table of marginal tax rates below.

tax rate	Single	married filing jointly	married filing separately	head of household
10%	up to $7000	up to $14,000	up to $7000	up to $10,000
15%	$7001 to $28,400	$14,001 to $56,800	$7001 to $28,400	$10,001 to $38,050
25%	$28,401 to $68,800	$56,801 to $114,650	$28,401 to $57,325	$38,051 to $98,250
28%	$68,801 to $143,500	$114,651 to $174,700	$57,326 to $87,350	$98,251 to $159,100
33%	$143,501 to $311,950	$174,701 to $311,950	$87,351 to $155,975	$159,101 to $311,950
35%	$311,951 or more	$311,951 or more	$155,976 or more	$311,951 or more

1. Roger is single and earned wages of $53,000 in 2006. He received $2700 in interest from savings accounts, he contributed $1500 to a tax-deferred retirement plan, and he had itemized deductions totaling $5320. Find his gross income, adjusted gross income, and taxable income.

_____

_____

_____

2. A married couple who itemize deductions are in the 33% marginal tax bracket. How much will their tax bill be reduced if they make a donation of $2000 to charity?

_____

_____

_____

3. Suppose that you are single with no dependents, and you had a taxable income of $51,600 in 2006. How much income tax did you pay?

_____

_____

_____

4. Suppose that you are married filing separately with two dependent children, and you had a taxable income of $56,500 in 2006. Assuming that you are entitled to a tax credit of $700 per child, how much income tax did you pay?

_____

_____

_____

Unit 4E Test 1 *(continued)*

Name:_____

5. In 2006, Wendy and John had adjusted gross incomes of $18,000 and $23,200, respectively. They had no dependents and they claimed standard deductions. Find the amount of their combined income tax if they were each single and if they were married filing jointly.

_____

_____

_____

6. Suppose that you were a self-employed single taxpayer, and you earned $52,500 from your business in 2006. You had no other income, you made no contributions to retirement plans, and you took the standard deduction. How much did you owe in FICA and income taxes combined? (Since your earnings are under $87,000, your FICA taxes are calculated at the rate of 15.3%; half of this self-employment tax should be taken as an adjustment to gross income.)

_____

_____

_____

7. In 2006, Jocelino was a single taxpayer whose income consisted solely of $390,000 in long term capital gains. He claimed $32,000 in itemized deductions, but he was not eligible to claim any personal exemption. How much tax did he owe?

_____

_____

_____

8. Suppose that, in 2006, you are single and have a taxable income of $15,000. How will your monthly take-home pay be affected if you make monthly contributions of $200 to a tax-deferred savings plan?

_____

_____

_____

Unit 4E Test 2

Name:_____

Date:_____

In the following problems, assume 2006 values for the personal exemption ($3050) and standard deductions ($4750 single, $9500 married filing jointly, $4750 married filing separately, and $7000 head of a household). When necessary, use the table of marginal tax rates below.

tax rate	Single	married filing jointly	married filing separately	head of household
10%	up to $7000	up to $14,000	up to $7000	up to $10,000
15%	$7001 to $28,400	$14,001 to $56,800	$7001 to $28,400	$10,001 to $38,050
25%	$28,401 to $68,800	$56,801 to $114,650	$28,401 to $57,325	$38,051 to $98,250
28%	$68,801 to $143,500	$114,651 to $174,700	$57,326 to $87,350	$98,251 to $159,100
33%	$143,501 to $311,950	$174,701 to $311,950	$87,351 to $155,975	$159,101 to $311,950
35%	$311,951 or more	$311,951 or more	$155,976 or more	$311,951 or more

1. Diana is married, but she and her husband filed separate income taxes in 2006. She earned wages of $32,000, and she received $800 in interest from savings accounts. She also contributed $1200 to a tax-deferred retirement plan, and had itemized deductions totaling $7220. Find her gross income, adjusted gross income, and taxable income.

_____

_____

_____

2. A single taxpayer who itemizes deductions is in the 28% marginal tax bracket. How much will his tax bill be reduced if he qualifies for a $650 tax credit?

_____

_____

_____

3. Suppose a married couple with no dependents filed jointly and had a taxable income of $56,400 in 2006. How much income tax did they pay?

_____

_____

_____

4. Suppose that you are a head of household with three dependent children, and you had a taxable income of $93,600 in 2006. Assuming you are entitled to a tax credit of $700 per child, how much income tax did you pay?

_____

_____

_____

5. In 2006, Jerry and Penny had adjusted gross incomes of $15,800 and $22,100, respectively. They had no dependents and they claimed standard deductions. Find the amount of their combined income tax if they were each single and if they were married filing jointly.

_____

_____

_____

6. Suppose that you were a self-employed single taxpayer, and you earned $41,500 from your business in 2006. You had no other income, you made no contributions to retirement plans, and you took the standard deduction. How much did you owe in FICA and income taxes combined? (Since your earnings are under $87,000, your FICA taxes are calculated at the rate of 15.3%; half of this self-employment tax should be taken as an adjustment to gross income.)

_____

_____

_____

7. In 2006, Joyce was a single taxpayer whose income consisted solely of $420,000 in long term capital gains. She claimed $52,000 in itemized deductions, but she was not eligible to claim any personal exemption. How much tax did she owe?

_____

_____

_____

8. Suppose that, in 2006, you are single and have a taxable income of $125,500. How will your monthly take-home pay be affected if you make monthly contributions of $900 to a tax-deferred savings plan?

_____

_____

_____

Unit 4E Test 3

Choose the correct answer to each problem.

In the following problems, assume 2006 values for the personal exemption ($3050) and standard deductions ($4750 single, $9500 married filing jointly, $4750 married filing separately, and $7000 head of a household). When necessary, use the table of marginal tax rates below.

tax rate	Single	married filing jointly	married filing separately	head of household
10%	up to $7000	up to $14,000	up to $7000	up to $10,000
15%	$7001 to $28,400	$14,001 to $56,800	$7001 to $28,400	$10,001 to $38,050
25%	$28,401 to $68,800	$56,801 to $114,650	$28,401 to $57,325	$38,051 to $98,250
28%	$68,801 to $143,500	$114,651 to $174,700	$57,326 to $87,350	$98,251 to $159,100
33%	$143,501 to $311,950	$174,701 to $311,950	$87,351 to $155,975	$159,101 to $311,950
35%	$311,951 or more	$311,951 or more	$155,976 or more	$311,951 or more

1. Mark is single and earned wages of $52,000 in 2006. He received $4300 in interest from savings accounts, he contributed $1200 to a tax-deferred retirement plan, and he took the standard deduction. Find his adjusted gross income.

    (a) $51,550   (b) $55,100   (c) $52,050   (d) $47,300

2. A married couple who claim the standard deduction are in the 28% marginal tax bracket. Which of the following will reduce their tax bill by $280?

    (a) They make a $1000 donation to charity.   (b) They make a $280 donation to charity.
    (c) They qualify for a $1000 tax credit.   (d) They qualify for a $280 tax credit.

3. Suppose a married couple with no dependents filed jointly and had a taxable income of $102,000 in 2006. How much income tax did they pay?

    (a) $15,220   (b) $19,120   (c) $21,600   (d) $25,500

4. Suppose that you are married filing separately with two dependent children, and you had a taxable income of $42,400 in 2006. Assuming you are not entitled to a tax credit for either child, how much income tax did you pay?

    (a) $3500   (b) $7410   (c) $8672.50   (d) $10,600

5. In 2006, Sid and Myra had adjusted gross incomes of $16,200 and $20,300, respectively. They had no dependents and they filed jointly as a married couple, claiming the standard deduction. Find the amount of their marriage penalty—that is, the amount of additional tax that they paid over what they would have paid if each had been single.

    (a) $0   (b) $180   (c) $218   (d) $240

6. Suppose that you were a self-employed single taxpayer, and you earned $54,500 from your business in 2006. You had no other income, you made no contributions to retirement plans, and you took the standard deduction. How much did you owe in FICA and income taxes combined? (Since your earnings are under $87,000, your FICA taxes are calculated at the rate of 15.3%; half of this self-employment tax should be taken as an adjustment to gross income.)

    (a) $7442.69   (b) $15,781.19   (c) $18,971.19   (d) $21,963.50

Unit 4E Test 3 *(continued)*

7. In 2006, Gina was a single taxpayer whose income consisted solely of $370,000 in long term capital gains. She claimed $18,000 in itemized deductions, but she was not eligible to claim any personal exemption. How much tax did she owe?

   (a) $49,960   (b) $52,800   (c) $55,500   (d) $104,532

8. Suppose that, in 2006, you are single and have a taxable income of $42,000. By how much will your monthly take-home pay be reduced if you make monthly contributions of $300 to a tax-deferred savings plan?

   (a) $75   (b) $150   (c) $200   (d) $225

Unit 4E Test 4

Name:_____

Date:_____

Choose the correct answer to each problem.

In the following problems, assume 2006 values for the personal exemption ($3050) and standard deductions ($4750 single, $9500 married filing jointly, $4750 married filing separately, and $7000 head of a household). When necessary, use the table of marginal tax rates below.

tax rate	Single	married filing jointly	married filing separately	head of household
10%	up to $7000	up to $14,000	up to $7000	up to $10,000
15%	$7001 to $28,400	$14,001 to $56,800	$7001 to $28,400	$10,001 to $38,050
25%	$28,401 to $68,800	$56,801 to $114,650	$28,401 to $57,325	$38,051 to $98,250
28%	$68,801 to $143,500	$114,651 to $174,700	$57,326 to $87,350	$98,251 to $159,100
33%	$143,501 to $311,950	$174,701 to $311,950	$87,351 to $155,975	$159,101 to $311,950
35%	$311,951 or more	$311,951 or more	$155,976 or more	$311,951 or more

1. Walter is married, but he and his wife filed separate income taxes in 2006. He earned wages of $62,000, and he received $4200 in interest from savings accounts. He also contributed $2500 to a tax-deferred retirement plan, and he took the standard deduction. Find his adjusted gross income.

    (a) $68,700   (b) $58,950   (c) $63,700   (d) $66,200

2. A single taxpayer who itemizes deductions is in the 33% marginal tax bracket. Which of the following will reduce her tax bill by $500?

    (a) She makes a $500 donation to charity.   (b) She makes a $165 donation to charity.
    (c) She qualifies for a $500 tax credit.   (d) She qualifies for a $165 tax credit.

3. Suppose that you are single with no dependents, and you had a taxable income of $87,300 in 2006. How much income tax did you pay?

    (a) $17,006   (b) $19,190   (c) $22,260   (d) $24,444

4. Suppose that you are a head of household with one dependent child, and you had a taxable income of $48,200 in 2006. Assuming you are not entitled to an additional tax credit for the child, how much income tax did you pay?

    (a) $5065   (b) $5565   (c) $7530   (d) $7745

5. In 2006, Felice and Stan had adjusted gross incomes of $17,500 and $24,300, respectively. They had no dependents and they filed jointly as a married couple, claiming the standard deduction. Find the amount of their marriage penalty—that is, the amount of additional tax that they paid over what they would have paid if each had been single.

    (a) $0   (b) $185   (c) $320   (d) $457.50

6. Suppose that you were a self-employed single taxpayer, and you earned $43,500 from your business in 2006. You had no other income, you made no contributions to retirement plans, and you took the standard deduction. How much did you owe in FICA and income taxes combined? (Since your earnings are under $87,000, your FICA taxes are calculated at the rate of 15.3%; half of this self-employment tax should be taken as an adjustment to gross income.)

    (a) $4903.06   (b) $6853.06   (c) $8528.53   (d) $11,558.56

Unit 4E Test 4 *(continued)*

Name:_____

7. In 2006, Patrick was a single taxpayer whose income consisted solely of $410,000 in long term capital gains. He claimed $24,000 in itemized deductions, but he was not eligible to claim any personal exemption. How much tax did he owe?

   (a) $55,060   **(b)** $78,245   **(c)** $116,432   **(d)** $135,100

8. Suppose that, in 2006, you are single and have a taxable income of $200,000. How will your monthly take-home pay be reduced if you make monthly contributions of $800 to a tax-deferred savings plan?

   (a) $332   **(b)** $536   **(c)** $718   **(d)** $734

Unit 4F Test 1

Name:_____

Date:_____

1. Give one reason why the national gross debt will continue to increase in the future even if there are several years of net surplus.

   _____

   _____

   _____

2. Briefly describe the two main categories of federal spending.

   _____

   _____

   _____

3. How does the government borrow money from the public?

   _____

   _____

   _____

4. If you wanted to start a small business that manufactures widgets, give examples of the kinds of outlays there would be: 2 that are in your control and 2 that are to some extent out of your control.

   _____

   _____

   _____

U.S. Federal Budget summary for 2005 and 2006
(all amounts in $ billions)

	2005	2006
Total Receipts	1259	1352
Total Outlays	1462	1516
Net Interest on the Debt	203	232
Gross Federal Debt	–4644	–4921

5. Calculate the interest rate paid on the debt in 2006.

   _____

   _____

   _____

Unit 4F Test 1 *(continued)*

6. Calculate the change in the gross debt from 2005 to 2006. What is the deficit for 2006? Which is the amount the government must repay?

_____

_____

_____

7. In 1999, total federal receipts were $1827 billion. In 2000, total federal receipts increased by about 10.2%. If receipts had increased by the same percentage in 2001, what would the total receipts have been?

_____

_____

_____

8. Assume that the budget balances each year so the national debt does not increase. If the government could raise $95 million per week in a national lottery and all of this money goes toward reducing the national debt, when will the debt be retired? Use the 2000 gross debt of $7 trillion.

_____

_____

_____

9. In 2000 the federal debt was $6 trillion. If there were 69 million people under the age of 18, what was the federal debt per person in the age group?

_____

_____

_____

10. Suppose the government cuts 2001 spending to 90% of the 2000 levels. If receipts in 2001 are $2100 billion and spending in 2000 was $1802 billion, what will the 2001 deficit be?

_____

_____

_____

Unit 4F Test 2

Name:_____

Date:_____

1. Explain one way the government can increase the yearly net surplus in the budget.

   _____

   _____

   _____

2. Briefly explain the difference between the deficit and the debt.

   _____

   _____

   _____

3. Give two examples of federal discretionary spending.

   _____

   _____

   _____

4. What would be an example of discretionary spending for a company such as the Wonderful Widget Company?

   _____

   _____

   _____

U.S. Federal Budget summary for 2003 and 2004
(all amounts in $ billions)

	2003	2004
Total Receipts	1154	1259
Total Outlays	1409	1462
Net Interest on the Debt	199	203
Gross Federal Debt	–4351	–4644

5. Calculate the interest rate paid on the debt in 2003.

   _____

   _____

   _____

Unit 4F Test 2 *(continued)*

6. Calculate the change in the gross debt from 2003 to 2004. What is the net deficit for 2004? Which is the amount the government must repay?

_____

_____

_____

7. In 1999, total federal outlays were $1707 billion. In 2000, total federal outlays increased by about 5.6%. If outlays increased by the same percentage in 2001, what would the total outlays have been?

_____

_____

_____

8. Assume that the budget balances each year so the national debt does not increase. If the government could raise $80 million per week in a national lottery and all of this money goes toward reducing the national debt, when will the debt be retired? Use the 2000 gross debt of $6 trillion.

_____

_____

_____

9. In 2000 the federal debt was $6 trillion. If there were 36 million people over the age of 65, what was the federal debt per person in this age group?

_____

_____

_____

10. Suppose the government cuts 2001 spending to 95% of the 2000 levels. If receipts in 2001 are $2300 billion and spending in 2000 was $1810 billion what will the 2001 deficit be?

_____

_____

_____

Unit 4F Test 3

Name:_____

Date:_____

Choose the correct answer to each problem.

1. Which of the following defines net income?

    (a) surplus – receipts   (b) receipts – outlays   (c) debt – outlays   (d) debt + receipts

2. Which of the following will <u>not</u> contribute to maintaining a balanced federal budget?

    (a) large tax increases
    (c) reducing discretionary spending

    (b) increasing Social Security benefits
    (d) balancing yearly receipts and outlays

3. What type of spending is easiest for the government to control?

    (a) interest payments on the debt
    (c) entitlement spending

    (b) Medicare
    (d) discretionary spending

4. Which of the following will allow the federal debt to be retired?

    (a) zero gross deficit
    (c) zero net deficit

    (b) zero gross debt
    (d) zero net surplus

5. If the gross federal debt at the end of 2003 was about $5500 billion and the interest rate was 5.2%, what was the interest due on this debt?

    (a) $286 billion   (b) $2860 billion   (c) $28.6 billion   (d) $2.86 billion

6. In 1997, total federal outlays were $1601 billion. If outlays increase by 6% per year, how would we forecast outlays in 2007?

    (a) $1601 \times (10 + 1.06)$
    (c) $1601 \times (1 + 10)^{0.06}$

    (b) $1601 \times (1 + 0.06)^{10}$
    (d) $1601 \times (1 + 0.60)^{10}$

7. Assume that the budget balances each year so the national debt does not increase beyond the 2000 gross debt of $6 trillion. If the government wanted to retire the debt in 50 years, how much money would need to be raised per week to be put toward reducing the debt?

    (a) $2.3 million   (b) $5.6 million   (c) $2.3 billion   (d) $5.6 billion

8. In 2001 the federal debt was $5182 billion. If there were 100 million people under the age of 18 or 65 and older and 5% of these people worked, then out of this age group what was the federal debt per laborer?

    (a) $1036   (b) $10,364   (c) $1,036,400   (d) $103,640

9. If the government cuts 2001 spending to 95% of the 2000 level of $1840 billion, and receipts in 2001 are $2300 billion, what will the net result be?

    (a) There will be a $552 billion net surplus for 2001.
    (c) The gross debt will increase by $552 billion.

    (b) There will be a $552 billion net deficit for 2001.
    (d) The gross debt will decrease by $552 billion.

Unit 4F Test 3 *(continued)*

10. Which of the following combinations will make it impossible to ever retire the federal debt?

   (a) Increase receipts by 1% and increase outlays by 1% (each year).
   (b) Increase receipts by 2% and increase outlays by 1% (each year)
   (c) Increase receipts by 1% and increase outlays by 0% (each year)
   (d) Increase receipts by 1% and decrease outlays by 1% (each year)

Unit 4F Test 4

Name:_____

Date:_____

Choose the correct answer to each problem.

1. Which term describes the actual amount the government is obligated to repay someday?

    (a) gross debt   (b) net deficit   (c) net debt   (d) gross deficit

2. What is the primary mandatory expense in the federal budget?

    (a) national defense   (b) education
    (c) interest on the debt   (d) Social Security payments

3. Which of the following combinations may allow the federal debt to be retired?

    (a) Increasing receipts by 1% and increasing outlays by 2% (each year).
    (b) Increasing receipts by 2% and increasing outlays by 2% (each year).
    (c) Increasing receipts by 1% and decreasing outlays by 0% (each year).
    (d) Decreasing receipts by 1% and increasing outlays by 2% (each year).

4. Which of the following is <u>not</u> a way the government borrows money from the public?

    (a) selling bonds to investors   (b) raising taxes
    (c) selling Treasury notes

5. If the gross federal debt at the end of 2003 was about $5800 billion and the interest rate was 4.6%, what was the interest due on this debt?

    (a) $26.68 billion   (b) $2668 billion   (c) $2.668 billion   (d) $266.8 billion

6. In 1997, total federal receipts were $1579 billion. If receipts increase by 2.5% per year, how would we forecast receipts in 2007?

    (a) $1579 \times (1+0.025)^{10}$ (b) $1579 \times (1+0.25)^{10}$
    (c) $1579 \times (1+10)^{0.025}$ (d) $1579 \times (1+10)^{0.25}$

7. Assume that the budget balances each year so the national debt does not increase beyond the 2000 gross debt of $6 trillion. If the government wanted to retire the debt in 70 years, how much money would need to be raised per week to be put toward reducing the debt?

    (a) $1.6 million   (b) $1.6 billion   (c) $1.6 trillion   (d) $4.01 billion

8. In 2000, the federal debt was $5435 billion. Suppose two-thirds of the population ages 18 to 64 was employed in 2000. Out of this age group, what was the 2000 federal debt per laborer if there were 170 million people age 18 to 64?

    (a) $31,971   (b) $47,956   (c) $3198   (d) $4796

Unit 4F Test 4 *(continued)*

9. If the government cuts 2001 spending to 90% of the 1999 level of $1764 billion, and receipts in 2001 are $2400 billion, what will the net result be?

   (a) The gross debt will decrease by $812 billion.

   (b) The gross debt will increase by $812 billion.

   (c) There will be a $812 billion net surplus for 2001.

   (d) There will be a $812 billion net deficit for 2001.

10. Which of the following will contribute to an increased federal debt?

   (a) raising taxes

   (b) decreasing Social Security benefits

   (c) increasing receipts

   (d) increasing international aid

Unit 5A Test 1

1. Explain what is meant by the placebo effect.

   _____

   _____

   _____

2. Explain what is meant by an experiment.

   _____

   _____

   _____

3. Explain the difference between a population and a sample.

   _____

   _____

   _____

4. Give an example of raw data.

   _____

   _____

   _____

5. Give an example of a sample statistic.

   _____

   _____

   _____

6. Give an example of a question that can be addressed with an observational study.

   _____

   _____

   _____

7. For the following question identify which type of statistical study is most likely to lead to an answer. Explain. *Can eating oatmeal every day reduce cholesterol levels?*

_____

_____

_____

8. For the following question identify which type of statistical study is most likely to lead to an answer. Explain. *Does a new drug lower blood pressure in hypertensive patients?*

_____

_____

_____

9. For the following question identify which type of statistical study is most likely to lead to an answer. Explain. *Which political party do most nurses belong to?*

_____

_____

_____

10. A survey finds that 45% of Americans spend less than 2 hours a day watching television, with a margin of error of 5%. Interpret these results.

_____

_____

_____

Unit 5A Test 2

Name:_____

Date:_____

1. Explain what is meant by raw data.

   _____

   _____

   _____

2. Explain what is meant by a sample statistic.

   _____

   _____

   _____

3. Explain what is meant by an observational study.

   _____

   _____

   _____

4. Give an example of the placebo effect.

   _____

   _____

   _____

5. Give an example of a population and a sample.

   _____

   _____

   _____

6. Give an example of a question that can be addressed with an experiment.

   _____

   _____

   _____

Unit 5A Test 2 *(continued)*

Name:_____

7. For the following question identify which type of statistical study is most likely to lead to an answer. Explain. *Does taking a zinc tablet reduce the duration of a cold?*

_____

_____

_____

8. For the following question identify which type of statistical study is most likely to lead to an answer. Explain.
Is the middle child usually more independent?

_____

_____

_____

9. For the following question identify which type of statistical study is most likely to lead to an answer. Explain. *Who will win the academy award for best supporting actor?*

_____

_____

_____

10. A survey finds that 65% of Americans watched the Academy Awards, with a margin of error of 5%. Interpret the survey results.

_____

_____

_____

Unit 5A Test 3

Choose the correct answer to each problem.

1. Which of the following describes a study in which the researchers do not know which participants are in the control group?

   (a) Single-blind experiment   (b) Observational experiment
   (c) Double-blind study   (d) Case-control study

2. Which of the following describes a study in which the participants naturally form groups by choice?

   (a) Single-blind experiment   (b) Case-control study
   (c) Double-blind experiment   (d) Observational study

3. A random sample of dog owners revealed that 72% of them walked their dog at least 3 times a week, with a margin of error of 8%. Which of the following can be stated with 95% confidence?

   (a) The actual percentage of dog owners who walk their dog at least 3 times a week is between 64% and 80%
   (b) The actual percentage of dog owners who walk their dog at least 3 times a week is between 72% and 80%
   (c) The actual percentage of dog owners who walk their dog at least 3 times a week is between 64% and 72%
   (d) The actual percentage of dog owners who walk their dog at least 3 times a week is 72%

4. There is a 95% chance that between 53% and 59% of voters will vote for Senator Sam in the next election. What do you know about the sample statistics and the margin of error of the survey?

   (a) 53% of the voters surveyed stated that they will vote for Senator Sam, and the margin of error is 6%
   (b) 59% of the voters surveyed stated that they will vote for Senator Sam, and the margin of error is 6%
   (c) 56% of the voters surveyed stated that they will vote for Senator Sam, and the margin of error is 3%
   (d) 53% of the voters surveyed stated that they will vote for Senator Sam, and the margin of error is 3%

5. In a study to determine the most popular automobile on the road, which of the following is the best sample?

   (a) The cars parked at an airport   (b) The cars parked at a local high school
   (c) The cars that drive by your house   (d) The cars driving on the highway

6. In a study to determine the percentage of college students who read the newspaper, which of the following is the best sample?

   (a) The students in a math class   (b) The freshman at a particular school
   (c) The first 50 students who arrive at a movie   (d) A group of seniors from a variety of high schools

7. *Does garlic lower cholersterol?*
   This question would best be answered by which of the following types of studies?

   (a) Single-blind experiment   (b) Case-control study
   (c) Observational study

Unit 5A Test 3 *(continued)*

8. *How many words can you write with a gel-pen?*
This question would best be answered by which of the following types of studies?

   (a) Single-blind experiment   **(b)** Double-blind experiment
   (c) Observational study

9. *Does caffeine cause birth defects?*
This question would best be answered by which of the following types of studies?

   (a) Single-blind experiment   **(b)** Case-control study
   (c) Double-blind experiment

10. *Will Proposition 222 be passed by the voters in the next election?*
This question would best be answered by which of the following types of studies?

   (a) Observational study   **(b)** Double-blind experiment
   (c) Case-control study

Unit 5A Test 4

Name:_____

Date:_____

Choose the correct answer to each problem.

1. Which of the following describes a study in which the researchers know which group of participants is receiving a placebo?

   (a) Double-blind experiment   (b) Observational study
   (c) Single-blind experiment   (d) Case-control study

2. Which of the following describes a study in which the researchers do not attempt to change the characteristics of those being studied.

   (a) Single-blind experiment   (b) Observational study
   (c) Double-blind experiment   (d) Case-control study

3. A random sample of high school students found that 17% chose History as their favorite subject, with a margin of error of 6%. Which of the following can be stated with 95% confidence?

   (a) The actual percentage of high school students whose favorite class is History is between 17% and 23%.
   (b) The actual percentage of high school students whose favorite class is History is between 11% and 17%.
   (c) The actual percentage of high school students whose favorite class is History is between 11% and 23%.
   (d) The actual percentage of high school students whose favorite class is History is 17%.

4. There is a 95% chance that between 42% and 46% of voters will vote for Congressman Bob in the next election. What do you know about the sample statistics and the margin of error of the survey?

   (a) 42% of the voters surveyed stated that they will vote for Congressman Bob, and the margin of error is 4%.
   (b) 44% of the voters surveyed stated that they will vote for Congressman Bob, and the margin of error is 2%.
   (c) 46% of the voters surveyed stated that they will vote for Congressman Bob, and the margin of error is 4%.
   (d) 44% of the voters surveyed stated that they will vote for Congressman Bob, and the margin of error is 4%.

5. In a study to determine the average weight of a house cat, which of the following is the best sample?

   (a) All of the cats that a pet groomer sees in one week   (b) All of the cats that a veterinarian sees in one week

   (c) All of the cats in your neighborhood   (d) Some of the cats in each of several neighborhoods

6. In a study to determine which airline has the friendliest flight attendants, which of the following is the best sample?

   (a) Flight attendants at several airlines   (b) All business travelers traveling in a certain week

   (c) All airline passengers traveling on a certain day   (d) Shoppers at a grocery store

Unit 5A Test 4 (continued)

7. *The Acme Soda Company wants to know if their soda tastes better than Cooky Cola.*
   This question would best be answered by which of the following types of studies?

   (a) Single-blind experiment   **(b)** Double-blind study
   (c) Case-control study

8. *Does a new sugar substitute taste the same as regular sugar?*
   This question would best be answered by which of the following types of studies?

   (a) Single-blind experiment   **(b)** Case-control study
   (c) Observational study

9. *Does exercising three hours per week lower blood pressure?*
   This question would best be answered by which of the following types of studies?

   (a) Single-blind experiment   **(b)** Case-control study
   (c) Observational study

10. *Are men teachers paid more than women teachers?*
    This question would best be answered by which of the following types of studies?

    (a) Double-blind experiment   **(b)** Case-control study
    (c) Observational study

Unit 5B Test 1

1. Give an example of a peer review.

_____

_____

_____

2. Explain what is meant by selection bias.

_____

_____

_____

3. Why is it important to consider the source of a study?

_____

_____

_____

4. Give an example that illustrates the meaning of availability error. Explain your example.

_____

_____

_____

5. Give an example of participation bias. Explain your example.

_____

_____

_____

6. In what way might the following study be flawed?
   The engineers who designed Vangard tires tested their reliability at high driving speeds by doing their own test driving using various vehicle makes and models.

_____

_____

_____

Unit 5B Test 1 *(continued)*

7. In what way might the following study be flawed?
   9 out of 10 dentists surveyed agree that chewing Dentamint sugarless gum after eating will help prevent tooth decay.

   _____

   _____

   _____

8. How would you select an unbiased sample for the following study?
   Which candidate for governor is most likely to win the next election?

   _____

   _____

   _____

9. Why do you think it is sometimes difficult to define the quantities of interest of a study? Give an example of a quantity of interest that is difficult to define.

   _____

   _____

   _____

Unit 5B Test 2

Name:_____

Date:_____

1. Explain what is meant by participation bias.

   _____

   _____

   _____

2. Explain what is meant by availability error.

   _____

   _____

   _____

3. Does a peer review guarantee the validity of a study? What does a study gain from a peer review?

   _____

   _____

   _____

4. Give an example of selection bias. Explain your example.

   _____

   _____

   _____

5. Give an example of a study conducted by an inappropriate source. Explain your example.

   _____

   _____

   _____

6. In what way might the following study be flawed?
   A group of high school students are asked if they would oppose the repeal of a school policy that currently does not allow students to wear shorts to school.

   _____

   _____

   _____

Unit 5B Test 2 (continued)   Name:_____

7. In what way might the following study be flawed?
   A scientist is studying the appetite of cats. He quietly holds a kitty treat ten feet in front of a cat and the cat runs forward to eat the treat. He tries this several times with several cats, and the cat always runs for the treat. He tries the experiment again after blindfolding the cats. The cats no longer run for the treat. He concludes that cats are only hungry when they see food.

   _____

   _____

   _____

8. How would you select an unbiased sample for the following study?
   Do the citizens of Redwood County support spending $5,000,000to construct a new school building?

   _____

   _____

   _____

9. Why do you think it is sometimes difficult to measure the quantities of interest of a study? Give an example of a quantity of interest that is difficult to measure.

   _____

   _____

   _____

Unit 5B Test 3

Choose the correct answer to each problem.

1. Which of the following describes the process by which scientists examine each others' research?

   (a) Participation review
   (c) Considering the conclusion

   (b) Peer review
   (d) Interpretation

2. Which of the following describes the bias that occurs when researchers select their sample in such a way that it is unlikely to be representative of the population?

   (a) Participation bias   (b) Availability bias   (c) Double-blind bias   (d) Selection bias

3. *As voters leave various polls across the city, every tenth voter at each polling place is asked who they chose to be the next mayor.*
   This study may suffer from what type of bias?

   (a) Selection Bias   (b) Participation Bias   (c) No Bias

4. *You hand a customer satisfaction questionnaire to every customer at a video store and ask them to fill it out and place it in a box after they check out.*
   This study may suffer from what type of bias?

   (a) Selection Bias   (b) Participation Bias   (c) No Bias

5. A recent magazine article determined that the Gemini is the most popular car on the road. A TV journalist decided to test the accuracy of the article with a survey. Which of the following survey questions will give the journalist the most accurate results?

   (a) What kind of car do you drive?
   (b) What do you think is the most popular car on the road?
   (c) Do you agree that the Gemini is the most popular car on the road?
   (d) What kind of car do you recall seeing advertised most often?

6. If you wanted to determine if your customers are satisfied with the selection in your store, which of the following survey questions would give you the most accurate results?

   (a) Is there anything you would have purchased if our stock was not without it?
   (b) Are you satisfied with the selection at this store?
   (c) Do you agree that our selection is better then our competition?
   (d) Is our selection as good as the selection of our competition?

7. Which of the following study results implies that there is a problem with the quality of education at Rydell High?

   (a) 25% of the senior class scored was accepted at an ivy league school.
   (b) 53% of the senior class was accepted for admission to Valley State College in the fall.
   (c) 83% of the seniors who applied for admission to Valley State College were accepted.
   (d) 30% of the senior class scored above average on the writing portion of a national aptitude test.

Unit 5B Test 3 *(continued)*

Name:_____

8. Which of the following quantities of interest would be the most difficult to define?

   (a) The levels of lead in various brands of paint
   (b) The least expensive brand of paint
   (c) The paint with the best looking finish
   (d) How water resistant a brand of paint is

9. Which of the following quantities of interest would be the most difficult to measure?

   (a) The average height of a volleyball team
   (b) The team member with the highest salary
   (c) The team member with the longest hair
   (d) The most outgoing team member

Unit 5B Test 4

Choose the correct answer to each problem.

1. Which of the following describes what scientists are attempting to measure in a particular statistical study?

   (a) Quantity of interest   **(b)** Quality of life   **(c)** Participation   **(d)** Peer review

2. Which of the following describes the bias that can occur when members of a study's sample are volunteers?

   (a) Single-blind bias   **(b)** Sample bias   **(c)** Participation bias   **(d)** Selection bias

3. *A telephone poll in the New York metropolitan area asks which film should win the Academy Award for best picture this year.*
   This study may suffer from what type of bias?

   (a) Selection bias   **(b)** Participation bias   **(c)** No bias

4. *The manager at a video store asks every customer if they were able to find the video they wanted to rent.*
   This study may suffer from what type of bias?

   (a) Selection bias   **(b)** Participation bias   **(c)** No bias

5. A recent newspaper article stated that Snazzy's is the most popular restaurant in the city. The city council decided to sponsor its own survey to determine the accuracy of the article. Which of the following survey questions will give them the most accurate survey results?

   (a) Which restaurant do you think is the most popular in the city?
   (b) Which restaurant in the city do you visit most often?
   (c) Which restaurant in the city do you think is the most crowded?
   (d) Do you agree that Snazzy's is the most popular restaurant in the city?

6. Proposition EZ proposes to raise the state sales tax by one quarter of a percent. The proceeds will be earmarked for music education in the public schools. If you want to determine whether or not it will pass, which of the following survey questions will give you the most accurate results?

   (a) Do you know which proposition will raise state sales tax and fund music education?
   (b) Will you vote for proposition EZ which will raise the amount of state sales tax that you pay every year?
   (c) Do you believe that music education is important?
   (d) Are you planning to vote for Proposition EZ which will raise state sales taxes and support music education?

7. Which of the following study results implies that there may be a problem with the health of newborn babies at Doctor's Hospital?

   (a) 25% of the newborns had genetic defects.
   (b) 53% of the newborns were born within one week of their due date.
   (c) 50% of the newborns were above average in weight.
   (d) 83% of the newborns were born with hepatitis.

Unit 5B Test 4 *(continued)*

8. Which of the following quantities of interest would be most difficult to define?

   (a) The number of children not counted in the last census
   (b) The number of children living below the poverty line
   (c) The percentage of children who brush their teeth at least twice a day
   (d) The percentage of second graders who read above grade level

9. Which of the following quantities of interest would be the most difficult to measure?

   (a) The levels of pesticides in a tomato crop   (b) The best tasting tomato crop
   (c) The largest crop of tomatoes   (d) The crop with the highest acid level

Unit 5C Test 1

Name:_____

Date:_____

1. Explain what is meant by a bin.

_____

_____

_____

2. Give an example of qualitative data.

_____

_____

_____

The following table shows the top selling personal computers in the U.S in 2005 as a percentage of all personal computers sold. Use it to answer questions 3, 4 and 5.

Apple	IBM	Compaq	Other
17%	21%	25%	37%

3. If 6.3 million computers were sold in 2005, how many were in each category? Show your work.

_____

_____

_____

_____

4. In a pie chart of this data, what angle should be used to represent each of the four categories? Show your work.

_____

_____

_____

_____

Unit 5C Test 2 *(continued)*

5. Make a pie chart for this data.

The following table shows the age distribution of Representatives in the US Congress in 2005. Use it to answer questions 6 and 7.

Under 40	40-49	50-59	60-69	70-79	80 and over
47	151	128	89	12	3

6. How many Representatives were there in the US Congress in 2005? What percentage of them were at least 70 years old?

_____

_____

_____

7. Draw a histogram of this data and superimpose a line chart over it.

Unit 5C Test 2 *(continued)*

Name:_____

8. On April 1st, Rachel purchased 50 shares of ACME stock for $4 per share. The following is a time-series diagram showing the price of ACME stock during the month of April:

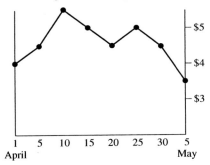

Use this time-series diagram to fill in the following table.

	April 5	April 15	April 25	May 5
Stock Price				
Value of Rachel's Investment				

Unit 5C Test 2 *(continued)*

Name:_____

1. Explain what is meant by quantitative data.

   _____

   _____

   _____

2. Suppose we have data on the number of minivans sold in the U.S. in 2004, 2005, and 2006. If you were to draw a histogram of this data, what would the label be on each bin?

   _____

   _____

   _____

The following table shows the average number of hours Americans sleep each night. Use it to answer questions 3, 4 and 5.

Less than 6	6	7	8	More than 8
12%	26%	30%	28%	4%

3. If there are 260 million Americans, how many sleep 6 hours, how many sleep 7 hours, and how many sleep 8 hours a night? Show your work.

   _____

   _____

   _____

   _____

4. In a pie chart of this data, what angle should be used to represent each of the five categories? Show your work.

   _____

   _____

   _____

   _____

Unit 5C Test 2 *(continued)*

5. Make a pie chart for this data.

The following table shows the age distribution of internet users in millions in 2005. Use it to answer

questions 6 and 7.

Under 20	20-25	26-30	31-35	36-40	Over 40
0.8	3.9	3.6	2.3	1.5	1.4

6. How many internet users were there in 2005? What percentage of them were between the ages of 26 and 35?

_____

_____

_____

7. Draw a histogram of these data and superimpose a line chart over it.

Unit 5C Test 2 (continued)

8. On June 1st, Staci purchased 40 shares of B&B stock for $7 per share. The following is a time-series diagram showing the price of B&B stock during the month of June:

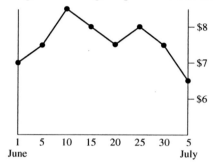

Use this time-series diagram to fill in the following table.

	June 5	June 15	June 25	July 5
Stock Price				
Value of Staci's Investment				

Unit 5C Test 3

Name:_____

Date:_____

Use the following table, which describes the age distribution of U.S. senators in 1994, to answer questions 1 and 2.

Under 50	50–59	60–69	70 and over
30	40	22	8

1. Which region of this pie chart represents the number of senators between the ages of 50 and 59?

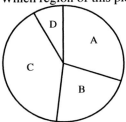

   (a) A   **(b)** B   **(c)** C   **(d)** D

2. What is the angle measure of the region that represents ages 50-69?

   (a) 167.4°   **(b)** 223.2°   **(c)** 42°   **(d)** 139.5°

The following bar graph shows the grades Ms. Muckluck gave the students in her English classes last year. Use it to answer questions 3–5.

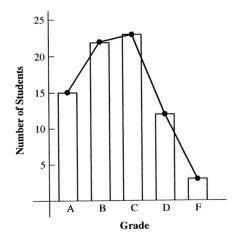

3. If one centimeter represents 5 students, how much taller is the bar for a C grade than the bar for a D grade?

   (a) 3.5 cm   **(b)** 3 cm   **(c)** 2.2 cm   **(d)** 1.4 cm

4. How many more students received a C than received a D or an F?

   (a) 11   **(b)** 2   **(c)** 20   **(d)** 8

Unit 5C Test 3 *(continued)*

Name:_____

5. How many students were in Ms. Muckluck's classes last year?

(a) 75   (b) 23   (c) 57   (d) 45

The following histogram shows how much money the Nelson family has spent on tuition between 2000 and 2007.
Use it to answer questions 6 and 7.

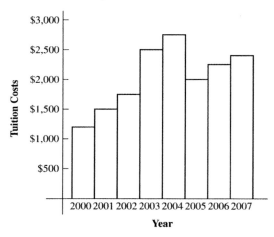

6. How much did the Nelsons spend on tuition between 2003 and 2005?

(a) $4,750   (b) $4,500   (c) $7,250   (d) $2,750

7. What was the first year that the Nelson's tuition declined?

(a) 2003   (b) 2004   (c) 2005   (d) 2006

8. The following time-series diagram tracks the performance of two mutual funds (Fund 1 and Fund 2) in the month of August.

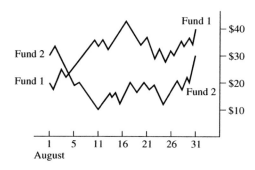

If $1000 was invested in Fund 1 and $2000 was invested in Fund 2 on August 1st, what would the combined value of the investments be on August 31?

(a) $3,000   (b) $4,000   (c) $5,000   (d) $6,000

Unit 5C Test 4

Use the following table, which describes the education level of smokers in the U.S., to answer questions 1 and 2.

Less than high school diploma	High school graduate	Some College	College graduate
35%	28%	20%	17%

1. Which region of this pie chart represents the percentage of smokers with less than a high school diploma?

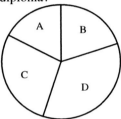

(a) A   (b) B   (c) C   (d) D

2. What is the angle measure of the region that represents college graduates?

(a) 72°   (b) 61.2°   (c) 54°   (d) 100°

The following bar graph shows the grades Mr. Mulligan gave the students in his History classes last year. Use it to answer questions 3–5.

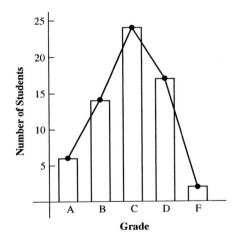

3. If one centimeter represents 5 students, how much taller is the bar for a B grade than the bar for an A grade?

(a) 1.5 cm   (b) 2.8 cm   (c) 1.2 cm   (d) 1.6 cm

4. How many more students received a C than received an A or a B?

(a) 10   (b) 8   (c) 4   (d) 6

5. How many students were in Mr. Mulligan's classes last year?

(a) 60   (b) 63   (c) 68   (d) 70

The following histogram shows how much money the Ricardo family has spent on orthodontia between 2000 and 2007. Use it to answer questions 6 and 7.

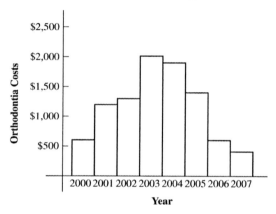

6. How much did the Ricardos spend on orthodontia between 2004 and 2006?

(a) $5,300   (b) $3,400   (c) $2,400   (d) $3,900

7. In what year did the Ricardos' orthodontia expenditures fall the most?

(a) 2006   (b) 2005   (c) 2004   (d) 2007

8. The following time-series diagram tracks the performance of two stocks (Stock 1 and Stock 2) in the month of October.

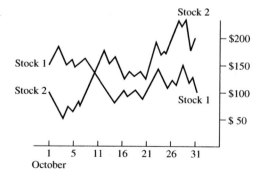

If $5000 was invested in Stock 1 and $10,000 was invested in Stock 2 on October 1st, what would the combined value of the investments be on October 31?

(a) $8333   (b) $10,666   (c) $16,667   (d) $25,000

Unit 5D Test 1

Name:_____

Date:_____

1. Explain what is meant by a contour map.

   _____

   _____

   _____

2. Explain what is meant by a three dimensional graph.

   _____

   _____

   _____

3. Why is it sometimes difficult to read a stack plot?

   _____

   _____

   _____

4. When is data displayed more clearly on an exponential scale? Give an example.

   _____

   _____

   _____

5. A recent study has just rated the 5 most popular brands of toothpaste. If you were to display the findings of this study in a pictograph, what sort of artwork would you use? Be specific.

   _____

   _____

   _____

6. Explain what is meant by inflation.

   _____

   _____

   _____

Unit 5D Test 1 *(continued)*

7. Using only the information in this graph, what can you determine about the real cost of a candy bar between 1985 and 2005?

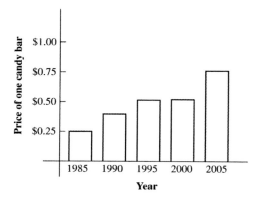

_____

_____

_____

8. In a percent change graph of an average teacher's annual salary the bars representing successive years are either unchanged or decreasing in size. Does this mean that the teacher's salary is going down every year? Explain.

_____

_____

_____

9. The following graphic describes the most popular pizza toppings at Pisano Pizzeria. This graphic is an example of two types of statistical graphs. What are they?

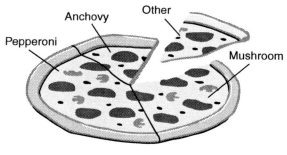

_____

_____

_____

Unit 5D Test 2

1. Explain what is meant by a stack plot.

   _____

   _____

   _____

2. Explain what is meant by a multiple bar graph.

   _____

   _____

   _____

3. Why is it sometimes difficult to interpret a three dimensional graph?

   _____

   _____

   _____

4. What sort of data can be displayed clearly with color coding? Give an example.

   _____

   _____

   _____

5. A recent study has just rated the 5 most popular brands of soda. If you were to display the findings of this study in a pictograph, what sort of artwork would you use? Be specific.

   _____

   _____

   _____

6. Explain what is meant by real cost.

   _____

   _____

   _____

Unit 5D Test 2 *(continued)*

Name:_____

7. The following graph shows the change in the price of greeting cards between 2002 and 2006. What other information do you need to determine the change in the real cost of greeting cards?

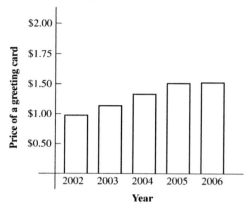

_____

_____

_____

8. How would a decrease in the price per gallon of milk be represented on a percent change graph? Explain.

_____

_____

9. The following chart describes the percentage of cigarette smokers in Gotham City. This chart is an example of two types of statistical graphs. What are they?

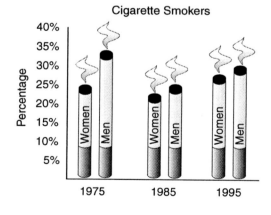

_____

_____

_____

Unit 5D Test 3

Name:_____

Date:_____

Choose the correct answer to each problem.

1. Which of the following describes a statistical graph where a quantity is represented by a curve and has the same value everywhere along the curve?

   (a) Stack plot   **(b)** Contour map   **(c)** Multiple bar graph   **(d)** Pictograph

2. Which of the following describes a statistical graph where each category has its own wedge and the wedges are displayed on top of one another?

   (a) Stack plot   **(b)** Contour map   **(c)** Multiple bar graph   **(d)** Pictograph

3. Which of the following describes a statistical graph that is embellished with additional art work?

   (a) Stack plot   **(b)** Contour map   **(c)** Multiple bar graph   **(d)** Pictograph

4. The difference in strength of the last 5 major earthquakes to hit California have varied by factors of 10. If you were to display data describing the strengths of these earthquakes what could you use to make the graph more readable?

   (a) A three dimensional graph   **(b)** A stack plot
   (c) A color coded map   **(d)** An exponential scale

5. Which of the following types of graphs can be difficult to interpret because of visual distortion on a flat page?

   (a) Stack plot   **(b)** Contour map
   (c) Multiple bar graph   **(d)** Three dimensional graph

6. Which of the following describes the tendency for prices to rise over time?

   (a) Real cost   **(b)** Percent change
   (c) Inflation   **(d)** Adjusted dollars

7. The price of a refrigerator is $1,200. If the rate of inflation in the next three years averages 4% per year and the real cost of the refrigerator remains unchanged in that time, what will the price of the refrigerator be in three years?

   (a) $1,337   **(b)** $1,200   **(c)** $1,344   **(d)** $1,350

8. In a graph that describes the percent rise in the price of grain over 5 years, what does it mean for the value at one year to be less than that value the next year?

   (a) The price of grain has gone down   **(b)** The rate at which the price is rising has gone down

   (c) The real cost of grain has gone down   **(d)** Inflation has gone down

Unit 5D Test 4

Name:_____

Date:_____

Choose the correct answer to each problem.

1. Which of the following describes a statistical graph that plots three or more related quantities simultaneously?

   (a) Contour map   (b) Three dimensional graph
   (c) Multiple bar graph   (d) Pictograph

2. Which of the following describes a statistical graph that plots two or more sets of related data on the same graph to facilitate comparison?

   (a) Contour map   (b) Three dimensional graph
   (c) Multiple bar graph   (d) Pictograph

3. In which of the following types of graphs can it be difficult to interpret the precise thickness of a wedge at a given data point?

   (a) Color coded map   (b) Stack plot
   (c) Multiple bar graph   (d) Exponential Scale

4. Which of the following types of statistical graphs are very common in the media, but are often hard to read due to their cosmetic embellishments?

   (a) Contour map   (b) Three dimensional graph
   (c) Multiple bar graph   (d) Pictograph

5. You have collected regional data showing the percentage of smokers in every state in the nation. Which of the following is a common method of representing this type of geographical data?

   (a) Stack plot   (b) Contour map
   (c) Multiple bar graph   (d) Color coded map

6. Which of the following describes the price of an item after it has been adjusted for inflation?

   (a) Real cost   (b) Economic data
   (c) Inflated cost   (d) Percent change

7. The price of a mountain bike is $1,500. If the rate of inflation in the next two years averages 5% per year and the real cost of the bike remains unchanged in that time, what will the price of the bike be in two years?

   (a) $1,650   (b) $1,500   (c) $1,654   (d) $1,600

8. In a graph that describes the percent rise in the price of gasoline over 10 years, what does it mean for the value at one year to be greater than the value the next year?

   (a) The rate at which the price is rising has gone down (b) The price of gasoline has gone up
   (c) The real cost of gasoline has gone up   (d) Inflation has gone up

Unit 5E Test 1

Name:_____

Date:_____

1. What condition constitutes a correlation between two variables?

_____

_____

_____

2. Would you expect a positive correlation, a negative correlation, or no correlation between the variables *number of calories burned and the number of hours spent exercising*? Explain.

_____

_____

_____

3. Would you expect a positive correlation, a negative correlation, or no correlation between the variables *a student's weight* and *his score on the SAT*? Explain.

_____

_____

_____

4. Do you think that the following correlation is an example of coincidence, a common cause, or causality? *When I flip the switch, the light comes on.*

_____

_____

_____

5. Do you think that the following correlation is an example of coincidence, a common cause, or causality? *Whenever I wash my car, it rains.*

_____

_____

_____

6. Give a physical model for the following cause-and-effect relationship. *Since the tax increase, retail sales have fallen.*

_____

_____

_____

Unit 5E Test 1 *(continued)*

7. Explain what is meant by *cause beyond a reasonable doubt.*

_____

_____

_____

In the following questions, refer to the data given below about average gasoline and diesel prices for the week of 2/26/06 according to region.

Retail Fuel Prices (per gallon)

Region	Gasoline	Diesel
East Coast	$1.424	$1.469
Midwest	$1.393	$1.428
Gulf Coast	$1.375	$1.392
Rocky Mountain	$1.433	$1.504
West Coast	$1.608	$1.557

Source: Energy Information Administration

8. Draw a scatter diagram for the data. Use the horizontal axis for gasoline prices and the vertical axis for diesel prices.

9. Does a correlation exist between gasoline prices and diesel prices? If so, is it positive or negative?

_____

_____

_____

10. Is the relationship between gasoline and diesel prices a coincidence, the result of some common underlying cause, or the result of one of the prices actually being the cause of the other? Explain.

_____

_____

_____

Unit 5E Test 2

Name:_____

Date:_____

1. What is meant by *positive correlation*?

   _____

   _____

   _____

2. Would you expect a positive correlation, a negative correlation, or no correlation between the variables *waist size* and *IQ*? Explain.

   _____

   _____

   _____

3. Would you expect a positive correlation, a negative correlation, or no correlation between the variables *high-school GPA and college GPA*? Explain.

   _____

   _____

   _____

4. Do you think that the following correlation is an example of coincidence, a common cause, or causality? *Whenever the windmill is turning, I hear a rustling noise in the trees.*

   _____

   _____

   _____

5. Do you think that the following correlation is an example of coincidence, a common cause, or causality? *People who smoke frequently have a higher instance of lung cancer.*

   _____

   _____

   _____

Unit 5E Test 2 *(continued)*

6. Give a physical model for the following cause-and-effect relationship.
   In countries where private ownership of handguns is illegal, there is higher frequency of violent crimes.

_____

_____

_____

7. Explain what is meant by *possible cause.*

_____

_____

_____

In the following questions, refer to the data given below about height and GPA for five students.

Student	Height	GPA
Maria	68 inches	3.75
Nancy	62 inches	2.10
Owen	67 inches	3.40
Paul	78 inches	4.00
Quincy	72 inches	3.75

8. Draw a scatter diagram for the data. Use the horizontal axis for height and the vertical axis for GPA.

9. Does a correlation exist between the two variables? If so, is it positive or negative?

_____

_____

_____

10. Is the relationship between height and GPA a coincidence, the result of some common underlying cause, or the result of one of the variables actually being the cause of the other? Explain.

_____

_____

_____

Unit 5E Test 3

Name:_____

Date:_____

Choose the correct answer to each problem.

1. Which of the following is a graph in which each point represents the values of two variables?

   (a) Histogram   (b) Scatter diagram   (c) Pie chart   (d) Bar graph

2. Which of the following exists when two variables tend to change in opposite directions, with one increasing while the other decreases?

   (a) No correlation
   (c) Negative correlation
   (b) Positive correlation
   (d) Perfect correlation

3. Which of the following pairs of variables is likely to have a negative correlation?

   (a) The price of jet fuel and the price of an airline ticket
   (b) A person's height and the same person's weight
   (c) The unemployment rate and the number of homeless people
   (d) Price of gasoline and the number of SUVs sold

4. Which of the following pairs of variables is likely to have no correlation?

   (a) The amount of time studying math and the grade on a math test
   (b) The amount of rainfall and the height of the grass
   (c) The temperature in Tempe, Arizona and the cost of tuition at Yale University
   (d) The unemployment rate and the number of home foreclosures

5. Which of the following relationships between pairs of variables is likely a coincidence?

   (a) Higher energy levels among children who eat more sugar
   (b) Higher test scores among students who dye their hair red
   (c) Higher income levels among people with more education
   (d) Fewer medical problems among people who exercise more often

6. Which of the following is likely the result of some common underlying cause?

   (a) Whenever I eat dessert, my weight increases.
   (b) Whenever I get 8 hours of sleep at night, I don't get sleepy during the day.
   (c) Whenever I get some cash at the ATM, my account balance decreases.
   (d) Whenever I see snowmen, I also see smoke coming out of chimneys.

7. Which of the following is likely a cause-and-effect relationship?

   (a) When the temperature drops, consumption of heating oil rises.
   (b) When the rooster crows, the morning glories open.
   (c) When I drive to work, the sun rises.
   (d) When I see stars, I also see the moon.

Unit 5E Test 3 *(continued)*

8. Which of the following is **not** a guideline for establishing causality?

   (a) Consider only the suspected cause, ignoring other potential causes.
   (b) Find a physical model that explains how the cause produces the effect.
   (c) If possible, test the suspected cause with an experiment.
   (d) Seek evidence that larger amounts of the cause produce larger amounts of the effect.

9. In studying the relationship between abortion and breast cancer, researchers have identified a hormone that they believe explains how having an abortion can lead to the development of breast cancer. This explanation is an example of which of the following?

   (a) A common underlying cause of abortion and breast cancer
   (b) A physical model demonstrating how abortion can cause breast cancer
   (c) Negative correlation between numbers of abortions and instances of breast cancer
   (d) Pure coincidence that many women who have abortions get breast cancer

10. Which of the following best describes our level of confidence in causality when we have discovered a correlation but cannot yet determine whether the correlation implies causality?

    (a) Possible cause
    (c) Cause beyond reasonable doubt
    (b) Probable cause
    (d) Absolute certainty

Unit 5E Test 4

Name:_____

Date:_____

Choose the correct answer to each problem.

1. When all the data points in a scatter diagram fall on a straight line, which of the following is present?

   (a) No correlation
   (c) Negative correlation

   (b) Positive correlation
   (d) Perfect correlation

2. Which of the following exists when two variables tend to increase together?

   (a) No correlation
   (c) Negative correlation

   (b) Positive correlation
   (d) Perfect correlation

3. Which of the following pairs of variables is likely to have a positive correlation?

   (a) The price of gasoline and the price of groceries
   (b) A person's height and the same person's body temperature
   (c) The price of DVD players and the number of DVD players sold
   (d) Interest rates and the number of real estate transactions

4. Which of the following pairs of variables is likely to have a negative correlation?

   (a) The amount of time studying math and the grade on a math test
   (b) The number of miles driven and the tread depth on your tires
   (c) The temperature in Tempe, Arizona and the cost of tuition at Yale University
   (d) The unemployment rate and the number of home foreclosures

5. Which of the following is likely a coincidence?

   (a) Higher real estate prices in cities with more employment opportunities
   (b) More crime in neighborhoods with fewer streetlights
   (c) Higher annual rainfall in states with stricter gun control laws
   (d) More instances of skin cancer in regions with more sunshine

6. Which of the following is likely the result of some common underlying cause?

   (a) Patients who eat a lot of salt often have high blood pressure.
   (b) Patients who have runny noses often have watery eyes as well.
   (c) Patients who eat more vegetables often have better eyesight.
   (d) Patients who exercise regularly often have better cholesterol levels.

7. Which of the following is likely a cause-and-effect relationship?

   (a) I washed dishes, and then I did laundry.
   (b) It was hot and humid, and then it stormed.
   (c) The dog barked, and then the clock chimed.
   (d) The phone rang, and then someone knocked on the door.

8. Which of the following is a guideline for establishing a causality?

   (a) Consider only the suspected cause, ignoring other potential causes.
   (b) Proceed only if the suspected cause-and-effect is politically correct.
   (c) If possible, test the suspected cause with an experiment.
   (d) Seek to discredit evidence that suggests that there is no causality.

9. Investigating a homeowner's complaints against the homebuilder, an inspector finds that all the reported problems can be explained by poor drainage. This explanation is an example of which of the following?

   (a) A common underlying cause
   (b) A physical model demonstrating causality
   (c) Positive correlation
   (d) Coincidence

10. Which of the following best describes our level of confidence in causality when we have found a physical model that is so successful in explaining how one thing causes another that it seems unreasonable to doubt the causality?

    (a) Possible cause
    (b) Probable cause
    (c) Cause beyond reasonable doubt
    (d) Absolute certainty

Unit 6A Test 1

1. Define the *distribution* of a variable.

_____

_____

_____

2. Explain what is meant by an outlier.

_____

_____

_____

3. How many peaks would you expect for the distribution of the results of rolling a fair die 1000 times? Why?

_____

_____

_____

4. State whether you expect the distribution of shoe sizes in a sample of 100 men to be symmetric, left-skewed or right-skewed. Explain.

_____

_____

_____

5. Find the mode of the following set of data.
   8, 3, 3, 17, 9, 22, 19

_____

_____

_____

6. Find the mean of the following data set.
   2, 7, 5, 7, 14

_____

_____

_____

7. Find the median of the following set of data.
   3, 5, 7, 3, 1, 2, 2, 6, 5, 4, 3, 4

   _____

   _____

   _____

8. Consider the distribution graphed below.

   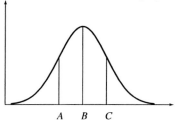

   A   B   C

   Determine whether each of the mean, median, and mode is represented by *A*, *B*, or *C*.

   _____

   _____

   _____

9. Suppose there are 300 students enrolled in the introductory geology course this semester. Each of these students is enrolled in one of three lecture sections of 100 students each and one of 15 laboratory sections of 20 students each. A student reports that the average size of his geology classes is 60 students, while the chairperson of the department claims that the average size of an introductory geology class is approximately 33 students. How can they both be right?

   _____

   _____

   _____

10. The median price of a new home is reported to be $172,400, and the mean price is reported to be $196,000. Describe the distribution of new home prices, explaining the relationship between the given median and mean.

   _____

   _____

   _____

Unit 6A Test 2

1. Give an example of a data set that you would expect to have a symmetric distribution.

   _____

   _____

   _____

2. Explain what is meant by a uniform distribution.

   _____

   _____

   _____

3. How many peaks would you expect for the distribution of the weights of all students at your college? Why?

   _____

   _____

   _____

4. State whether you expect the distribution of the ages of students at your college to be symmetric, left-skewed or right-skewed. Explain.

   _____

   _____

   _____

5. Find the mode of the following set of data.
   65, 78, 53, 96, 87, 96, 34, 46, 85

   _____

   _____

   _____

6. Find the mean of the following data set.
   11, 8, 2, 5, 17, 39, 52, 42

   _____

   _____

   _____

Unit 6A Test 2 *(continued)*

7. Find the median of the following set of data.
   3, 2, 1, 1, 3, 1, 2, 1

   _____

   _____

   _____

8. Consider the distribution graphed below.

   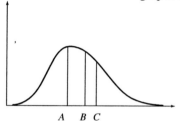

   A   B C

   Determine whether each of the mean, median, and mode is represented by *A*, *B*, or *C*.

   _____

   _____

   _____

9. A small company has 20 employees of which 9 earn $40,000 per year, 3 earn $39,000 per year, and 8 earn $19,000 per year. The owner reports the average salary of his employees as $39,000 per year, while an unhappy employee claims the average is only $31,450 per year. How can they both be right?

   _____

   _____

   _____

10. The median score on a test is reported to be 79, and the mean score is reported to be 72. Describe the distribution of test scores, explaining the relationship between the given median and mean.

    _____

    _____

    _____

Unit 6A Test 3

Name:_____

Date:_____

Choose the correct answer to each problem.

1. Which measure of the center of a distribution is most affected by an outlier?

   (a) Mean   **(b)** Median   **(c)** Mode   **(d)** Variation

2. Which best describes the shape of a unimodal distribution?

   (a) No peaks   **(b)** One peak
   (c) Two peaks   **(d)** More than two peaks

3. Which quantity describes how widely data values are spread about the center of a distribution?

   (a) Mean   **(b)** Variation
   (c) Skewness   **(d)** Number of peaks

4. Which measure of center would you expect to be the largest in a left-skewed distribution?

   (a) Mean   **(b)** Median   **(c)** Mode   **(d)** Variation

5. Which of the following distributions is most likely to be uniform?

   (a) The distribution of the heights of a sample of 100 college students
   (b) The distribution of the last digits of ID numbers in a sample of 100 college students
   (c) The distribution of the scores on a mathematics exam taken by 100 college students
   (d) The distribution of the GPAs of a sample of 100 college students

6. Find the mean of the following set of data.

   101, 88, 74, 60, 12, 94, 74, 85

   (a) 73.5   **(b)** 79.5   **(c)** 84   **(d)** 73

7. Find the median of the following data set.

   4, 8, 1, 14, 9, 21, 12

   (a) 12   **(b)** 9   **(c)** 8   **(d)** 10.5

8. Find the mode of the following set of data.

   1, 2, 2, 3, 3, 3, 4, 4, 5, 5, 6, 7

   (a) 3   **(b)** 3.5   **(c)** 3.75   **(d)** 4

Unit 6A Test 3 *(continued)*

9. Consider the distribution graphed below.

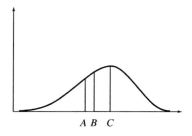

   A B   C

   Which are most likely to be the values of *A*, *B*, and *C*?

   (a) *A* = mode, *B* = median, *C* = mean
   (b) *A* = mode, *B* = mean, *C* = median
   (c) *A* = median, *B* = mean, *C* = mode
   (d) *A* = mean, *B* = median, *C* = mode

10. Which best describes the distribution graphed below?

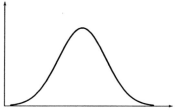

   (a) Uniform and left-skewed   **(b)** Uniform and symmetric
   (c) Unimodal and symmetric   **(d)** Bimodal and right-skewed

Unit 6A Test 4

Choose the correct answer to each problem.

1. Which best describes the shape of a uniform distribution?

   (a) No peaks
   (c) Two peaks
   (b) One peak
   (d) More than two peaks

2. Which measure of center is at the peak of a right-skewed distribution?

   (a) Mean   (b) Median   (c) Mode   (d) Variation

3. Which of the following is **not** used to describe the shape of a distribution?

   (a) Number of Peaks
   (c) Variation
   (b) Symmetry or skewness
   (d) Mean, median, and mode

4. Which measure of center would you expect to be the smallest in a left-skewed distribution?

   (a) Mean   (b) Median   (c) Mode   (d) Variation

5. Which of the following distributions is most likely to be bimodal?

   (a) The distribution of the heights of a sample of 100 female college students
   (b) The distribution of the last digits of ID numbers in a sample of 100 college students
   (c) The distribution of the weights of 100 dogs, where 50 are poodles and 50 are huskies
   (d) The distribution of the shoe sizes of a sample of 100 male college students

6. Find the median of the following set of data.

   14, 27, 3, 82, 64, 34, 8, 51

   (a) 71   (b) 30.5   (c) 87   (d) 32.5

7. Find the mode of the following data set.

   2.1, 1.8, 3.5, 2.1, 1.9, 1.7

   (a) 1.8   (b) 2.0   (c) 2.1   (d) 2.2

8. Find the mean of the following set of data.

   1, 2, 2, 3, 3, 3, 4, 4, 5, 5, 6, 7

   (a) 3   (b) 3.5   (c) 3.75   (d) 4

Unit 6A Test 4 *(continued)*

9. Consider the distribution graphed below.

    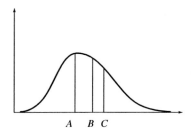

    Which are most likely to be the values of *A*, *B*, and *C*?

    (a) *A* = mode, *B* = median, *C* = mean
    (b) *A* = mode, *B* = mean, *C* = median
    (c) *A* = median, *B* = mean, *C* = mode
    (d) *A* = mean, *B* = median, *C* = mode

10. Which best describes the distribution graphed below?

    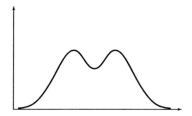

    (a) Uniform and symmetric   (b) Unimodal and right-skewed
    (c) Unimodal and symmetric   (d) Bimodal and symmetric

Unit 6B Test 1

Name:_____

Date:_____

1. Explain the meaning of the lower quartile of a set of numerical data.

   _____

   _____

   _____

2. What commonly used measure of variation describes how far data values are spread around the mean of a data set?

   _____

   _____

   _____

3. The monthly incomes of 20 employees working for a certain company are as follows:

   2300, 3400, 2400, 2600, 1800, 2500, 4700, 3200, 2400, 3100,
   2000, 2600, 2700, 3300, 1900, 4200, 3100, 1700, 2800, 2900.

   Find the range of the data.

   _____

   _____

   _____

4. The prices of a gallon of regular gasoline at 10 stations within a mile of one another are as follows:

   $1.59, $1.61, $1.63, $1.63, $1.65, $1.67, $1.69, $1.71, $1.79, $1.85.

   Find the upper quartile of the prices.

   _____

   _____

   _____

5. A set of data consists of the numbers:

   5.7, 8.3, 8.9, 8.9, 9.4, 9.7, 10.4, 10.6, 12.6, 13.8.

   Find the five-number summary for the data.

   _____

   _____

   _____

Unit 6B Test 1 *(continued)*

6. The heights, in inches, of fourteen students are:

$$62, 62, 63, 64, 65, 65, 66, 67, 68, 68, 69, 70, 71, 73.$$

Make a box plot for the data.

7. The weights, in pounds, of a group of dogs are:

$$3, 4, 7, 11, 12, 12, 15, 16.$$

Calculate the standard deviation.

_____

_____

_____

8. The scores on a mathematics test are:

$$59, 72, 73, 73, 78, 81, 85, 88, 88, 93, 97, 103.$$

Estimate the standard deviation of the scores using the range rule of thumb.

_____

_____

_____

Unit 6B Test 2

1. Explain the meaning of the upper quartile of a set of numerical data.

_____

_____

_____

2. From which measure of center is the standard deviation calculated?

_____

_____

_____

3. The monthly incomes of 20 employees working for a certain company are as follows:

    2600, 1800, 2500, 4400, 3200, 2400, 3100, 2000, 2600, 2700,
    2300, 2300, 3400, 2400, 1900, 3700, 3100, 1800, 2800, 2300.

   Find the range of the data.

_____

_____

_____

4. The prices, in dollars, of a pound of onions at 10 local stores are:

    0.29, 0.29, 0.39, 0.59, 0.59, 0.59, 0.59, 0.69, 0.69, 0.79.

   Find the lower quartile of the prices.

_____

_____

_____

5. A set of data consists of the numbers:

    4.3, 5.2, 5.4, 5.5, 5.7, 6.1, 6.1, 7.3, 7.5, 8.2.

   Find the five-number summary for the data.

_____

_____

_____

Unit 6B Test 2 *(continued)*

6. The heights, in inches, of fourteen students are:

$$42, 44, 44, 45, 46, 47, 48, 49, 50, 51, 54, 56, 58, 60.$$

Make a box plot for the data.

_____

_____

_____

7. The weights, in pounds, of a group of dogs are:

$$11, 4, 19, 6, 22, 24, 20, 21, 26.$$

Calculate the standard deviation.

_____

_____

_____

8. The prices, in dollars, of a gallon of regular gasoline at 5 gas stations at the same freeway exit are:

$$2.41, 2.43, 2.43, 2.47, 2.51.$$

Estimate the standard deviation of the prices using the range rule of thumb.

_____

_____

_____

Unit 6B Test 3

Name:_____

Date:_____

Choose the correct answer to each problem.

1. Which of the following is **not** a measure of variation?

   (a) Five-number summary   (b) Range
   (c) Mean   (d) Standard deviation

2. In a typical set of numerical data, what fraction of the data values lie at or above the upper quartile?

   (a) 0 (i.e., none of the data)   (b) $\frac{1}{4}$

   (c) $\frac{1}{2}$ (d) $\frac{3}{4}$

3. Find the range of the following data set.
   15.1, 13.7, 15.3, 18.9, 17.4

   (a) 1.2   (b) 3.6   (c) 5.2   (d) 6.1

4. Find the lower quartile of the following data set.
   14.1, 14.9, 15.0, 15.2, 15.5, 15.8

   (a) 14.9   (b) 14.95   (c) 15.0   (d) 15.1

5. A set of data consists of the numbers:

   $$1.2, 1.4, 1.6, 1.6, 1.7, 1.9, 2.1, 2.6, 2.7, 3.2.$$

   Find the five-number summary for the data.

   (a) 1.2, 1.6, 1.6, 2.6, 3.2   (b) 1.2, 1.5, 1.7, 2.6, 3.2
   (c) 1.2, 1.6, 2.0, 2.6, 3.2   (d) 1.2, 1.6, 1.8, 2.6, 3.2

6. The box plot shown represents the heights of 100 students. Approximately how many of these students are between 60.5 and 64.5 inches tall?

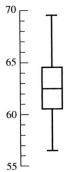

Height (inches)

   (a) 25 students   (b) 40 students   (c) 50 students   (d) 75 students

Unit 6B Test 3 *(continued)*

7. The weights, in pounds, of a group of dogs are

$$34, 37, 42, 57, 64, 82.$$

Calculate the standard deviation.

(a) 16.9 pounds **(b)** 18.5 pounds **(c)** 24.8 pounds **(d)** 343 pounds

8. The ages, in days, of a group of infants, are: 3, 3, 4, 7, 10, 19.
Estimate the standard deviation of the ages using the range rule of thumb.

(a) 4 days **(b)** 6.2 days **(c)** 5.5 days **(d)** 7 days

Unit 6B Test 4

Name:_____

Date:_____

Choose the correct answer to each problem.

1. Which of the following is **not** part of the five-number summary?

   (a) High   (b) Lower quartile   (c) Median   (d) Mode

2. In a typical set of numerical data, what fraction of the data values lie at or above the lower quartile?

   (a) $\dfrac{1}{4}$ (b) $\dfrac{1}{2}$

   (c) $\dfrac{3}{4}$ (d) 1 (i.e., all of the data)

3. Find the range of the following set of data.
   0.9, 1.7, 1.2, 0.7, 1.5

   (a) 0.6   (b) 1.0   (c) 1.2   (d) 1.7

4. Find the upper quartile of the following data set.
   59, 65, 70, 71, 71, 74, 75, 78, 80, 83, 84, 87, 91, 98

   (a) 83.5   (b) 84   (c) 85.5   (d) 87

5. A set of data consists of the numbers:

   $$3.5, 3.7, 3.8, 4.2, 4.6, 4.8, 4.8, 5.3, 5.6, 5.7.$$

   Find the five-number summary for the data.

   (a) 3.5, 3.8, 4.7, 5.3, 5.7   (b) 3.5, 4.0, 4.8, 5.45, 5.7
   (c) 3.5, 3.8, 4.6, 5.3, 5.7   (d) 3.5, 3.8, 4.8, 5.3, 5.7

6. The box plot shown represents the heights of 160 students. Approximately how many of these students are between 43.5 and 46.5 inches tall?

Height (inches)

   (a) 40 students   (b) 60 students   (c) 80 students   (d) 120 students

7. The weights, in pounds, of a group of dogs are:

$$8, 14, 26, 56, 72, 90.$$

Calculate the standard deviation.

(a) 27.3 pounds   (b) 31.0 pounds   (c) 33.4 pounds   (d) 1155 pounds

8. The lengths, in inches, of ten baguettes are:
17.2, 17.9, 17.9, 18.0, 18.0, 18.0, 18.1, 18.1, 18.2, 18.6
Estimate the standard deviation of the lengths using the range rule of thumb.

(a) 0.04   (b) 0.35   (c) 0.17   (d) 0.60

Unit 6C Test 1

Where appropriate, you may use the following abbreviated table of z-scores and percentiles.

z-score	−3.0	−2.0	−1.5	−1.0	−0.9	−0.8	−0.7	−0.6	−0.5
percentile	0.13	2.28	6.68	15.87	18.41	21.19	24.20	27.43	30.85

z-score	−0.4	−0.3	−0.2	−0.1	0.0	0.1	0.2	0.3	0.4
percentile	34.46	38.21	42.07	46.02	50.00	53.98	57.93	61.79	65.54

z-score	0.5	0.6	0.7	0.8	0.9	1.0	1.5	2.0	3.0
percentile	69.15	72.57	75.80	78.81	81.59	84.13	93.32	97.72	99.87

1. Bob took a standardized test, and his score was in the 79th percentile. Explain the meaning of this statement.

   _____

   _____

   _____

2. Assume that a set of test scores is normally distributed with a mean of 70 and a standard deviation of 15. What percentage of scores lie between 55 and 70?

   _____

   _____

   _____

3. Assume that a set of test scores is normally distributed with a mean of 820 and a standard deviation of 35. In what percentile is a score of 750?

   _____

   _____

   _____

4. Suppose a data set has a mean of 126 and a standard deviation of 4. Find the z-score for a data value of 133.

   _____

   _____

   _____

Unit 6C Test 1 *(continued)*

5. What is the *z*-score of a data value that is 0.2 standard deviations below the mean? In what percentile is that data value?

_____

_____

_____

6. About how many standard deviations above or below the mean is a data value in the 69th percentile?

_____

_____

_____

7. Suppose that, in a company with 3000 employees, the monthly salaries are normally distributed. The mean salary is $2700, with a standard deviation of $400. About how many of the employees earn more than $2460 per month?

_____

_____

_____

8. Prior to recentering in 1995, the mean SAT verbal score was about 430. Assume that the standard deviation was 100 points. Find the *z*-score and the percentile for a student who scored 580.

_____

_____

_____

9. After recentering in 1995, the mean SAT math score was about 500. Assume that the standard deviation was 100 points. Find the *z*-score and the percentile for a student who scored 520.

_____

_____

_____

10. The average person has an IQ of 100, and scores are normally distributed with a standard deviation of 15 points. What percentage of people have an IQ between 85 and 100?

_____

_____

_____

Unit 6C Test 2

Where appropriate, you may use the following abbreviated table of z-scores and percentiles.

z-score	−3.0	−2.0	−1.5	−1.0	−0.9	−0.8	−0.7	−0.6	−0.5
percentile	0.13	2.28	6.68	15.87	18.41	21.19	24.20	27.43	30.85

z-score	−0.4	−0.3	−0.2	−0.1	0.0	0.1	0.2	0.3	0.4
percentile	34.46	38.21	42.07	46.02	50.00	53.98	57.93	61.79	65.54

z-score	0.5	0.6	0.7	0.8	0.9	1.0	1.5	2.0	3.0
percentile	69.15	72.57	75.80	78.81	81.59	84.13	93.32	97.72	99.87

1. Carol took a standardized test, and her score was in the 34th percentile. Explain the meaning of this statement.

_____

_____

_____

2. Assume that a set of test scores is normally distributed with a mean of 55 and a standard deviation of 10. What percentage of scores lie between 55 and 75?

_____

_____

_____

3. Assume that a set of test scores is normally distributed with a mean of 630 and a standard deviation of 15. In what percentile is a score of 615?

_____

_____

_____

4. Suppose a data set has a mean of 104 and a standard deviation of 10. Find the z-score for a data value of 110.

_____

_____

_____

Unit 6C Test 2 *(continued)*

Name:_____

5. What is the z-score of a data value that is 0.6 standard deviations below the mean? In what percentile is that data value?

_____

_____

_____

6. About how many standard deviations above or below the mean is a data value in the 24th percentile?

_____

_____

_____

7. Suppose that, in a company with 4000 employees, the monthly salaries are normally distributed. The mean salary is $3500, with a standard deviation of $500. About how many of the employees earn more than $3750 per month?

_____

_____

_____

8. Prior to recentering in 1995, the mean SAT verbal score was about 430. Assume that the standard deviation was 100 points. Find the z-score and the percentile for a student who scored 370.

_____

_____

_____

9. After recentering in 1995, the mean SAT math score was about 500. Assume that the standard deviation was 100 points. Find the z-score and the percentile for a student who scored 460.

_____

_____

_____

10. The average person has an IQ of 100, and scores are normally distributed with a standard deviation of 15 points. What percentage of people have an IQ between 70 and 100?

_____

_____

_____

Unit 6C Test 3

Choose the correct answer to each problem.

Where appropriate, you may use the following abbreviated table of z-scores and percentiles.

z-score	−3.0	−2.0	−1.5	−1.0	−0.9	−0.8	−0.7	−0.6	−0.5
percentile	0.13	2.28	6.68	15.87	18.41	21.19	24.20	27.43	30.85

z-score	−0.4	−0.3	−0.2	−0.1	0.0	0.1	0.2	0.3	0.4
percentile	34.46	38.21	42.07	46.02	50.00	53.98	57.93	61.79	65.54

z-score	0.5	0.6	0.7	0.8	0.9	1.0	1.5	2.0	3.0
percentile	69.15	72.57	75.80	78.81	81.59	84.13	93.32	97.72	99.87

1. Ted took a standardized test. If 24% of the students scored below Ted, 3% had the same score, and 73% had a higher score, what percentile was Ted in?

   (a) 24th percentile   **(b)** 27th percentile   **(c)** 73rd percentile   **(d)** 78th percentile

2. Assume that a set of test scores is normally distributed with a mean of 545 and a standard deviation of 30. What percentage of scores lie between 515 and 545?

   (a) 34%   **(b)** 47.5%   **(c)** 68%   **(d)** 95%

3. Assume that a set of test scores is normally distributed with a mean of 65 and a standard deviation of 10. In what percentile is a score of 85?

   (a) 65th percentile   **(b)** 85th percentile   **(c)** 95th percentile   **(d)** 97.5th
   percentile

4. Suppose a data set has a mean of 136 and a standard deviation of 8. Find the z-score for a data value of 121.

   (a) −1.875   **(b)** −0.75   **(c)** 0.75   **(d)** 1.875

5. In what percentile is a data value that is 0.8 standard deviation above the mean?

   (a) 21.19th percentile   **(b)** 34.46th percentile   **(c)** 65.54th percentile   **(d)** 78.81th
   percentile

6. About how many standard deviations above or below the mean is a data value in the 62nd percentile?

   (a) 0.6 standard deviation below the mean   **(b)** 0.3 standard deviation below the mean
   (c) 0.3 standard deviation above the mean   **(d)** 0.6 standard deviation above the mean

7. Suppose that, in a company with 5000 employees, the monthly salaries are normally distributed. The mean salary is $3300, with a standard deviation of $600. About how many of the employees earn more than $3060 per month?

   (a) 1723 employees   **(b)** 2104 employees   **(c)** 2897 employees   **(d)** 3277
   employees

Unit 6C Test 3 *(continued)*

8. Prior to recentering in 1995, the mean SAT verbal score was about 430. Assume that the standard deviation was 100 points. Find the *z*-score for a student who scored 490.

   (a) −0.6   (b) −0.1   (c) 0.1   (d) 0.6

9. After recentering in 1995, the mean SAT math score was about 500. Assume that the standard deviation was 100 points. Find the percentile for a student who scored 570.

   (a) 24.20th percentile   (b) 38.21st percentile   (c) 61.79th percentile   (d) 75.80th percentile

10. The average person has an IQ of 100, and scores are normally distributed with a standard deviation of 15 points. What percentage of people have an IQ below 115?

    (a) 34%   (b) 47.5%   (c) 68%   (d) 84%

Unit 6C Test 4

Choose the correct answer to each problem.

Where appropriate, you may use the following abbreviated table of z-scores and percentiles.

z-score	−3.0	−2.0	−1.5	−1.0	−0.9	−0.8	−0.7	−0.6	−0.5
percentile	0.13	2.28	6.68	15.87	18.41	21.19	24.20	27.43	30.85
z-score	−0.4	−0.3	−0.2	−0.1	0.0	0.1	0.2	0.3	0.4
percentile	34.46	38.21	42.07	46.02	50.00	53.98	57.93	61.79	65.54
z-score	0.5	0.6	0.7	0.8	0.9	1.0	1.5	2.0	3.0
percentile	69.15	72.57	75.80	78.81	81.59	84.13	93.32	97.72	99.87

1. Alice took a standardized test. If 58% of the students scored below Alice, 5% had the same score, and 37% had a higher score, what percentile was Alice in?

    (a) 37th percentile
    (c) 58th percentile
    (b) 42nd percentile
    (d) 63rd percentile

2. Assume that a set of test scores is normally distributed with a mean of 480 and a standard deviation of 20. What percentage of scores lie between 440 and 480?

    (a) 34%
    (b) 47.5%
    (c) 68%
    (d) 95%

3. Assume that a set of test scores is normally distributed with a mean of 55 and a standard deviation of 15. In what percentile is a score of 70?

    (a) 68th percentile
    (b) 70th percentile
    (c) 84th percentile
    (d) 95th percentile

4. Suppose a data set has a mean of 117 and a standard deviation of 10. Find the z-score for a data value of 103.

    (a) −7
    (b) −1.4
    (c) 1.4
    (d) 7

5. In what percentile is a data value that is 0.6 standard deviation above the mean?

    (a) 21.19th percentile
    (b) 34.46th percentile
    (c) **72.57**th percentile
    (d) 78.81st
    percentile

6. About how many standard deviations above or below the mean is a data value in the 21st percentile?

    (a) 0.8 standard deviation below the mean
    (c) 0.4 standard deviation above the mean
    (b) 0.4 standard deviation below the mean
    (d) 0.8 standard deviation above the mean

7. Suppose that, in a company with 6000 employees, the monthly salaries are normally distributed. The mean salary is $2900, with a standard deviation of $300. About how many of the employees earn more than $3170 per month?

    (a) 1104 employees
    (c) 3932 employees
    (b) 2068 employees
    (d) 4896 employees

Unit 6C Test 4 *(continued)*

8. Prior to recentering in 2000, the mean SAT verbal score was about 440. Assume that the standard deviation was 100 points. Find the z-score for a student who scored 410.

   (a) −1.0　　　　　**(b)** −0.3　　　　　**(c)** 0.3　　　　　**(d)** 1.0

9. After recentering in 1995, the mean SAT math score was about 500. Assume that the standard deviation was 100 points. Find the percentile for a student who scored 420.

   (a) 21.19th percentile　　**(b)** 34.46th percentile　　**(c)** 65.54th percentile　　**(d)** 78.81st percentile

10. The average person has an IQ of 100, and scores are normally distributed with a standard deviation of 15 points. What percentage of people have an IQ below 130?

    (a) 68%　　　　　**(b)** 84%　　　　　**(c)** 95%　　　　　**(d)** 97.5%

Unit 6D Test 1

1. What does it mean for an observed difference to be statistically significant at the 0.05 level?

   _____

   _____

   _____

2. According to the Central Limit Theorem, what is the mean of a sampling distribution?

   _____

   _____

   _____

3. Suppose you draw a single sample of size 1600 from a large population and measure its sample proportion. What is the margin of error for 95% confidence?

   _____

   _____

   _____

4. Suppose that you take a random sample of 400 people who voted in the last election in a heavily populated county and you find that 21% of those people voted illegally. Find a 95% confidence interval for the actual percentage of people who voted illegally in that county.

   _____

   _____

   _____

5. Should a presidential candidate conclude that his popularity is dwindling because a poll shows his approval rating to be 61% one day and 59% the next day? Explain.

   _____

   _____

   _____

6. A school claims that 99% of its graduates obtain jobs in their field of study within one year of graduation. In a sample of 1600 graduates out of school more than one year, a researcher finds that 289 graduates of the school have never worked in their field of study. Discuss the school's claim in light of this sample.

   _____

   _____

   _____

Unit 6D Test 1 *(continued)*

The following questions refer to a (hypothetical) study of 400 people that was designed to determine whether a certain drug was effective in treating arthritis pain. The results are summarized in the following contingency table.

	Severe pain	Mild or no pain	Total
Drug	60	140	200
Placebo	80	120	200
Total	140	260	400

7. Construct an alternative hypothesis and a null hypothesis for this study.

_____

_____

_____

8. Briefly describe the results expected in this study if the *null hypothesis* is true.

_____

_____

_____

9. Briefly describe the results expected in this study if the *alternative hypothesis* is true.

_____

_____

_____

10. In terms of percentages, how do the actual results compare to the results expected according to the alternative hypothesis or the null hypothesis?

_____

_____

_____

Unit 6D Test 2

Name:_____

Date:_____

1. What does it mean for an observed difference to be statistically significant at the 0.01 level?

   _____

   _____

   _____

2. What is a sampling distribution?

   _____

   _____

   _____

3. The actual proportion of students living in residence halls at a large university is 0.38. Several samples of 100 students each yield proportions of 0.28, 0.30, 0.31, and 0.39 residence hall students. According to the Central Limit Theorem, what is the mean of these sample proportions?

   _____

   _____

   _____

4. If you take samples of size 64 from a large population, what is the standard deviation of the sampling distribution?

   _____

   _____

   _____

5. Of what are you 95% confident when you give a 95% confidence interval?

   _____

   _____

   _____

6. Suppose you draw a single sample of size 1,000,000 from a large population and measure its sample proportion. What is the margin of error for 95% confidence?

   _____

   _____

   _____

Unit 6D Test 2 (continued)

Name:_____

The following questions refer to a (hypothetical) study of 500 people that was designed to determine whether a certain drug was effective in reducing the number of pimples. The results are summarized in the following contingency table.

	Reduced pimples	No reduction	Total
Drug	205	95	300
Placebo	145	55	200
Total	350	150	500

7. Construct an alternative hypothesis and a null hypothesis for this study.

_____

_____

_____

8. Briefly describe the results expected in this study if the *null hypothesis* is true.

_____

_____

_____

9. Briefly describe the results expected in this study if the *alternative hypothesis* is true.

_____

_____

_____

10. In terms of percentages, how do the actual results compare to the results expected according to the alternative hypothesis or the null hypothesis?

_____

_____

_____

Unit 6D Test 3

Name:_____

Date:_____

Choose the correct answer to each problem.

1. The actual proportion of students living in residence halls at a university with 20,000 students is 0.28. Five samples of 100 university students yield proportions of 0.27, 0.31, 0.26, 0.33, and 0.33 residence hall students. According to the Central Limit Theorem, what is the mean of this sampling distribution?

   (a) 0.28   (b) 0.30   (c) 0.31   (d) 0.33

2. If you take samples of size 625 from a large population, what is the standard deviation of the sampling distribution?

   (a) 0.02   (b) 0.04   (c) 0.4   (d) 0.95

3. Suppose you draw a single sample of size 100 from a large population and measure its sample proportion. What is the margin of error for 95% confidence?

   (a) 0.05   (b) 0.1   (c) 0.5   (d) 0.95

4. Suppose that you take a random sample of 1600 people who voted in the last U.S. presidential election and you find that 13% of those people voted illegally. Find a 95% confidence interval for the actual percentage of people who voted illegally in that election.

   (a) 8% to 18%   (b) 9.75% to 16.25%   (c) 10.5% to 15.5%   (d) 11.75% to 14.25%

5. A poll shows the approval rating of a senator to be 45% one day and 42% the next day. Which of the following is most likely the reason for the discrepancy in these sample statistics?

   (a) 3% of the population who approved of the senator at the time of the first poll disapproved at the time of the second poll.
   (b) The percentage of the population who approves of the senator didn't change; the difference in the statistics is due to chance.
   (c) Between the times of the polls, a news story was released alleging that the senator who claims to be "for the children" is a pedophile.
   (d) The senator's staff paid the polling organization more for the first poll than for the second poll.

6. An environmentalist group seeking millions of federal dollars to clean up a polluted lake states in its report to the U.S. Congress that 75% of the fish in the lake have dangerous levels of toxins. The bipartisan committee reviewing the report hires an independent research group to test this claim. In a random sample of 280 fish from the lake, the independent group finds 35 fish that contain toxins. Which of the following is most likely true?

   (a) The difference in the two statistics is due to chance, and the population parameter is close to 75% as reported by the environmentalist group.
   (b) The fish with dangerous levels of toxins are smarter than other fish, so they were able to avoid being caught by the independent research group.
   (c) Since cleaning up the lake is a good idea, Congress should have given the group the money without questioning its claims.
   (d) The statistic of 75% reported by the environmentalist group is wrong, and the true population parameter is close to 12.5%.

Unit 6D Test 3 *(continued)*

7. In what circumstance is a result said to have high statistical significance?

    (a) It is very likely to have occurred by chance.
    (b) It is very unlikely to have occurred by chance.
    (c) It supports the alternative hypothesis of an experiment.
    (d) It supports the null hypothesis of an experiment.

The following questions refer to a (hypothetical) study of 600 people that was designed to determine whether a certain drug was effective in curing cold sores. The results are summarized in the following contingency table.

	Cured	Not cured	Total
Drug	190	110	300
Placebo	160	140	300
Total	350	250	600

8. Which of the following would be a reasonable alternative hypothesis for this study?

    (a) The drug was at least as effective as the placebo at curing cold sores.
    (b) The drug was more effective than the placebo at curing cold sores.
    (c) The drug was no more effective than the placebo at curing cold sores.
    (d) The drug was less effective than the placebo at curing cold sores.

9. Which of the following would be a reasonable null hypothesis for this study?

    (a) The drug was at least as effective as the placebo at curing cold sores.
    (b) The drug was more effective than the placebo at curing cold sores.
    (c) The drug was no more effective than the placebo at curing cold sores.
    (d) The drug was less effective than the placebo at curing cold sores.

10. Using the percentages of cured patients among drug-taking patients and placebo-taking patients, how do the actual results compare to the results expected according to the alternative hypothesis or the null hypothesis?

    (a) The results agree with the null hypothesis only.
    (b) The results agree with the alternative hypothesis only.
    (c) The results agree with both the null hypothesis and the alternative hypothesis.
    (d) The results do not agree with either the null hypothesis or the alternative hypothesis.

Unit 6D Test 4

Name:_____

Date:_____

Choose the correct answer to each problem.

1. The actual proportion of students living in residence halls at a university with 18,000 students is 0.42. Six samples of 100 university students yield proportions of 0.39, 0.40, 0.40, 0.42, 0.43, and 0.45 residence hall students. According to the Central Limit Theorem, what is the mean of this sampling distribution?

   (a) 0.40   (b) 0.41   (c) 0.415   (d) 0.42

2. If you take samples of size 16 from a large population, what is the standard deviation of the sampling distribution?

   (a) 0.05   (b) 0.125   (c) 0.25   (d) 0.5

3. Suppose you draw a single sample of size 64 from a large population and measure its sample proportion. What is the margin of error for 95% confidence?

   (a) 5%   (b) 6.25%   (c) 12.5%   (d) 95%

4. Suppose that you take a random sample of 100 people who voted in the last U.S. presidential election and you find that 17% of those people voted illegally. Find a 95% confidence interval for the actual percentage of people who voted illegally in that election.

   (a) 0% to 34%   (b) 7% to 27%
   (c) 10% to 20%   (d) 14.5% to 19.5%

5. A poll of 750 registered voters shows the support for a proposed tax increase to build new schools to be 65% one week and 21% the next week. Which of the following is a reasonable explanation for the discrepancy in these sample statistics?

   (a) The percentage of the population who supports the tax increase didn't change; the difference in the statistics is due to chance.
   (b) The proportion of the population who supports a tax increase dropped significantly during the week between the two polls.
   (c) The margin of error is so large that the difference is not statistically significant; the two sample statistics are estimates of the same population parameter.
   (d) The organization seeking the tax increase paid the polling organization 44% more for the first poll than for the second poll.

6. An organization of psychologists seeking millions of federal dollars to treat adults who were abused as children states in its report to the U.S. Congress that an estimated 45% of adults in the United States suffered some form of abuse during their childhood. The bipartisan committee reviewing the report hires an independent research group to test this claim. In a random sample of 144 adults, the independent group finds 9 adults who believe they were abused as children. Which of the following is **not** a reasonable explanation for the difference in the statistics?

   (a) The difference in the two statistics is due to chance, so that the difference is not statistically significant.
   (b) The organization seeking the money exaggerated in their report in order to make their cause seem more urgent.
   (c) The organization of psychologists used a sample of convicted felons to find its statistic, while the independent research group used a sample of the entire U.S. population.
   (d) The statistic of 45% reported by the organization of psychologists is wrong, and the true population parameter is close to 6.25%.

Unit 6D Test 4 *(continued)*

7. In what circumstance is a result said to have low statistical significance?

    (a) It is very likely to have occurred by chance.
    (b) It is very unlikely to have occurred by chance.
    (c) It supports the alternative hypothesis of an experiment.
    (d) It supports the null hypothesis of an experiment.

The following questions refer to a (hypothetical) study of 450 people that was designed to determine whether a certain drug was effective in relieving arthritis symptoms. The results are summarized in the following contingency table.

	Relieved symptoms	**Not relieved**	**Total**
Drug	190	110	300
Placebo	100	50	150
Total	290	160	450

8. Which of the following would be a reasonable alternative hypothesis for this study?

    (a) The drug was no more effective than the placebo at relieving arthritis symptoms.
    (b) The drug was at least as effective as the placebo at relieving arthritis symptoms.
    (c) The drug was more effective than the placebo at relieving arthritis symptoms.
    (d) The drug was less effective than the placebo at relieving arthritis symptoms.

9. Which of the following would be a reasonable null hypothesis for this study?

    (a) The drug was no more effective than the placebo at relieving arthritis symptoms.
    (b) The drug was at least as effective as the placebo at relieving arthritis symptoms.
    (c) The drug was more effective than the placebo at relieving arthritis symptoms.
    (d) The drug was less effective than the placebo at relieving arthritis symptoms.

10. Using the percentages of drug-taking patients and placebo-taking patients who experienced a relief of symptoms, how do the actual results compare to the results expected according to the alternative hypothesis or the null hypothesis?

    (a) The results agree with the null hypothesis only.
    (b) The results agree with the hypothesis only.
    (c) The results agree with both the null hypothesis and the hypothesis.
    (d) The results do not agree with either the null hypothesis or the hypothesis.

Unit 7A Test 1

Name:_____

Date:_____

1. Define *event*.

_____

_____

_____

2. What is the probability of an event that is impossible?

_____

_____

_____

3. Name the method of estimating probabilities based on experience or intuition.

_____

_____

_____

4. Jeanne rolled a die 100 times and 12 of those times got a 6. She concludes that the probability of getting 6 on a roll of her die is 0.12. Which method of determining probabilities did Jeanne use?

_____

_____

_____

5. Li noted that there are six possible outcomes when you roll a die and 6 is one of those outcomes. He concluded that the probability of getting 6 on a roll of his die is 1/6. Which method of determining probabilities did Li use?

_____

_____

_____

6. Suppose that you roll two six-sided dice. How many possible outcomes are there?

_____

_____

_____

Unit 7A Test 1 *(continued)*

Name:_____

7. Suppose that you roll two six-sided dice. How many of the outcomes have a sum of 6?

_____

_____

_____

8. Suppose that you roll two six-sided dice and then add the numbers on the dice. Make a probability distribution table listing all the possible events and their probabilities.

_____

_____

_____

9. The probability that a student chosen at random from your class is an art major is 0.32. What is the probability that a student chosen at random from your class is **not** an art major?

_____

_____

_____

10. The probability that our team will finish first in the relay race is 0.25. What are the odds of our team winning the race?

_____

_____

_____

Unit 7A Test 2

1. What are the most basic possible results of observations or experiments?

   _____

   _____

   _____

2. What is the probability of an event that is certain?

   _____

   _____

   _____

3. Name the method of determining probabilities based on observations or experiments.

   _____

   _____

   _____

4. In a particular class, there are 3 freshman, 5 sophomores, 11 juniors, and 2 seniors. If the instructor randomly chooses a student to answer a question in class, what is the probability that the student chosen will be a freshman?

   _____

   _____

   _____

5. Suppose that you flip five coins. How many possible outcomes are there?

   _____

   _____

   _____

6. Suppose that you flip four coins. How many of the outcomes have exactly 2 heads?

   _____

   _____

   _____

Unit 7A Test 2 *(continued)*

Name:_____

7. Suppose that you flip four coins and then count the number of heads. Make a probability distribution table listing all the possible events and their probabilities.

_____

_____

_____

8. Suppose that you have red, green, and yellow marbles in a bag and that you draw one without looking at its color. The following probability distribution lists the events of this experiment and their probabilities. Explain why this probability distribution is not valid.

Event	Probability
Red	$\dfrac{5}{16}$
Green	$\dfrac{7}{16}$
Yellow	$\dfrac{5}{16}$

_____

_____

_____

9. The probability that a student chosen at random from your class is an English major is 0.27. What is the probability that a student chosen at random from your class is **not** an English major?

_____

_____

_____

10. The probability that our team will finish first in the relay race is 0.40. What are the odds of our team losing the race?

_____

_____

_____

Unit 7A Test 3

Name:_____

Date:_____

Choose the correct answer to each problem.

1. Given that $P(E) = 0$, what must be true about the event E?

   (a) The event E is impossible.
   (c) The event E is probable but not certain.

   (b) The event E is possible but not likely.
   (d) The event E is certain.

2. Which method of determining probabilities is also known as the relative frequency method?

   (a) Theoretical method   (b) Empirical method   (c) Subjective method   (d) Classical method

3. Sean flipped a coin 100 times and got heads 42 times. He concludes that the probability of getting heads on a flip of his coin is 0.42. Which method did Sean use?

   (a) Theoretical method
   (c) Subjective method

   (b) Empirical method
   (d) Monte Carlo method

4. Chantal noted that there are two possible outcomes when you flip a coin and heads is one of those outcomes. She concluded that the probability of getting heads on a flip of her coin is 1/2 or 0.5. Which method did Chantal use?

   (a) Theoretical method   (b) Empirical method   (c) Subjective method   (d) Monte Carlo method

5. There are 2 red marbles, 3 yellow marbles, and 5 blue marbles in a bag. Determine the probability of drawing a red marble from the bag.

   (a) 0.2   (b) 0.25   (c) 0.4   (d) 0.5

6. Determine the probability of obtaining a sum of 9 on a single roll of two fair dice.

   (a) $\dfrac{1}{6}$ (b) $\dfrac{1}{9}$ (c) $\dfrac{1}{11}$ (d) $\dfrac{1}{12}$

7. A quality control agent tested 10 parts produced by a single machine during the past hour. She found that 3 of the parts are defective. What is the probability that another part made by the same machine will be defective?

   (a) 0.03   (b) 0.15   (c) 0.30   (d) 0.43

8. What number correctly completes the following probability distribution?

Result	Probability
3 boys	0.25
2 boys	0.35
1 boy	0.30
0 boys	

   (a) 0.0   (b) 0.1   (c) 0.2   (d) 0.3

9. The probability that a student chosen at random from your class is a French major is 0.04. What is the probability that a student chosen at random from your class is **not** a French major?

   (a) 0.04   **(b)** 0.40   **(c)** 0.96

   (d) Cannot be determined from the information given.

10. The probability that our team will finish first in the relay race is 0.20. What are the odds of our team winning the race?

   (a) 1 to 2   **(b)** 1 to 4   **(c)** 1 to 5   **(d)** 2 to 5

Unit 7A Test 4

Name:_____

Date:_____

Choose the correct answer to each problem.

1. What are the most basic possible results of observations or experiments?

    (a) Events   **(b)** Outcomes   **(c)** Probabilities   **(d)** Distributions

2. Given that $P(E) = 1$, what must be true about the event E?

    (a) The event E is impossible.   **(b)** The event E is possible but not likely.
    (c) The event E is probable but not certain.   **(d)** The event E is certain.

3. In which method of determining probabilities is it important that all outcomes be equally likely?

    (a) Theoretical method   **(b)** Empirical method   **(c)** Subjective method   **(d)** Monte Carlo
    method

4. Which method of determining probabilities is essentially the empirical method except that it uses computer simulations?

    (a) Theoretical method   **(b)** Empirical method   **(c)** Subjective method   **(d)** Monte Carlo
    method

5. Roger conducted a survey in his math class and found that 15% of the students are international students. He concludes that the probability of a student in his math class being an international student is 0.15. Which method did Roger use?

    (a) Theoretical method   **(b)** Empirical method   **(c)** Subjective method   **(d)** Monte Carlo
    method

6. There are 3 red marbles, 3 yellow marbles, and 4 blue marbles in a bag. Determine the probability of drawing a yellow red from the bag.

    (a) 0.3   **(b)** 0.4   **(c)** 0.5   **(d)** 0.75

7. Determine the probability of obtaining a sum of 10 on a single roll of two fair dice.

    (a) $\frac{1}{3}$ **(b)** $\frac{1}{6}$ **(c)** $\frac{1}{11}$ **(d)** $\frac{1}{12}$

8. What number correctly completes the following probability distribution?

Result	Probability
3 girls	0.1
2 girls	0.3
1 girl	0.4
0 girls	

    (a) 0.0   **(b)** 0.1   **(c)** 0.2   **(d)** 0.3

9. The probability that a student chosen at random from your class is a music major is 0.15. What is the probability that a student chosen at random from your class is **not** a music major?

    (a) 0.15   **(b)** 0.85   **(c)** 0.75
    (d) Cannot be determined from the information given

Unit 7A Test 4 *(continued)*

10. The probability that our team will finish first in the relay race is 0.60. What are the odds of our team winning the race?

   (a) 1 to 6   (b) 6 to 1   (c) 3 to 2   (d) 6 to 10

Unit 7B Test 1

Name:_____

Date:_____

1. Are doing well on a midterm exam and on the comprehensive final exam for the same class independent or dependent events? Explain.

   _____

   _____

   _____

2. The probability of one stapler jamming on a given try is 0.05. The probability of another stapler jamming on a given try is 0.06. What is the probability that when each is used once, both will jam?

   _____

   _____

   _____

3. Two pools, maintained by different companies, are inspected for bacteria levels. Are the test results for the two pools independent or dependent events? Explain.

   _____

   _____

   _____

4. Two cards are drawn from a 52-card deck. What is the probability of drawing a pair of kings?

   _____

   _____

   _____

5. A voter may be registered as a Democrat. A voter may be registered as a Republican. Are these two events mutually exclusive? Why or why not?

   _____

   _____

   _____

6. A power drill in use is running at high speed 60% of the time, at low speed 20% of the time, and in reverse 20% of the time. What percentage of the time is it running either at high speed or in reverse?

   _____

   _____

   _____

7. An engine may be overheating. It may also be stalling. Are these events mutually exclusive? Why or why not?

    _____

    _____

    _____

8. In a wood pile of 39 pieces, 12 are rotten, 23 are too short to use, and 5 are both rotten and too short. What is the probability that a piece is either rotten or too short?

    _____

    _____

    _____

9. An erratic floppy disk drive has a history of one error in every 21 tries. What is the probability of at least one read error in the next 5 tries? Give the answer as a decimal rounded to three places.

    _____

    _____

    _____

10. A careless automobile driver runs out of gas once every 930 trips. What are the chances that he will run out of gas at least once in the next 20 trips? Give the answer as a decimal rounded to three places.

    _____

    _____

    _____

Unit 7B Test 2

Name:_____

Date:_____

1. Two circuits, working together to supply power to the same electric motor, can each overload and shut down. Are these events independent or dependent? Explain.

_____

_____

_____

2. A certain newborn panda in one zoo has 0.80 chance of survival, and a newborn panda in a different zoo has a 0.60 chance of survival. What is the probability that both turtles will survive?

_____

_____

_____

3. Are the failures of two hard disk drives on different computers, in different locations, independent or dependent events? Explain.

_____

_____

_____

4. Of seven coastal lighthouses in the same area, two are designed by a certain well-known architect. A tour group randomly picks two to visit, one on Monday and one on Tuesday. What is the chance that both lighthouses by the famous architect are chosen?

_____

_____

_____

5. A person can have red hair. A person can have blue eyes. Are these two events mutually exclusive? Why or why not?

_____

_____

_____

Unit 7B Test 2 *(continued)*

6. 81 students in a class bought two books by the same author. 62 students read the first book, 54 read the second book, and 39 read both. What is the probability that a randomly selected student read at least one of the two books?

_____

_____

_____

7. A voter can vote for a certain candidate for President. The voter can also vote for a different candidate. Are the two events mutually exclusive? Why or why not?

_____

_____

_____

8. A pen manufacturing assembly line is operating at high output 15% of the time, at medium output 40% of the time, and 45% of the time it is idle. What percentage of the time is the line either running at medium output or sitting idle?

_____

_____

_____

9. A little boy loses his shoe once in every three trips to the backyard. What is the probability that he will lose his shoe at least once in the next six trips? Give the answer as a decimal rounded to three places.

_____

_____

_____

10. A rug weaver's thread accidentally breaks, on average, once every 42 passes. What is the probability that the thread will break at least once in the next 12 passes?

_____

_____

_____

Unit 7B Test 3

Name:_____

Date:_____

Choose the correct answer to each problem.

1. Which of the following are examples of independent events?

   (a) Two consecutive victories by the same army
   (b) Two archeological discoveries at different locations in the same country, at the same time
   (c) Two people in the same family falling ill in the same week
   (d) Two laughs by different people watching the same movie in a theater

2. A televised debate is being taped using two independent sound systems. The first has a 0.03 probability of failure during taping; the second has a 0.05 probability of failure. What is the probability that both will fail during taping?

   (a) 0.080   (b) 0.020   (c) 0.0042   (d) 0.0015

3. A music fan randomly selects 4 CDs from a stack of 35, where 6 are by the same country-western artist. What is the probability that all of the CDs chosen are by that artist?

   (a) 0.00013   (b) 0.00021   (c) 0.00029   (d) 0.00037

4. Three soccer teams will finish first, second, and third in a field of 12 evenly-matched teams, which includes 5 European teams. What are the chances of a European medal sweep?

   (a) 0.04545   (b) 0.03535   (c) 0.06193   (d) 0.07788

5. A knight may win a tournament. He may also fail to win the love of his lady. Are these events mutually exclusive? Why or why not?

   (a) Yes, because all ladies love all winners   (b) Yes, because not all ladies love all winners
   (c) No, because all ladies love all winners   (d) No, because not all ladies love all winners

6. The welds done in a certain factory are all inspected by two inspectors working separately. 95% are passed by inspector A, 92% are passed by inspector B, and 87% are passed by both. What percent of welds are passed by at least one inspector?

   (a) 97%   (b) 95%   (c) 93%   (d) 87%

7. A job for one person could be filled by a man. It could also be filled by a woman. Are these events mutually exclusive? Why or why not?

   (a) Yes, because the job could be filled by either   (b) Yes, because nobody is both a man and a woman
   (c) No, because the job could be filled by either   (d) No, because nobody is both a man and a woman

8. At most one of three ships will be sent on a certain mission. The Diego Garcia has a 15% chance of being sent, the Jorge Sanchez has a 20% chance, and the Franco Rivera has a 10% chance. What is the percent chance that at least one ship is sent?

   (a) 30%   (b) 35%   (c) 45%   (d) 55%

9. In a certain country, there is a bank failure once every six years, on average. What is the probability of at least one bank failure in the next 30 years?

    (a) 0.992   **(b)** 0.994   **(c)** 0.996   **(d)** 0.998

10. A plant has a pollution-control system shutdown once every 75 days, on average. What is the probability of at least one shutdown in the next year? Give the answer to one decimal place.

    (a) 96.9%   **(b)** 97.2 %   **(c)** 98.6%   **(d)** 99.3%

Unit 7B Test 4

Name:_____

Date:_____

Choose the correct answer to each problem.

1. Which of the following are examples of independent events?

   (a) Two travelers from the same family, but in different countries, catching local diseases at the same time
   (b) Two people in different places getting mugged by the same man on the same afternoon
   (c) Two baseball players getting salaries over $10 million during the same preseason negotiations
   (d) Two bids at an open auction, for the same painting, by different people

2. A certain wrench has a 5% breakage rate in normal use. Another brand of wrench has a 2% breakage rate. What is the percent chance that a person who uses both wrenches moderately often will break both during normal use?

   (a) 0.096%   (b) 0.024%   (c) 0.012%   (d) 0.1%

3. Two whirlpool spas by different manufacturers are subjected to government safety tests. The first has a 0.86 probability of passing without modification; the second has a 0.88 probability. What is the probability that both spas will pass without modification?

   (a) 0.7568   (b) 0.7812   (c) 0.8302   (d) 0.8466

4. Two friends compete with each other and five other, equally good violinists for first and second chair in an orchestra, in a blind competition. What is the probability that the two friends end up as first and second chair together?

   (a) 0.0255   (b) 0.0476   (c) 0.0598   (d) 0.0784

5. A stitch may hold or unravel under stress. Are these events mutually exclusive?

   (a) Yes, because a stitch may also break, instead
   (b) Yes, because if a stitch unravels it does not hold
   (c) No, because a stitch may also break, instead
   (d) No, because if a stitch unravels it does not hold

6. The soldiers in a battalion are all inspected by two inspectors, working separately. 87% of the men are passed by inspector A, 89% are passed by inspector B, and 80% are passed by both. What percent of soldiers are passed by at least one inspector?

   (a) 92%   (b) 94%   (c) 96%   (d) 98%

7. A hijacked plane may land in Greece. It may also land in Cuba. Are these events mutually exclusive? Why or why not?

   (a) No, because the plane might land in two places
   (b) No, because the plane can only land in one place
   (c) Yes, because the plane might land in two places
   (d) Yes, because the plane can only land in one place

8. Cindy has money for at most one craft kit. There is a 25% chance she will buy a moccasin kit, a 30% chance that she will be a beaded belt kit, and a 15% chance that she will buy a beaded purse kit. What is the percent chance that she will buy at least one of the three?

   (a) 65%   (b) 70%   (c) 85%   (d) 90%

9. In a certain city, there is a suicide twice a week, on average. What is the probability of at least one suicide in the next two weeks?

    (a) 0.991   **(b)** 0.994   **(c)** 0.997   **(d)** 0.999

10. A bicycle rider has a spill once every 25 days, on average. What is the probability of at least one fall in the next 30 days?

    (a) 68.2%   **(b)** 70.5%   **(c)** 70.6%   **(d)** 82.6%

Unit 7C Test 1

1. A surgical procedure has a 46% chance of helping the average cancer patient it is performed on. If the operation is done on 43,500 patients, how many may it be expected to help?

_____

_____

_____

2. A new style of policing is thought to give a city a 3 in 5 chance of reducing crime by 15%. If the style is adopted by 30 cities, about how many can be expected to achieve that result?

_____

_____

_____

3. A particular kind of loan, to a certain kind of person, has an estimated 15% chance of not being repaid, a 25% chance of being repaid with difficulty, and a 60% chance of being repaid without incident. If this kind of loan is granted to 38,000 people, how many people in each category may one expect?

_____

_____

_____

4. A golfer, who keeps missing crucial putts, bets his friend that he will sink the next one, because "I'm due for a good putt." This is an example of what is called ...

_____

_____

_____

5. A private pilot buys a plane with possible mechanical trouble. There is a 20% chance that the plane is in good condition and worth $43,000, there is a 50% chance that it needs a complete systems overhaul and is worth $26,000, and there is a 30% chance that the plane needs only minor repairs and is worth $35,000. What is the plane's expected value?

_____

_____

_____

Unit 7C Test 1 *(continued)*

6. Cold weather threatens an orange grove. If the weather passes without dropping the temperatures too far, the crop will be worth \$320,000, but there is a 20% chance that the oranges will freeze and become worthless. What is the expected value of the crop?

_____

_____

_____

7. A hacker breaking into a computer system has a 10% chance of being in after 3 minutes, a 30% chance of being in after 10 minutes, and a 60% chance of being in after 30 minutes. (Assume it takes him either 3, 10, or 30 minutes.) What is the expected time will take the hacker to get in?

_____

_____

_____

8. A painting has a 0.80 probability of being genuine and a 0.20 probability of being a forgery. If it is genuine, it is worth \$3.6 million; if it is a forgery, it is worth \$20,000. What is the painting's expected value?

_____

_____

_____

9. A casino card game takes \$5 bets. Players have a 24% chance of winning and winning back their bets plus \$15, and they have a 76% chance of losing their bets. What is the house edge?

_____

_____

_____

10. A game consists of laying a bet of \$1 and taking a single card from a dealer (the house). If the card is a face card, the player wins and collects \$3.00 plus the original bet; otherwise, the player loses the \$1. What is the house edge in this game?

_____

_____

_____

Unit 7C Test 2

1. A radiation treatment for tumors has a 59% chance of helping the average cancer patient it is performed on. If the operation is done on 42,100 patients, how many may it be expected to help?

_____

_____

_____

2. A new hairstyle is all the rage, and a hairstylist figures that about one in five women coming into the salon request this style. If the salon expects about 600 women during the next week, how many times will the hairstyle be recreated at the salon that week?

_____

_____

_____

3. A criminal investigation into a department of the government suggests that for any given worker, there is a chance of about 1 in 30 that this person is involved in questionable but criminally minor activities of some kind or other, while 1 in 120 is involved in a serious crime. The rest are innocent. If the department contains 5400 workers, how many may be expected to be innocent, how many involved in minor shady dealings, and how many in serious crime?

_____

_____

_____

4. A smoker whose friend urges him to quit refuses, saying "My grandfather and father both died of lung cancer; I figure my family's run of bad luck is due to change." This is an example of what is called ...

_____

_____

_____

5. An recently excavated skull is being bought, sight unseen, by an antiquities dealer. There is a 30% chance that the skull is in good condition and worth $5900; there is a 20% chance that it is heavily damaged and worth only $850, and there is a 50% chance that it suffers from only minor damage and is worth $3400. What is the skull's expected value?

_____

_____

_____

6. Humid weather threatens to cause an increase of insects at a popular tourist destination. If the weather stays dry, the locals expect tourist revenues of $360,000 during the season. However, there is a 25% chance that humid weather will cause an insect outbreak that cuts tourist revenues to $280,000. What are the expected revenues for the season?

_____

_____

_____

7. A piece of antique furniture has an 80% chance of being a genuine article 300 years old, a 10% chance of being a 150-year-old forgery, and a 10% chance of being a 50-year-old forgery. What is the expected age of the piece?

_____

_____

_____

8. A lawyer considering taking a case figures that there is a 40% chance of winning the case in court and earning his firm $400,000, a 50% chance of losing and costing his firm $150,000, and a 10% chance of settling out of court and bringing in $200,000. What is the expected payoff of the case for the firm?

_____

_____

_____

9. A casino card game takes $5 bets. Players have a 19% chance of winning and winning back their bets plus $20, and they have an 81% chance of losing their bets. What is the house edge?

_____

_____

_____

10. A game consists of laying a $1 bet and taking a single card from a dealer (the house) working with a 54-card deck, which includes two jokers. If the card is hearts or spades, the player wins and gets the $1 back plus another $1; otherwise, the player loses the $1. What is the house edge in this game?

_____

_____

_____

Unit 7C Test 3

Name:_____

Date:_____

Choose the correct answer to each problem.

1. A movie critic gives a single star (worst rating) to one movie in eight that he reviews. If he expects to review 160 movies during the summer season, how many one-star movies can the readers expect?

   (a) 20   (b) 24   (c) 32   (d) 48

2. A certain religious denomination sends one out of every seven of its missionaries to Asia. If the denomination is sending 476 missionaries next year, how many are likely to go to Asia?

   (a) 55   (b) 68   (c) 73   (d) 91

3. A copier jams about once in 45 copies. If a person is planning to copy 624 pages, how many jams can she expect?

   (a) 12   (b) 14   (c) 16   (d) 18

4. A woman, buying a computer of the same brand her friends have had trouble with, figures that the company is overdue to have a satisfied customer, and she figures to be it. This is a case of the gambler's fallacy because ...

   (a) The satisfied customer could be someone else.   (b) She is relying on chance, which is unwise.
   (c) Her experiences will probably match her friends'.   (d) Her friends aren't a large sample of users.

5. Twenty bearded men gather. Ten have eight-inch beards, six have ten-inch beards, and four have twelve-inch beards. What is the expected length of a randomly selected man from this group?

   (a) 9.4 inches   (b) 10.2 inches   (c) 10.8 inches   (d) 11. inches

6. Of eight dresses on a rack, two have a 1-inch hem, five have a 2-inch hem, and one has a 3-inch hem. What is the expected hem of a dress randomly selected from this set?

   (a) $1\frac{5}{8}$ inches   (b) $1\frac{1}{2}$ inches   (c) $1\frac{3}{4}$ inches   (d) $1\frac{7}{8}$ inches

7. A CD has a 5% chance of being a smash hit and earning $5.2 million, a 40% chance of being a modest success and earning $1.1 million, and a 55% chance of being a flop and breaking even. What is the expected earnings value of the CD?

   (a) $100,000   (b) $300,000   (c) $500,000   (d) $700,000

8. A child has a 35% chance of being sent to a day-care facility that charges $400 per month and a 65% chance of being sent to one that charges $700. What is the expected cost of the child's day care?

   (a) $520   (b) $595   (c) $540   (d) $550

9. A casino card game takes $4 bets. Players have a 32% chance of winning and winning back their bets plus $8, and they have a 68% chance of losing their bets. What is the house edge?

   (a) 1 cent per dollar   (b) 2 cents per dollar   (c) 3 cents per dollar   (d) 4 cents per dollar

Unit 7C Test 3 *(continued)*

10. A game consists of laying a $1 bet and taking a single card from a dealer (the house) working with a 54-card deck, which includes two jokers. If the card is clubs, the player wins and gets the $1 back plus another $3; otherwise, the player loses the $1. What is the house edge in this game?

(a) 2.95 cents per dollar   **(b)** 3.28 cents per dollar   **(c)** 3.70 cents per dollar   **(d)** 4.22 cents per dollar

Unit 7C Test 4

Choose the correct answer to each problem.

1. A magazine auto critic gives a single star (worst rating) to about one car in twelve that he reviews. If he expects to review 216 cars during the next season, how many one-star cars can the readers expect?

   (a) 14   (b) 16   (c) 18   (d) 20

2. A certain college tries to accept the top 4 percent of applicants. If it expects 6400 applicants for next year, how many students should it plan on accepting?

   (a) 228   (b) 240   (c) 256   (d) 264

3. Suppose a motorcycle rider has 1 chance in 3 of falling sometime during a year of driving. If there are 2,700 motorcycle riders in a certain area, about how many will fall in the next year?

   (a) 700   (b) 900   (c) 1100   (d) 1300

4. A soldier takes cover in a shell hole, on the grounds that the chances of another shell striking in the same place are astronomically small. This is a case of the gambler's fallacy because ...

   (a) The enemy is obviously aiming for the hole.   (b) He is relying on chance, which is unwise.
   (c) The soldier hasn't seen enough shells to know.   (d) The hole is just as likely to be hit as any spot is.

5. A silicon wafer is produced by a process that has a 20% chance of producing material of 100% purity, a 35% chance of producing material of 99% purity, and a 45% chance of producing material of 96% purity. What is the expected purity of a randomly selected wafer?

   (a) 97.85%   (b) 98.5%   (c) 99%   (d) 99.5%

6. A chimp learning sign language is judged by the trainer to have 1 chance in 4 of learning 50 words, 1 chance in 2 of learning 35, and 1 chance in 4 of learning only 20. What is the expected number of words the chimp will learn?

   (a) 32   (b) 35   (c) 38   (d) 41

7. An insurance company is about to collect a one-time premium of $25,000 to insure an object for $1.5 million. The object has a 0.015 probability of being stolen. What is the value of the transaction to the insurer?

   (a) $1900   (b) $2100   (c) $2300   (d) $2500

8. A credit card company issues a credit card to a person for whom there is a likelihood of 0.7 that he will borrow on the card and pay a steady flow of interest of $6 per month, and a likelihood of 0.3 that he will pay all his borrowings promptly and incur no interest. What is the expected flow of interest payments to the company?

   (a) $4.20 per month   (b) $3.00 per month
   (c) $3.20 per month   (d) $3.30 per month

9. A casino card game takes $10 bets. Players have a 33% chance of winning and winning back their bets plus $20, and they have a 67% chance of losing their bets. What is the house edge?

   (a) 0.5 cent per dollar   **(b)** 1 cent per dollar
   (c) 2 cents per dollar   **(d)** 3 cents per dollar

10. A game consists of laying a $1 bet and taking a single card from a dealer (the house) working with a 52-card deck. If the card is clubs, the player wins and gets the $1 back plus another $2; otherwise, the player loses the $1. What is the house edge in this game?

    (a) 10 cents per dollar   **(b)** 13 cents per dollar
    (c) 18 cents per dollar   **(d)** 25 cents per dollar

Unit 7D Test 1

Name:_____

Date:_____

1. Suppose that in a country of 35 million people, about 266,000 are victims of violent crime each year. What is the percent chance that a person will be a violent crime victim in a given year?

_____

_____

_____

2. South Africa has a population of 46 million people. About 250,000 South Africans die of AIDS each years. What is the percent chance that a person will die of AIDS in a given year?

_____

_____

_____

In the following problems, consider that in 1995, 90 million American men drove about 1530 billion miles and about 10.6 million were involved in accidents.

3. How many miles did the average man drive?

_____

_____

_____

4. How many men per 1000 were involved in accidents? What was the risk for a given man of being in an accident that year?

_____

_____

_____

5. What was the accident rate per 10 million miles driven?

_____

_____

_____

Unit 7D Test 1 *(continued)*

Name:_____

In the following problems, consider the following table, showing firearm deaths among American females in 2004. The total number of American females that year was about 130 million.

Type of death	Total number
Accident	193
Suicide	2559
Homicide	3025

6. What was the firearm homicide rate per 100,000 females? What was the probability that a female was the victim of a firearm homicide?

_____

_____

_____

7. What was the probability of a female's dying through either a firearm suicide or a firearm accident?

_____

_____

_____

8. What is the probability that an American female is killed by a firearm?

_____

_____

_____

Unit 7D Test 2

1. Suppose that in a country of 28 million people, about 487,000 are victims of violent crime each year. What is the percent chance that a person will be a violent crime victim in a given year?

_____

_____

_____

2. In a country of 26 million people, about 55,000 die of AIDS each year. What is the percent chance that a person will die of AIDS in a given year?

_____

_____

_____

In the following problems, consider that in 2005, 87 million American women drove about 850 billion miles and about 7.0 million were involved in accidents.

3. How many miles did the average woman drive?

_____

_____

_____

4. How many women per 1000 were involved in accidents? What was the risk for a given woman of being in an accident that year?

_____

_____

_____

5. What was the accident rate per 10 million miles driven?

_____

_____

_____

Unit 7D Test 2 *(continued)*

In the following problems, consider the following table, showing firearm deaths among American males in 2005. The total number of American males that year was about 120 million.

Type of death	Total number
Accident	1328
Suicide	16,381
Homicide	15,228

6. What was the firearm homicide rate per 100,000 males? What was the probability that a male was the victim of a firearm homicide?

_____

_____

_____

7. What was the probability of a male's dying through either a firearm suicide or a firearm accident?

_____

_____

_____

8. What is the probability that an American male is killed by a firearm?

_____

_____

_____

Unit 7D Test 3

Name:_____

Date:_____

1. Suppose that in a country of 72 million people, about 3600 die from drowning each year. What is the percent chance that a person will drown in a given year?

   (a) 0.002%   **(b)** 0.003%   **(c)** 0.004%   **(d)** 0.005%

2. In a country of 48 million people, about 27,000 die from AIDS each year. What is the percent chance that a person will die of AIDS in a given year?

   (a) 0.035%   **(b)** 0.04%   **(c)** 0.56%   **(d)** 0.056%

   For the following problems, consider that in 2005, 87 million American women drove about 860 billion miles and about 13,000 were involved in fatal accidents.

3. How many miles did the average woman drive?

   (a) 9900   **(b)** 12,300   **(c)** 14,600   **(d)** 16,100

4. What was the risk for a given woman of being involved in a fatal accident that year?

   (a) 0.008%   **(b)** 0.011%   **(c)** 0.015%   **(d)** 0.018%

5. What was the fatal accident rate per billion miles driven?

   (a) 11   **(b)** 15   **(c)** 19   **(d)** 27

   For the following problems, consider the following table, showing some infant mortality data for America in 1995. The total number of births that year was about 3.9 million.

Cause of death	Total number, deaths under 1 yr
Congenital	6010
Premature/low birthweight	3390
Sudden Infant Death (SIDS)	2900

6. What was the percent chance that an infant died of a congenital defect?

   (a) 0.055%   **(b)** 0.062%   **(c)** 0.154%   **(d)** 0.093%

7. What was the percent chance of an infant's dying either from prematurity/low birthweight or from a congenital condition?

   (a) 0.12%   **(b)** 0.15%   **(c)** 0.19%   **(d)** 0.24%

8. How many deaths per 100,000 births resulted from one of the three causes?

   (a) 280   **(b)** 315   **(c)** 472   **(d)** 511

Unit 7D Test 4

1. Suppose that in a country of 64 million people, about 3200 die from drowning each year. What is the percent chance that a person will drown in a given year?

   (a) 0.002%   **(b)** 0.003%   **(c)** 0.005%   **(d)** 0.007%

2. In a country of 37 million people, about 16,000 die from AIDS each year. What is the percent chance that a person will die of AIDS in a given year?

   (a) 0.021%   **(b)** 0.032%   **(c)** 4.32%   **(d)** 0.043%

For the following problems, consider that in 2005, 90 million American men drove about 1530 billion miles and about 37,500 were involved in fatal accidents.

3. How many miles did the average man drive?

   (a) 17,000   **(b)** 18,500   **(c)** 19,600   **(d)** 22,000

4. What was the risk for a given man of being involved in a fatal accident that year?

   (a) 0.028%   **(b)** 0.042%   **(c)** 0.065%   **(d)** 0.088%

5. What was the fatal accident rate per billion miles driven?

   (a) 14.5   **(b)** 19   **(c)** 21   **(d)** 24.5

For the following problems, consider the following table, showing some infant mortality data for America in 1995. The total number of births that year was about 3.9 million.

Cause of death	Total number, deaths under 1 yr
Congenital	6010
Premature/low birthweight	3390
Sudden Infant Death (SIDS)	2900

6. What was the percent chance that an infant died of SIDS?

   (a) 0.087%   **(b)** 0.074%   **(c)** 0.106%   **(d)** 0.144%

7. What was the percent chance of an infant's dying either from SIDS or from a congenital condition?

   (a) 0.14%   **(b)** 0.18%   **(c)** 0.23%   **(d)** 0.27%

8. How many deaths per 100,000 births resulted from one of the three causes?

   (a) 266   **(b)** 290   **(c)** 315   **(d)** 374

Unit 7E Test 1

Name:_____

Date:_____

1. A frozen yogurt shop offers eight flavors and twelve toppings. How many ways of choosing one flavor and one topping are there?

   _____

   _____

   _____

2. A brand of ballpoint pen comes in five colors, with fine or regular point, and with standard, deluxe, or executive styling. How many different versions does the pen come in?

   _____

   _____

   _____

3. A six-character license plate can be any three letters of the alphabet, followed by any three numerical digits. How many different license plates are possible?

   _____

   _____

   _____

4. A seven-character computer password can be any three letters of the alphabet, followed by two numerical digits, followed by two more letters. How many different passwords are possible?

   _____

   _____

   _____

5. Evaluate the expression $\dfrac{19!}{16!}$ without using the factorial key on a calculator.

   _____

   _____

   _____

Unit 7E Test 1 *(continued)*

6. Evaluate the expression $\dfrac{5!}{2!3!}$ without using the factorial key on a calculator.

_____

_____

_____

7. Twenty people are choosing a president, a vice-president, and a secretary from among their ranks. How many ways are there to do this?

_____

_____

_____

8. From a normal deck of 52 playing cards, three cards are drawn and placed face up on a table, left to right. How many possible results are there of this procedure?

_____

_____

_____

9. How many different ways are there to order a medium two-topping pizza, given that there are nine toppings to choose from?

_____

_____

_____

10. A scholar is choosing six books to take on vacation, from a stack of 34. How many different combinations of books are there?

_____

_____

_____

Unit 7E Test 2

1. An auto dealer offers a compact car, a midsize, a sport utility vehicle, and a light truck, each either in standard, custom, or sport styling. How many ways of buying a vehicle from this dealer are there?

   _____

   _____

   _____

2. A cooking pot comes in blue, green or white enamel, with wood or synthetic handles, and with either a plain or a non-stick bottom. How many different versions does the pot come in?

   _____

   _____

   _____

3. A seven-character Internet address must be five letters of the alphabet followed by a two-digit number. How many different addresses of this kind are possible?

   _____

   _____

   _____

4. A corporate ID number consists of any five numerical digits, followed by any two letters of the alphabet, followed by two more digits. How many different ID numbers are possible?

   _____

   _____

   _____

5. Evaluate the expression $\dfrac{21!}{18!}$ without using the factorial key on a calculator.

   _____

   _____

   _____

Unit 7E Test 2 *(continued)*

6. Evaluate the expression $\dfrac{7!}{2!3!}$ without using the factorial key on a calculator.

_____

_____

_____

7. Eighteen people on an amateur sports team are choosing a captain, a vice-captain, and a social coordinator from among their ranks. How many ways are there to do this?

_____

_____

_____

8. From a normal deck of 54 playing cards (including two jokers, one red and one black), three cards are drawn and placed face up on a table, left to right. How many possible results are there of this procedure?

_____

_____

_____

9. How many different ways are there to order a three-flavor ice cream sundae, given that there are six flavors to choose from?

_____

_____

_____

10. A customer at a bookstore is choosing four paperback novels to take on a trip, from a shelf containing 42 books. How many different combinations of books are there?

_____

_____

_____

Unit 7E Test 3

Name:_____

Date:_____

Choose the correct answer to each problem.

1. A type of flowering tree comes in normal, giant, and dwarf sizes, and each size produces four different colors of flower. How many varieties of the tree are there?

    (a) 8   (b) 12   (c) 15   (d) 22

2. A company makes four specialized types of calculators, each in both battery and solar powered versions, and each in six designer colors. How many different kinds of calculator are there?

    (a) 25   (b) 32   (c) 48   (d) 80

3. A manufacturer's automobile serial number consists of two letters of the alphabet followed by six numerical digits. How many different serial numbers are possible?

    (a) 362 million   (b) 676 million   (c) 1.76 billion   (d) 2.53 billion

4. A magazine mailing code consists of two numerical digits, followed by four letters of the alphabet, followed by two more numerical digits. How many different mailing codes of this type are possible?

    (a) 248,483,900   (b) 873,800,000   (c) 2,662,730,000   (d) 4,569,760,000

5. Evaluate $\dfrac{35!}{32!}$.

    (a) 720   (b) 39,270   (c) 46,180   (d) 1,256,640

6. Evaluate $\dfrac{7!}{4!3!}$.

    (a) 35   (b) 48   (c) 72   (d) 154

7. In a sports event with eleven competitors, gold, silver, and bronze medals are given out for first, second, and third place, respectively. How many different medal outcomes are possible?

    (a) 990   (b) 2930   (c) 5360   (d) 8440

8. From a selection of sixteen courses fulfilling a certain breadth requirement, a student must pick any four to take, one in each of the next four terms. How many different sequences of courses are possible?

    (a) 1950   (b) 23,220   (c) 43,680   (d) 97,300

9. Five lotto numbers are to be picked at random from a collection of 100 numbers. Order does not matter. How many combinations of lotto numbers are there?

    (a) 722,370   (b) 960,030   (c) 46,894,440   (d) 75,287,520

10. An insurance fraud investigator chooses seven people to audit, from a pool of eighteen. How many combinations of people are possible?

    (a) 20,438   (b) 31,824   (c) 924,546   (d) 1,226,988

Unit 7E Test 4

Name:_____

Date:_____

Choose the correct answer to each problem.

1. A set of kitchen knives comes in normal, deluxe, or professional models, and each model comes with handles in one of six different colors. How many choices of kitchen knife are there?

   (a) 9   **(b)** 11   **(c)** 14   **(d)** 18

2. A wood products company produces paper in newsprint, standard bond, and glossy finish styles, each in one of four weights (thicknesses) and each in either white, yellow, pink, or powder blue. How many different kinds of paper are available?

   (a) 12   **(b)** 27   **(c)** 48   **(d)** 84

3. A mail-order catalog lists products using a catalog number consisting of four numerical digits followed by three letters of the alphabet. How many different catalogue numbers are possible?

   (a) 175,760,000   **(b)** 398,663,000   **(c)** 824,849,000   **(d)** 1,255,716,000

4. A corporate bank account code consists of a letter of the alphabet, followed by five numerical digits, followed by another letter. How many different account numbers of this type are possible?

   (a) 87,444,500   **(b)** 67,600,000   **(c)** 256,904,000   **(d)** 1,262,821,400

5. Evaluate $\dfrac{15!}{9!}$.

   (a) 805,520   **(b)** 3,603,600   **(c)** 9,243,438   **(d)** 28,894,780

6. Evaluate $\dfrac{8!}{4!4!}$.

   (a) 27   **(b)** 45   **(c)** 70   **(d)** 124

7. A crime victim is asked to pick, out of a lineup of ten people, the person she thinks did the crime, the person who drove the getaway car, and the person who stood and watched. How many different outcomes of this identification are possible?

   (a) 27   **(b)** 19683   **(c)** 729   **(d)** 720

8. A track athlete can compete in four events at a meet, one each day. There are ten events to choose from, and order is important. How many different schedules are there that the athlete could end up with?

   (a) 940   **(b)** 2580   **(c)** 3228   **(d)** 5040

9. Five spices are chosen from a rack of twenty-seven, to use in a salad. How many combinations of spices are possible?

   (a) 56,880   **(b)** 80,730   **(c)** 494,560   **(d)** 820,600

10. A tax auditor chooses seven people to audit, from a pool of twenty-four. How many combinations of people are possible?

    (a) 346,104   **(b)** 247,660   **(c)** 390,202   **(d)** 539,686

Unit 8A Test 1

Name:_____

Date:_____

1. The population of a certain city is decreasing at the rate of 17% per year. Explain whether this statement describes a linear or exponential relationship.

   _____

   _____

   _____

2. The price of gasoline is increasing at the rate of $0.06 per week. Explain whether this statement describes a linear or exponential relationship.

   _____

   _____

   _____

3. Suppose a chess board has one grain of wheat on the first square, two grains on the second square, four grains on the third square, eight grains on the fourth square, and so on. How many grains are on the 12th square?

   _____

   _____

   _____

4. Suppose a chess board has one grain of wheat on the first square, two grains on the second square, four grains on the third square, eight grains on the fourth square, and so on, up to and including the 18th square. Find the total number of grains on the board.

   _____

   _____

   _____

5. Suppose a leprechaun gives you a magic penny that doubles every night. How much money would you have after 12 days?

   _____

   _____

   _____

Unit 8A Test 1 (continued)

6. Suppose that a single bacterium is in a bottle at 11:00 am. It divides into two bacteria at 11:01, and the population continues to double every minute until the bottle is completely full at 12:00 noon. Find the population of bacteria at 11:25 am.

_____

_____

_____

7. Suppose that a single bacterium is in a bottle at 11:00 am. It divides into two bacteria at 11:01, and the population continues to double every minute until the bottle is completely full at 12:00 noon. Find the fraction of the bottle that is full at 11:51 am.

_____

_____

_____

8. Suppose that a single bacterium exists at 11:00 am. It divides into two bacteria at 11:01, and the population continues to double every minute. If each bacterium has a volume of 10^{-21} m^3, how deep would the bacteria be at 1:08 pm if they were spread in a uniform layer all over the surface of the Earth? (Assume that the surface area of the Earth is 5.1 x 10^{14} m^2, and show your work.)

_____

_____

_____

9. The population of a certain city is now 74,000 people. If the population doubles every 25 years, what will the population be after 125 years?

_____

_____

_____

Unit 8A Test 2

Name:_____

Date:_____

1. The price of a certain product is increasing at a rate of $2.30 per year. Explain whether this statement describes a linear or exponential relationship.

_____

_____

_____

2. The value of farm land in a certain state is increasing at a rate of 4% per year. Explain whether this statement describes a linear or exponential relationship.

_____

_____

_____

3. Suppose a chess board has one grain of wheat on the first square, two grains on the second square, four grains on the third square, eight grains on the fourth square, and so on. How many grains are on the 18th square?

_____

_____

_____

4. Suppose a chess board has one grain of wheat on the first square, two grains on the second square, four grains on the third square, eight grains on the fourth square, and so on, up to and including the 16th square. Find the total number of grains on the board.

_____

_____

_____

5. Suppose a leprechaun gives you a magic penny that doubles every night. How much money would you have after 9 days?

_____

_____

_____

Unit 8A Test 2 *(continued)*

6. Suppose that a single bacterium is in a bottle at 11:00 am. It divides into two bacteria at 11:01, and the population continues to double every minute until the bottle is completely full at 12:00 noon. Find the population of bacteria at 11:27 am.

_____

_____

_____

7. Suppose that a single bacterium is in a bottle at 11:00 am. It divides into two bacteria at 11:01, and the population continues to double every minute until the bottle is completely full at 12:00 noon. Find the fraction of the bottle that is full at 11:54 am.

_____

_____

_____

8. Suppose that a single bacterium exists at 11:00 am. It divides into two bacteria at 11:01, and the population continues to double every minute. If each bacterium has a volume of 10^{-21} m^3, how deep would the bacteria be at 1:10 pm if they were spread in a uniform layer all over the surface of the Earth? (Assume that the surface area of the Earth is 5.1 x 10^{14} m^2, and show your work.)

_____

_____

_____

9. Suppose the population of a certain city has been doubling every 30 years, and the population was 48,000 in 1850. Complete the table showing the growth of the population at 30-year intervals.

Year	1850	1880	1910	1940	1970
Population					

Unit 8A Test 3

Name:_____

Date:_____

Choose the correct answer to each problem.

1. Which of the following statements describes an exponential relationship?

   (a) The population of a certain city is increasing at the rate of 600 people per year.
   (b) The value of this rental property can be depreciated at the rate of $4300 per year.
   (c) The number of dogs is increasing at the rate of 40 dogs per year.
   (d) The price of a widget is increasing at the rate of 34% per year.

2. Which of the following statements describes a relationship that is *not* exponential?

   (a) The price of houses in this neighborhood is increasing at the rate of 12% per year.
   (b) The number of bacteria is increasing at the rate of 18% per minute.
   (c) The temperature is increasing at the rate of 7° per hour.
   (d) The number of cars in the parking lot is decreasing at the rate of 15% per hour.

3. Suppose a chess board has one grain of wheat on the first square, two grains on the second square, four grains on the third square, eight grains on the fourth square, and so on. How many grains are on the 12th square?

   (a) 2^9 (b) 2^{10} (c) 2^{11} (d) 2^{12}

4. Suppose a chess board has one grain of wheat on the first square, two grains on the second square, four grains on the third square, eight grains on the fourth square, and so on, up to and including the 19th square. Find the total number of grains on the board.

   (a) 2^{20} (b) $2^{20} - 1$ (c) 2^{19} (d) $2^{19} - 1$

5. Suppose a leprechaun gives you a magic penny that doubles every night. How much money would you have after 6 days?

   (a) $0.32   (b) $0.64   (c) $1.28   (d) $2.56

6. Suppose that a single bacterium is in a bottle at 11:00 am. It divides into two bacteria at 11:01, and the population continues to double every minute until the bottle is completely full at 12:00 noon. Find the population of bacteria at 11:32 am.

   (a) 2^{31} (b) 2^{32} (c) 2^{33} (d) 2^{34}

7. Suppose that a single bacterium is in a bottle at 11:00 am. It divides into two bacteria at 11:01, and the population continues to double every minute until the bottle is completely full at 12:00 noon. Find the fraction of the bottle that is full at 11:53 am.

   (a) $\dfrac{1}{32}$ (b) $\dfrac{1}{64}$ (c) $\dfrac{1}{128}$ (d) $\dfrac{1}{512}$

8. Suppose that a single bacterium exists at 11:00 am. It divides into two bacteria at 11:01, and the population continues to double every minute. If each bacterium has a volume of 10^{-21} m^3, approximately how deep would the bacteria be at 1:09 pm if they were spread in a uniform layer all over the surface of the Earth? (Assume that the surface area of the Earth is 5.1×10^{14} m^2, and show your work.)

   (a) 468 m   (b) 1334 m   (c) 589 m   (d) 1024 m

9. Suppose the population of a certain city doubles every 20 years, and the current population is 83,000. Make a table showing the population after 20 years, after 40 years, and so on. Use your table to find the population after 140 years.

   (a) 1,328,000   (b) 2,656,000   (c) 5,312,000   (d) 10,624,000

Unit 8A Test 4

Name:_____

Date:_____

Choose the correct answer to each problem.

1. Which of the following statements describes an exponential relationship?

   (a) The temperature is increasing at the rate of 3° per hour.
   (b) The population of your home town is decreasing at a rate of 7% per year.
   (c) The number of cars in the parking lot is decreasing at the rate of 5 cars per hour.
   (d) The price of houses in this neighborhood is increasing at the rate of $15,000 per year.

2. Which of the following statements describes a relationship that is *not* exponential?

   (a) The value of this rental property can be depreciated at the rate of $4300 per year.
   (b) The number of cats is decreasing at the rate of 8% per year.
   (c) The population of a certain city is increasing at the rate of 40% per year.
   (d) The price of a gizmo is increasing at the rate of 14% per year.

3. Suppose a chess board has one grain of wheat on the first square, two grains on the second square, four grains on the third square, eight grains on the fourth square, and so on. How many grains are on the 13th square?

   (a) 2^{12} (b) 2^{13} (c) 2^{14} (d) 2^{15}

4. Suppose a chess board has one grain of wheat on the first square, two grains on the second square, four grains on the third square, eight grains on the fourth square, and so on, up to and including the 16th square. Find the total number of grains on the board.

   (a) $2^{15} - 1$ (b) 2^{15} (c) $2^{16} - 1$ (d) 2^{16}

5. Suppose a leprechaun gives you a magic penny that doubles every night. How much money would you have after 6 days?

   (a) $0.32 (b) $0.64 (c) $1.28 (d) $2.56

6. Suppose that a single bacterium is in a bottle at 11:00 am. It divides into two bacteria at 11:01, and the population continues to double every minute until the bottle is completely full at 12:00 noon. Find the population of bacteria at 11:29 am.

   (a) 2^{27} (b) 2^{28} (c) 2^{29} (d) 2^{30}

7. Suppose that a single bacterium is in a bottle at 11:00 am. It divides into two bacteria at 11:01, and the population continues to double every minute until the bottle is completely full at 12:00 noon. Find the fraction of the bottle that is full at 11:55 am.

   (a) $\dfrac{1}{32}$ (b) $\dfrac{1}{64}$ (c) $\dfrac{1}{128}$ (d) $\dfrac{1}{512}$

8. Suppose that a single bacterium exists at 11:00 am. It divides into two bacteria at 11:01, and the population continues to double every minute. If each bacterium has a volume of 10^{-21} m^3, approximately how deep would the bacteria be at 1:07 pm if they were spread in a uniform layer all over the surface of the Earth? (Assume that the surface area of the Earth is 5.1×10^{14} m^2, and show your work.)

   (a) 64 m   (b) 76 m   (c) 108 m   (d) 334 m

9. Suppose the population of a certain city doubles every 15 years, and the current population is 69,000. Make a table showing the population after 15 years, after 30 years, and so on. Use your table to find the population after 90 years.

   (a) 1,104,000   (b) 2,208,000   (c) 4,416,000   (d) 8,832,000

Unit 8B Test 1

Name:_____

Date:_____

1. If a quantity quadruples every 16 days, what is its doubling time?

   _____

   _____

   _____

2. Suppose that a population has a doubling time of 18 years. By what factor will it grow in 72 years?

   _____

   _____

   _____

3. Suppose that you possess some of a radioactive substance that has a half-life of 31 days. What fraction of the substance will remain after 217 days?

   _____

   _____

   _____

4. If the doubling time of a state's population is 38 years, how long does it take for the population to increase by a factor of 8?

   _____

   _____

   _____

5. Suppose you deposit $800 in a bank account that has a doubling time of 16 years. What will your balance be after 36 years?

   _____

   _____

   _____

6. Suppose that a savings account increases its value by 6.3% per year (APY). Use the approximate doubling time formula to estimate the doubling time of the account.

   _____

   _____

   _____

7. If the half-life of a drug in the bloodstream is 6 hours, how much drug is left in the bloodstream 17 hours after a 280 milligram dose?

_____

_____

_____

8. Suppose that the consumer price index of a country is decreasing at the rate of 4.3% per year. Use the approximate half-life formula to estimate the half-life.

_____

_____

_____

9. Suppose that a quantity is halved every 20 years. Use the approximate half-life formula to estimate its decay rate.

_____

_____

_____

10. Suppose you are using the approximate half-life formula to determine the half-lives corresponding to several different decay rates. Will you obtain exact results? If not, explain when your results will be the *least* accurate.

_____

_____

_____

Unit 8B Test 2

1. If a quantity quadruples every 18 days, what is its doubling time?

2. Suppose that a population has a doubling time of 12 years. By what factor will it grow in 60 years?

3. Suppose that you possess some of a radioactive substance that has a half-life of 27 days. What fraction of the substance will remain after 216 days?

4. If the doubling time of a state's population is 13 years, how long does it take for the population to increase by a factor of 32?

5. Suppose you deposit $700 in a bank account that has a doubling time of 18 years. What will your balance be after 42 years?

6. Suppose that a savings account increases its value by 6.2% per year (APY). Use the approximate doubling time formula to estimate the doubling time of the account.

7. If the half-life of a drug in the bloodstream is 8 hours, how much drug is left in the bloodstream 14 hours after a 250 milligram dose?

_____

_____

_____

8. Suppose that the consumer price index of a country is decreasing at the rate of 6.1% per year. Use the approximate half-life formula to estimate the half-life.

_____

_____

_____

9. Suppose that a quantity is halved every 16 years. Use the approximate half-life formula to estimate its decay rate.

_____

_____

_____

10. Suppose you are using the approximate half-life formula to determine the half-lives corresponding to several different decay rates. Will you obtain exact results? If not, explain when your results will be the *most* accurate.

_____

_____

_____

Unit 8B Test 3

Name:_____

Date:_____

Choose the correct answer to each problem.

1. If a quantity quadruples every 24 days, what is its doubling time?

   (a) 6 days   **(b)** 8 days   **(c)** 12 days   **(d)** 16 days

2. Suppose that a population has a doubling time of 15 years. By what factor will it grow in 105 years?

   (a) 64   **(b)** 128   **(c)** 256   **(d)** 512

3. Suppose that you possess some of a radioactive substance that has a half-life of 21 days. What fraction of the substance will remain after 105 days?

   (a) 1/5   **(b)** 1/8   **(c)** 1/16   **(d)** 1/32

4. If the doubling time of a state's population is 42 years, how long does it take for the population to increase by a factor of 16?

   (a) 84 years   **(b)** 126 years   **(c)** 168 years   **(d)** 672 years

5. Suppose you deposit $800 in a bank account that has a doubling time of 23 years. To the nearest $100, what will your balance be after 41 years?

   (a) $1600   **(b)** $2700   **(c)** $2800   **(d)** $4300

6. Suppose that a savings account increases its value by 5.8% per year (APY). Use the approximate doubling time formula to estimate the doubling time of the account.

   (a) 11 years   **(b)** 12 years   **(c)** 13 years   **(d)** 14 years

7. If the half-life of a drug in the bloodstream is 7 hours, how much of the drug is left in the bloodstream 16 hours after a 320 milligram dose?

   (a) 66 milligrams   **(b)** 83 milligrams   **(c)** 140 milligrams   **(d)** 236 milligrams

8. Suppose that the consumer price index of a country is decreasing at the rate of 2.8% per year. Use the approximate half-life formula to estimate the half-life.

   (a) 25 years   **(b)** 24 years   **(c)** 26 years   **(d)** 28 years

9. Suppose that a quantity is halved every 18 years. Use the approximate half-life formula to estimate its decay rate.

   (a) 3.3% per year   **(b)** 3.5% per year   **(c)** 3.7% per year   **(d)** 3.9% per year

10. Suppose you use the approximate doubling time formula to determine the doubling time for each of the growth rates listed. For which growth rate would you expect your answer to be the *most* accurate?

    (a) 3% per week   **(b)** 6% per week   **(c)** 9% per week   **(d)** 12% per week

Unit 8B Test 4

Name:_____

Date:_____

Choose the correct answer to each problem.

1. If a quantity quadruples every 20 days, what is its doubling time?

   (a) 5 days   (b) 10 days   (c) 12 days   (d) 15 days

2. Suppose that a population has a doubling time of 14 years. By what factor will it grow in 112 years?

   (a) 64   (b) 128   (c) 256   (d) 512

3. Suppose that you possess some of a radioactive substance that has a half-life of 23 days. What fraction of the substance will remain after 69 days?

   (a) 1/4   (b) 1/8   (c) 1/16   (d) 1/32

4. If the doubling time of a state's population is 53 years, how long does it take for the population to increase by a factor of 8?

   (a) 106 years   (b) 159 years   (c) 212 years   (d) 424 years

5. Suppose you deposit $600 in a bank account that has a doubling time of 22 years. To the nearest $100, what will your balance be after 64 years?

   (a) $1700   (b) $3200   (c) $3700   (d) $4500

6. Suppose that a savings account increases its value by 4.7% per year (APY). Use the approximate doubling time formula to estimate the doubling time of the account.

   (a) 13 years   (b) 14 years   (c) 15 years   (d) 16 years

7. If the half-life of a drug in the bloodstream is 9 hours, how much of the drug is left in the bloodstream 20 hours after a 260 milligram dose?

   (a) 32 milligrams   (b) 56 milligrams   (c) 117 milligrams   (d) 190 milligrams

8. Suppose that the consumer price index of a country is decreasing at the rate of 3.8% per year. Use the approximate half-life formula to estimate the half-life.

   (a) 14 years   (b) 16 years   (c) 18 years   (d) 20 years

9. Suppose that a quantity is halved every 26 years. Use the approximate half-life formula to estimate its decay rate.

   (a) 2.7% per year   (b) 2.9% per year   (c) 3.1% per year   (d) 3.3 % per year

10. Suppose you use the approximate doubling time formula to determine the doubling time for each of the growth rates listed. For which growth rate would you expect your answer to be the *least* accurate?

    (a) 3% per week   (b) 6% per week   (c) 9% per week   (d) 12% per week

Unit 8C Test 1

1. Explain the meaning of *carrying capacity*.

   _____

   _____

   _____

2. For Australia in 2005, the birth rate was approximately 2.8 births per 100 people per year and the death rate was approximately 1.3 deaths per 100 people per year. Find the population growth rate as a percentage. (Neglect the effects of immigration and emigration.)

   _____

   _____

   _____

3. The population growth rate of Liberia has been estimated at 3.1% per year. What is the doubling time?

   _____

   _____

   _____

4. If the population of a country is now 300,000 and the population growth rate is 4.3% per year, what will the population be in 65 years?

   _____

   _____

   _____

5. Suppose that a country's population is 64 million and its population growth rate is 3.7% per year. If the population growth follows a logistic growth model with $r = 0.053$, what is the country's carrying capacity?

   _____

   _____

   _____

6. The table gives the birth and death rates for Greece between 1988 and 2005.

Year	Birth Rate (per 1000)	Death Rate (per 1000)	Growth Rate (% per year)
1988	15.4	9.1	
1998	10.2	9.3	
2005	10.0	10.0	

   a. Describe the general trend in the birth rate between 1988 and 2005.
   b. Describe the general trend in the death rate between 1988 and 2005.
   c. Complete the table to show the country's net growth rate due to births and deaths in 1988, 1998, and 2005. Neglect the effects of immigration.
   d. Based on your answers to parts (a) through (c), predict how the country's population will change over the next 20 years. Do you think your prediction is reliable? Explain.

   _____

   _____

   _____

7. Suppose the population of a country changes due to births, deaths, and immigration. The annual birth rate is 5.6 births per 1000 people, the death rate is 4.3 deaths per 1000 people, the immigration rate into the country is 7.8 per 1000, and the emigration rate out of the country is 2.4 per 1000. Find the net growth rate as a percentage.

   _____

   _____

   _____

8. Suppose a country currently has a population of 18 million and an annual growth rate of 2.50%. If the population growth follows a logistic growth model with a carrying capacity of 65 million, calculate the annual growth rate when the population is 32 million.

   _____

   _____

   _____

Unit 8C Test 2

Name:_____

Date:_____

1. Explain the meaning of *logistic growth model*.

   _____

   _____

   _____

2. For Ireland in 1997, the birth rate was approximately 1.3 births per 100 people per year and the death rate was approximately 0.9 deaths per 100 people per year. Find the population growth rate as a percentage. (Neglect the effects of immigration and emigration.)

   _____

   _____

   _____

3. The population growth rate of Kuwait has been estimated at 1.9% per year. What is the doubling time?

   _____

   _____

   _____

4. If the population of a country is now 500,000 and the population growth rate is 3.1% per year, what will the population be in 75 years?

   _____

   _____

   _____

5. Suppose that a country's population is 76 million and its population growth rate is 2.8% per year. If the population growth follows a logistic growth model with $r = 0.047$, what is the country's carrying capacity?

   _____

   _____

   _____

Unit 8C Test 2 *(continued)*

6. The table gives the birth and death rates for France between 1988 and 2005.

Year	Birth Rate (per 1000)	Death Rate (per 1000)	Growth Rate (% per year)
1988	14.8	10.2	
1998	13.5	9.3	
2005	11.0	9.0	

a. Describe the general trend in the birth rate between 1988 and 2005.

b. Describe the general trend in the death rate between 1988 and 2005.

c. Complete the table to show the country's net growth rate due to births and deaths in 1988, 1998, and 2005.
   Neglect the effects of immigration.

d. Based on your answers to parts (a) through (c), predict how the country's population will change over the next 20 years. Do you think your prediction is reliable? Explain.

_____

_____

_____

7. Suppose the population of a country changes due to births, deaths, and immigration. The annual birth rate is 3.5 births per 1000 people, the death rate is 7.2 deaths per 1000 people, the immigration rate into the country is 9.3 per 1000, and the emigration rate out of the country is 4.6 per 1000. Find the net growth rate as a percentage.

_____

_____

_____

8. Suppose a country currently has a population of 21 million and an annual growth rate of 4.20%. If the population growth follows a logistic growth model with a carrying capacity of 83 million, calculate the annual growth rate when the population is 32 million.

_____

_____

_____

Unit 8C Test 3

Name:_____

Date:_____

Choose the correct answer to each problem.

1. Real populations sometimes increase beyond their environment's carrying capacity in a relatively short period of time. What is the name of this phenomenon?

   (a) Logistic growth

   (b) Collapse

   (c) Overshoot

   (d) Annual growth rate

2. For Luxembourg in 2005, the birth rate was approximately 2.7 births per 100 people per year and the death rate was approximately 2.2 deaths per 100 people per year. Find the population growth rate. (Neglect the effects of immigration and emigration.)

   (a) 0.5%

   (b) 0.8%

   (c) 1.3%

   (d) 2.1%

3. The population growth rate of Laos has been estimated at 2.8% per year. What is the approximate doubling time?

   (a) 15 years

   (b) 20 years

   (c) 25 years

   (d) 30 years

4. If the population of a country is now 600,000 and the population growth rate is 2.7% per year, what will the approximate population be in 85 years?

   (a) 3,858,000

   (b) 4,738,000

   (c) 5,822,000

   (d) 9,372,000

5. The table gives the birth and death rates for Japan from 1988 to 2005. Determine the net growth rate due to births and deaths in each of the three years, and observe the general trend in the net growth rate. (Neglect the effects of immigration.) If the trend continues, which of the following predictions would be accurate?

Year	Birth Rate (per 1000)	Death Rate (per 1000)	Growth Rate (% per year)
1988	13.7	6.2	
1998	9.9	6.7	
2005	10.0	7.0	

   (a) The population will increase dramatically.

   (b) The population will continue to grow for some time, but may level off at some point in the future.

   (c) The population will level off in the next few years, and then begin to decrease.

   (d) The population is decreasing and will continue to do so.

6. Using the data in Exercise 5, what was Japan's growth rate in 1998?

   (a) 0.09% per year

   (b) 0.32% per year

   (c) 1.66% per year

   (d) 3.2% per year

7. Suppose the population of a country changes due to births, deaths, and immigration. The annual birth rate is 4.3 births per 1000 people, the death rate is 2.1 deaths per 1000 people, the immigration rate into the country is 7.2 per 1000, and the emigration rate out of the country is 5.1 per 1000. Find the net growth rate as a percentage.

   (a) 0.01% per year

   (b) 0.43% per year

   (c) 0.85% per year

   (d) 4.3% per year

Name:_____

8. Suppose a country currently has a population of 24 million and an annual growth rate of 3.4%. If the population growth follows a logistic growth model with a carrying capacity of 90 million, calculate the annual growth rate when the population is 32 million.

   (a) 2.2% (b) 2.6% (c) 3.0% (d) 3.4%

9. Suppose that a country's population is 90 million and its population growth rate is 5.3% per year. If the population growth follows a logistic growth model with $r = 0.083$, what is the country's carrying capacity?

   (a) 124 million (b) 141 million (c) 206 million (d) 249 million

Unit 8C Test 4

Name:_____

Date:_____

Choose the correct answer to each problem.

1. If a population has exceeded the carrying capacity of its environment, it may suffer a rapid and severe decrease in the population. What is the name of this type of population decrease?

   (a) Logistic growth
   (c) Overshoot
   (b) Collapse
   (d) Annual growth rate

2. For Singapore in 1997, the birth rate was approximately 1.9 births per 100 people per year and the death rate was approximately 1.4 deaths per 100 people per year. Find the population growth rate. (Neglect the effects of immigration and emigration.)

   (a) 0.6%   (b) 0.5 %   (c) 1.6%   (d) 2.1%

3. The population growth rate of Lebanon has been estimated at 3.1% per year. What is the approximate doubling time?

   (a) 18 years   (b) 23 years   (c) 28 years   (d) 39 years

4. If the population of a country is now 400,000 and the population growth rate is 3.4% per year, what will the approximate population be in 55 years?

   (a) 1,875,000   (b) 2,548,000   (c) 3,187,000   (d) 4,773,000

5. The table gives the birth and death rates for Portugal from 1988 to 2005. Determine the net growth rate due to births and deaths in each of the three years, and observe the general trend in the net growth rate. (Neglect the effects of immigration.) If the trend continues, which of the following predictions would be accurate?

Year	Birth Rate (per 1000)	Death Rate (per 1000)	Growth Rate (% per year)
1988	16.4	9.9	
1998	11.8	10.4	
2005	11.0	10.0	

   (a) The population will increase dramatically.
   (b) The population will continue to grow exponentially forever.
   (c) The population will level off in the next decade or two, and then may begin to decrease.
   (d) The population is now decreasing and will continue to do so.

6. Using the data in Exercise 5, what was Portugal's growth rate in 1998?

   (a) 0.14% per year   (b) 0.22% per year   (c) 1.4% per year   (d) 2.2% per year

7. Suppose the population of a country changes due to births, deaths, and immigration. The annual birth rate is 6.2 births per 1000 people, the death rate is 5.3 deaths per 1000 people, the immigration rate into the country is 8.4 per 1000, and the emigration rate out of the country is 3.9 per 1000. Find the net growth rate as a percentage.

   (a) −0.36% per year   (b) 0.08% per year   (c) 0.54% per year   (d) 5.4% per year

8. Suppose a country currently has a population of 28 million and an annual growth rate of 2.2%. If the population growth follows a logistic growth model with a carrying capacity of 74 million, calculate the annual growth rate when the population is 32 million.

   (a) 1.9%   **(b)** 2.0%   **(c)** 2.1%   **(d)** 2.2%

9. Suppose that a country's population is 57 million and its population growth rate is 1.6% per year. If the population growth follows a logistic growth model with $r = 0.035$, what is the country's carrying capacity?

   (a) 75 million   **(b)** 85 million   **(c)** 105 million   **(d)** 125 million

Unit 8D Test 1

1. Give one reason why earthquakes of the same magnitude may cause different amounts of damage.

   _____

   _____

   _____

2. Give a possible explanation for why the 1990 earthquake in Iran of magnitude 7.7 caused so many more deaths than the relatively comparable earthquake in 1997.

   _____

   _____

   _____

3. Compare the estimated energies released by the 1990 magnitude 7.7 and the 1997 magnitude 7.5 earthquakes in Iran. Show your work.

   _____

   _____

   _____

4. What is a sound of 0 decibels defined to be?

   _____

   _____

   _____

5. Suppose that a sound is 90 times as intense as the softest audible sound. What is its loudness, in decibels?

   _____

   _____

   _____

6. How much more intense is a 79 dB sound than a 17 dB sound?

   _____

   _____

   _____

Unit 8D Test 1 *(continued)*

7. The sound level from a television 1 meter away is 130 dB. How far away from the television should you be to avoid risking damage to your ears?

_____

_____

_____

8. Name something in a refrigerator that probably has a pH value lower than 7.

_____

_____

_____

9. What is the pH of a solution with a hydrogen ion concentration of 10^{-8} moles per liter?

_____

_____

_____

10. Name something that can cause acid rain.

_____

_____

_____

Unit 8D Test 2

1. Give a possible explanation for why the 1990 earthquake in Iran of magnitude 7.7 cause an estimated 40,000 deaths but the 1989 earthquake in San Francisco of magnitude 7.1 caused less than 100 deaths.

    _____

    _____

    _____

2. Explain how scientists compare earthquakes.

    _____

    _____

    _____

3. Compare the estimated energies released by the 1989 earthquake in San Francisco of magnitude 7.1 and the 1994 earthquake in Los Angeles of magnitude 6.7. Show your work.

    _____

    _____

    _____

4. Describe what happens mathematically to the intensity of a sound you hear as you move away from the source of the sound.

    _____

    _____

    _____

5. Suppose that a sound is 10,000 times as intense as the softest audible sound. What is its loudness, in decibels?

    _____

    _____

    _____

6. How much more intense is a 70 dB sound than a 40 dB sound?

    _____

    _____

    _____

Unit 8D Test 2 *(continued)*

7. The sound level from a siren 30 meters away is 100 dB. How close can you get to the siren before there is a strong risk of damage to your ears?

_____

_____

_____

8. Name something that probably has a pH value greater than 7.

_____

_____

_____

9. What is the pH of a solution with a hydrogen ion concentration of 10^{-3} moles per liter?

_____

_____

_____

10. Give an example of the effects of acid rain.

_____

_____

_____

Unit 8D Test 3

Name:_____

Date:_____

Choose the correct answer to each problem.

1. How much energy, in joules is released by an earthquake of magnitude 6?

   (a) 2.5×10^6 joules

   (c) 2.5×10^9 joules

   (b) 7.9×10^7 joules

   (d) 2.5×10^{13} joules

2. Earthquakes of what magnitude occur most frequently?

   (a) less than 3   (b) 5   (c) 7   (d) 8 and up

3. Earthquakes usually cause damage in all but which one of the following related ways?

   (a) Tsunamis

   (c) Collapsed building due to inferior construction

   (b) Fires caused by heat from the earth's interior.

   (c) Landslides

4. Which of the following sounds would you expect to have the highest decibel measurement?

   (a) Rustling leaves

   (c) Background noise in an average home

   (b) Ordinary conversation

   (d) Afternoon traffic in New York City

5. What is the loudness, in decibels, of a sound that is 500 times as intense as the softest audible sound?

   (a) 3 dB   (b) 27 dB   (c) 400 dB   (d) 60 dB

6. A sound of what loudness, in decibels, is 63 times as intense as a 13 dB sound?

   (a) 819 dB   (b) 14.8 dB   (c) 31 dB   (d) 122 dB

7. If you are 2 meters away from a sound of 90 dB, how far away should you move so that the intensity is decreased by a factor of 16?

   (a) 10 meters   (b) 8 meters   (c) 9 meters   (d) 6 meters

8. Which of the following probably has a pH value lower than 6?

   (a) orange juice   (b) tap water   (c) drain opener   (d) antacid tablets

9. What is the hydrogen ion concentration of a strong acid?

   (a) 10^{-1} moles per liter

   (c) 10^{-7} moles per liter

   (b) 10^{-6} moles per liter

   (d) 10^{-10} moles per liter

10. How much more acidic is acid rain with a pH of 3.5 than ordinary rain with a pH of 6?

    (a) 3 times more acidic   (b) 316 times more acidic   (c) 1.7 times more acidic   (d) 60 times more acidic

Unit 8D Test 4

Name:_____

Date:_____

Choose the correct answer to each problem.

1. How much energy, in joules, is released by an earthquake of magnitude 4?

   (a) 2.5×10^8 joules

   (b) 2.5×10^{10} joules

   (c) 7.9×10^5 joules

   (d) 2.5×10^{11} joules

2. Approximately how many times per year is there a major earthquake of magnitude 7-8?

   (a) more than 1

   (b) more than 50

   (c) more than 500

   (d) more than 1000

3. Which of the following are factors in the amount of damage caused by an earthquake?

   (a) The type of surface bedrock near the quake

   (b) The amount of energy released in surface waves as compared to interior waves

   (c) The economy of the region hit by the earthquake

   (d) All of the above

4. Which of the following decibel measurements corresponds to an inaudible sound?

   (a) 100 dB   (b) 0 dB   (c) −10 dB   (d) 140 dB

5. If a sound measures 80 dB, that sound is how many times as intense as the softest audible sound?

   (a) 100   (b) 10   (c) 10 thousand   (d) 100 million

6. A 92 dB sound is 50 times as intense as a sound of what loudness?

   (a) 90.3 dB   (b) 18.4 dB   (c) 75 dB   (d) 937 dB

7. If you are 15 meters away from a sound of 10 dB, how much more intense is the sound if you move 10 meters closer to it?

   (a) 3 times more intense

   (b) 9 times more intense

   (c) 10 times more intense

   (d) 25 times more intense

8. Which of the following probably has a pH value greater than 8?

   (a) lye   (b) pure water   (c) grapefruit juice   (d) vinegar

9. What is the hydrogen ion concentration of a strong base?

   (a) 10^{-1} moles per liter

   (b) 10^{-12} moles per liter

   (c) 10^{-8} moles per liter

   (d) 10^{-3} moles per liter

Unit 8-D Test 4 *(continued)*

10. How much more acidic is acid rain with a pH of 4 than ordinary rain with a pH of 6?

    (a) 1.5 times more acidic   **(b)** 100 times more acidic **(c)** 10 times more acidic   **(d)** $\frac{2}{3}$ more acidic

Unit 9A Test 1

Name:_____

Date:_____

1. What is benefit of representing a function with an equation?

   _____

   _____

   _____

2. Name the three basic ways to represent a function.

   _____

   _____

   _____

3. What is meant by the independent variable of a function?

   _____

   _____

   _____

4. In words, describe a function involving the altitude, over time, of a ball thrown into the air.

   _____

   _____

   _____

5. Use the notation (independent variable, dependent variable) to characterize the function in the previous question.

   _____

   _____

   _____

Unit 9A Test 1 *(continued)*

Name:_____

In the following problems, use the table below. It lists measurements of the concentration of a particular chemical in a public pool which is serviced every 2 weeks.

Days after regular maintenance	Concentration in parts per million (ppm)
2	7.5
8	6
12	5

6. Assuming that the complete function includes all other data values that make sense, draw the graph of the function.

7. What are the domain and range of this function?

_____

_____

_____

8. Use words to describe the function.

_____

_____

_____

9. Use the graph of the function to find the concentration on day 6.

_____

_____

_____

10. Use the graph to find the day on which the concentration is 5.25 ppm.

_____

_____

_____

Unit 9A Test 2

1. What is the benefit of representing a function with a graph?

   _____

   _____

   _____

2. What is meant by the dependent variable of a function?

   _____

   _____

   _____

3. What is a periodic function?

   _____

   _____

   _____

4. In words, describe a function involving the temperature, over time, of water being heated on a stove.

   _____

   _____

   _____

5. Use the notation (independent variable, dependent variable) to characterize the function in the previous question.

   _____

   _____

   _____

Unit 9A Test 2 *(continued)*

Name:_____

In the following problems, use the table below. It represents measurements of the concentration of a substance in a patient's bloodstream, after the start of treatment meant to boost the concentration.

Days after start of treatment	Concentration in parts per million (ppm)
2	5.4
5	6
10	7

6. Assuming that the complete function includes all other data values that make sense, draw the graph of the function.

7. What are the domain and range of this function?

_____

_____

_____

8. Use words to describe the function.

_____

_____

_____

9. Use the graph of the function to find the concentration on day 6.

_____

_____

_____

10. Use the graph to find the day on which the concentration is 6.6 ppm.

_____

_____

_____

Unit 9A Test 3

Name:_____

Date:_____

Choose the correct answer to each problem.

1. Which of the following is the most compact mathematical representation of a function?

   (a) Data table   **(b)** Graph   **(c)** Equation   **(d)** Domain

2. The domain of a function is the set of _____ values?

   (a) All numeral   **(b)** Dependent variable   **(c)** Independent variable   **(d)** Periodic

3. Which of the following most likely describes a periodic function?

   (a) (age of my 2001 truck, its value)   **(b)** (date, time of sunrise)
   (c) (age of a child, her height)   **(d)** (distance traveled, time elapsed)

4. Is the following a function: "The size of a pool , measured in square feet"? Why or why not?

   (a) Yes, because it relates two variables mentioned   **(b)** No, because only one variable is
   (c) Yes, because the area can change   **(d)** No, because the units are wrong

5. Use the notation (independent variable, dependent variable) to characterize the relationship between time and the elevation of a flying object.

   (a) (time and elevation, duration)   **(b)** (duration, time and elevation)
   (c) (elevation, time)   **(d)** (time, elevation)

For the following problems, use the table below. It lists measurements of the concentration of a particular chemical in a public pool.

Days after regular maintenance	Concentration in parts per million (ppm)
4	7
6	6.5
10	5.5

6. Assuming that the complete function includes all other data values that make sense, which is the graph of the function?

(a)
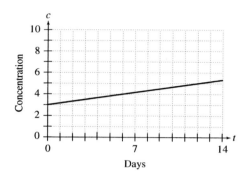

(b)
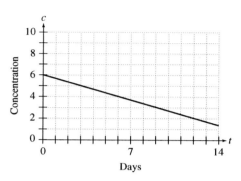

(c)
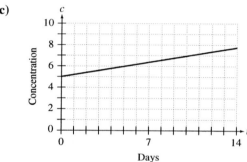

(d)
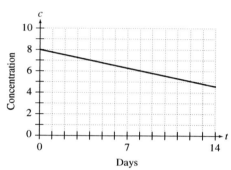

7. What are the domain and range of this function?

(a) Domain: $t \geq 0$; range: $c \geq 8$
(c) Domain: $t \geq 0$; range: $0 \leq c \leq 8$

(b) Domain: $c \geq 0$; range: $t \geq 8$
(d) Domain: $c \geq 0$; range: $t \geq 0$

8. Which is a reasonable guess about the chemical being measured?

(a) It is added during maintenance.
(c) It is caused by heavy pool usage.

(b) It is naturally occurring.
(d) It builds up over time.

9. Use the graph of the function to find the concentration on day 12.

(a) 5 ppm
(b) 6.5 ppm
(c) 8 ppm
(d) 9.75 ppm

10. Use the graph to find the day on which the concentration is 7.75 ppm.

(a) Day 1
(b) Day 3
(c) Day 5
(d) Day 7

Unit 9A Test 4

Choose the correct answer to each problem.

1. Which of the following is a mathematical representation of a function that provides detailed information but can become unwieldy?

   (a) Data table   (b) Graph   (c) Equation   (d) Domain

2. The range of a function is the set of _____ values?

   (a) All numerical   (b) Dependent variable   (c) Independent variable   (d) Periodic

3. Which of the following most likely describes a periodic function?

   (a) (age of my computer, its value)   (b) (date, your age)
   (c) (date, number of days until Friday)   (d) (Tom's age, his shoe size)

4. Is the following a function: "The volume of a soup can, measured in cubic ounces"? Why or why not?

   (a) No, because the units are wrong   (b) Yes, because the mass cannot change
   (c) No, because only one variable is mentioned   (d) Yes, because it relates two variables

5. Use the notation (independent variable, dependent variable) to characterize the relationship between time and the temperature of a cooling object.

   (a) (temperature, time)   (b) (time, temperature)
   (c) (temperature and time, rate of cooling)   (d) (rate of cooling, temperature and time)

For the following problems, use the table below. It represents measurements of the concentration of a substance in a patient's bloodstream, after the start of medical treatment.

Days after start of treatment	Concentration in parts per million (ppm)
3	5.6
8	6.6
10	7

Unit 9A Test 4 *(continued)*

6. Assuming that the complete function includes all other data values that make sense, which is the graph of the function?

(a)
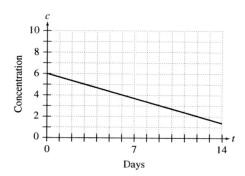

(b)
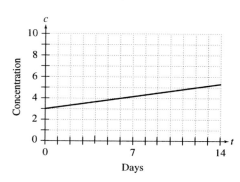

(c)
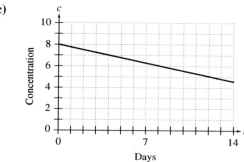

(d)
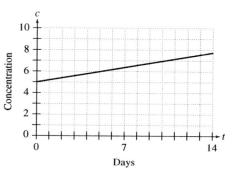

7. What are the domain and range of this function?

   (a) Domain: $t \geq 0$; range: $c \geq 5$
   (c) Domain: $t \geq 0$; range: $0 \leq c \leq 5$

   (b) Domain: $c \geq 0$; range: $t \geq 0$
   (d) Domain: $c \geq 0$; range: $0 \leq t \leq 5$

8. Which is a reasonable guess about the substance being measured?

   (a) It is harmful to the body in large amounts.
   (c) It is synthetic.

   (b) The body metabolizes it readily.
   (d) A certain amount of it is in the body naturally.

9. Use the graph of the function to find the concentration on day 13.

   (a) 6.5 ppm   (b) 7.6 ppm   (c) 8.1 ppm   (d) 9.2 ppm

10. Use the graph to find the day on which the concentration is 6 ppm.

   (a) Day 1   (b) Day 3   (c) Day 5   (d) Day 7

Unit 9B Test 1

For questions 1 through 6, use the graph shown, which shows the concentration of a substance, in parts per million (ppm), as a function of time, in days.

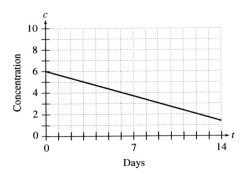

1. What is the concentration on day 9?

_____

_____

_____

2. What is the rate of change?

_____

_____

_____

3. By how much does the concentration drop over the space of 6 days?

_____

_____

_____

4. Find the initial value of the concentration.

_____

_____

_____

Unit 9B Test 1 *(continued)*

5. Write an equation representing concentration, c, as a function of time, t.

_____

_____

_____

6. Use the equation to predict the concentration on day 15.

_____

_____

_____

7. Solve the equation $y = -4x - 3$ for x.

_____

_____

_____

8. Create a linear function relating x and y which includes the points (4, 110) and (10, 302). Write y as a function of x.

_____

_____

_____

9. Use the function from the previous question to find y when $x = 3\ 1/2$.

_____

_____

_____

10. A new computer costs $1500 today and decreases in value at a constant rate of $300 per year. What will be the value of this computer in 2.5 years?

_____

_____

_____

Unit 9B Test 2

For questions 1 through 6, use the graph shown, which shows the concentration of a substance, in parts per million (ppm), as a function of time, in days.

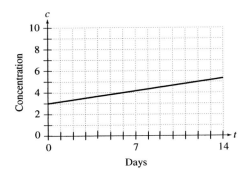

1. What is the concentration on day 9?

_____

_____

_____

2. What is the rate of change?

_____

_____

_____

3. By how much does the concentration rise over the space of 6 days?

_____

_____

_____

4. Find the initial value of the concentration.

_____

_____

_____

Name:_____

5. Write an equation representing concentration, c, as a function of time, t.

_____

_____

_____

6. Use the equation to predict the concentration on day 18.

_____

_____

_____

7. Solve the equation $y = 6x - 7$ for x.

_____

_____

_____

8. Create a linear function relating x and y which includes the points $(5, -45)$ and $(7, -65)$. Write y as a function of x.

_____

_____

_____

9. Use the function from the previous question to find y when $x = 2\ 1/2$.

_____

_____

_____

10. The price of a computer is \$1200 today, and its value decreases at the rate of \$30 per month. What will be the value of the computer in 1 year?

_____

_____

_____

Unit 9B Test 3

Name:_____

Date:_____

For questions 1 through 6, use the graph shown, which shows the concentration of a substance, in parts per million (ppm), as a function of time, in days.

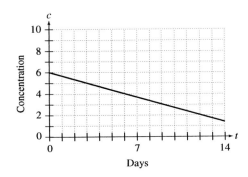

1. What is the concentration on day 12?

   (a) 0.5 ppm   **(b)** 2 ppm   **(c)** 3.5 ppm   **(d)** 5 ppm

2. What is the rate of change?

   (a) $-\dfrac{1}{4}$ ppm per day   **(b)** $\dfrac{1}{6}$ ppm per day   **(c)** $-\dfrac{1}{3}$ ppm per day   **(d)** $\dfrac{1}{5}$ ppm per day

3. By how much does the concentration drop over the space of 3 days?

   (a) 0.5 ppm   **(b)** 1 ppm   **(c)** 2 ppm   **(d)** 2.5 ppm

4. Find the initial value of the concentration.

   (a) 6 ppm   **(b)** 7.5 ppm   **(c)** 8.5 ppm   **(d)** 10 ppm

5. Which is an equation representing concentration, c, as a function of time, t?

   (a) $c = 8 - \dfrac{1}{4}t$ **(b)** $c = 6 - \dfrac{1}{3}t$ **(c)** $c = 5 + \dfrac{1}{5}t$ **(d)** $c = 3 + \dfrac{1}{6}t$

6. Use the equation to predict the concentration on day 18.

   (a) 0 ppm   **(b)** 1.5 ppm   **(c)** 2 ppm   **(d)** 2.5 ppm

7. Solve the equation $y = 3x + 2$ for x.

   (a) $x = \dfrac{y+3}{2}$ **(b)** $x = \dfrac{y-3}{2}$ **(c)** $x = \dfrac{y-2}{3}$ **(d)** $x = \dfrac{y+2}{3}$

8. Create a linear function relating x and y which includes the points $(8, 8)$ and $(12, 28)$. Write y as a function of x.

   (a) $y = 4x - 20$ **(b)** $y = 5x - 32$ **(c)** $y = 6x - 40$ **(d)** $y = 7x - 51$

9. Use the function from question 8 to find y when $x = 15$.

    (a) 40   **(b)** 43   **(c)** 50   **(d)** 54

10. The price of a computer is \$800 today, and its value decreases at the constant rate of \$250 per year. What will be the value of the computer after 3 months?

    (a) \$50   **(b)** \$300   **(c)** \$550   **(d)** \$738

Unit 9B Test 4

Name:_____

Date:_____

For questions 1 through 6, use the graph shown, which shows the concentration of a substance, in parts per million (ppm), as a function of time, in days.

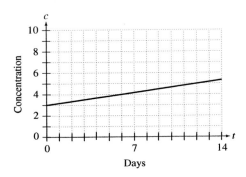

1. What is the concentration on day 6?

    (a) 2.5 ppm

    (b) 4 ppm

    (c) 5.5 ppm

    (d) 7 ppm

2. What is the rate of change?

    (a) $-\dfrac{1}{4}$ ppm per day

    (b) $\dfrac{1}{6}$ ppm per day

    (c) $-\dfrac{1}{3}$ ppm per day

    (d) $\dfrac{1}{5}$ ppm per day

3. How much does the concentration rise over the duration of 3 days?

    (a) 0.5 ppm

    (b) 1 ppm

    (c) 2 ppm

    (d) 2.5 ppm

4. Find the initial value of the concentration.

    (a) 3 ppm

    (b) 4.5 ppm

    (c) 6.5 ppm

    (d) 8 ppm

5. Which is an equation representing concentration, c, as a function of time, t?

    (a) $c = 8 - \dfrac{1}{4}t$

    (b) $c = 6 - \dfrac{1}{3}t$

    (c) $c = 5 + \dfrac{1}{5}t$

    (d) $c = 3 + \dfrac{1}{6}t$

6. Use the equation to predict the concentration on day 18.

    (a) 0 ppm

    (b) 3.5 ppm

    (c) 6 ppm

    (d) 7.5 ppm

7. Solve the equation $y = -4x + 7$ for x.

    (a) $x = \dfrac{y-7}{-4}$

    (b) $x = \dfrac{y+7}{4}$

    (c) $x = \dfrac{y+4}{7}$

    (d) $x = \dfrac{y-4}{7}$

8. Create a linear function relating x and y which includes the points $(8, 8)$ and $(12, 32)$. Write y as a function of x.

    (a) $y = 4x - 18$

    (b) $y = 5x - 32$

    (c) $y = 6x - 40$

    (d) $y = 7x - 48$

9. Use the function from question 8 to find *y* when *x* = 15.

   (a) 42   (b) 43   (c) 50   (d) 57

10. The price of a 3-day cruise is $1200 and increases at a constant rate of $60 per year. How much will the cruise cost in 4.5 years?

    (a) $1410   (b) $1440   (c) $1470   (d) $1500

Unit 9C Test 1

Name:_____

Date:_____

1. In 1970, the population of a certain city was 80,000, and it has been growing at a steady rate of 8% per year since then. Complete the table to show the population of the city each year from 1970 to 1985, and make a graph from the data.

Year	Population
1970	
1971	
1972	
1973	
1974	
1975	
1976	
1977	

Year	Population
1978	
1979	
1980	
1981	
1982	
1983	
1984	
1985	

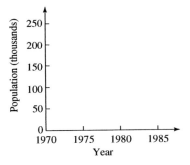

2. Linda placed $1000 in a brokerage account that has been increasing its value by 11% per year (i.e., APY = 11%). At the same time, John began placing $1000 under a mattress at the beginning of each year. Who had more money after 20 years, and by how much?

_____

_____

_____

Unit 9C Test 1 *(continued)*

Name:_____

3. The average price of a home in a certain town was $86,000 in 1990, but home prices have been *falling* by 4% per year. Create an exponential function of the form $Q = Q_0 \times (1 + r)^t$ to model this situation. Be sure to clearly identify each of the variables in your function. Then make a graph of the exponential function.

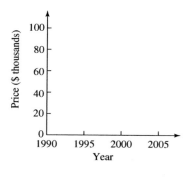

_____

_____

_____

4. In 1995, the enrollment at a certain university was 5200 students. If the enrollment increases by 9% per year, what will the enrollment be in the year 2010?

_____

_____

_____

5. Suppose that the average price for a certain product was $16.40 in 1990 and $22.80 in 1998. With an inflation rate of 3% per year, compare the inflation-adjusted prices of this product.

_____

_____

_____

6. If prices increase at a monthly rate of 1.5%, how much do they increase in a year?

_____

_____

_____

7. Suppose that poaching reduces the population of an endangered animal by 12% per year. Further, suppose that when the population of this animal falls below 45, its extinction is inevitable (owing to the lack of reproductive options without severe in-breeding). If the current population of this animal is 1400, in how many years will it face extinction?

8. A toxic radioactive substance with a density of 5 milligrams per square centimeter is detected in the ventilating ducts of an old nuclear processing building. If the half-life of the substance is 11 years, what was the density of the substance when it was deposited 38 years ago?

9. A fossilized bone contains about 62% of its original carbon-14. How old is the bone? (The half-life of carbon-14 is about 5700 years.)

10. Suppose $500 is invested in a bank account that increases its value annually by 8.3% (i.e., APY = 8.3%), while the inflation rate is 4.2% per year. Find the buying power (in today's dollars) of the account after 65 years.

Unit 9C Test 2

Name:_____

Date:_____

1. In 1970, the population of a certain city was 40,000, and it has been growing at a steady rate of 12% per year since then. Complete the table to show the population of the city each year from 1970 to 1985, and make a graph from the data.

Year	Population
1970	
1971	
1972	
1973	
1974	
1975	
1976	
1977	

Year	Population
1978	
1979	
1980	
1981	
1982	
1983	
1984	
1985	

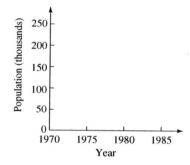

2. Peter placed $500 in a brokerage account that has been increasing its value by 14% per year (i.e., APY = 14%). At the same time, Paul began placing $500 under a mattress at the beginning of each year. Who had more money after 15 years, and by how much?

_____

_____

_____

Unit 9C Test 2 *(continued)*

Name:_____

3. The average price of a home in a certain town was $74,000 in 1990, but home prices have been *falling* by 8% per year. Create an exponential function of the form $Q = Q_0 \times (1+r)^t$ to model this situation. Be sure to clearly identify each of the variables in your function. Then make a graph of the exponential function.

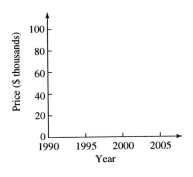

_____

_____

_____

4. In 1995, the enrollment at a certain university was 1800 students. If the enrollment increases by 7% per year, what will the enrollment be in the year 2010?

_____

_____

_____

5. Suppose that the average price for a certain product was $12.50 in 1990 and $14.25 in 1998. With an inflation rate of 3% per year, compare the inflation-adjusted prices of this product.

_____

_____

_____

6. If prices increase at a monthly rate of 1.2%, how much do they increase in a year?

_____

_____

_____

Unit 9C Test 2 *(continued)*

7. Suppose that poaching reduces the population of an endangered animal by 9% per year. Further, suppose that when the population of this animal falls below 15, its extinction is inevitable (owing to the lack of reproductive options without severe in-breeding). If the current population of this animal is 1800, in how many years will it face extinction?

_____

_____

_____

8. A toxic radioactive substance with a density of 8 milligrams per square centimeter is detected in the ventilating ducts of an old nuclear processing building. If the half-life of the substance is 13 years, what was the density of the substance when it was deposited 56 years ago?

_____

_____

_____

9. A fossilized bone contains about 56% of its original carbon-14. How old is the bone? (The half-life of carbon-14 is about 5700 years.)

_____

_____

_____

10. Suppose $300 is invested in a bank account that increases its value annually by 6.8% (i.e., APY = 6.8%), while the inflation rate is 5.3% per year. Find the buying power (in today's dollars) of the account after 85 years.

_____

_____

_____

Unit 9C Test 3

Name:_____

Date:_____

Choose the correct answer to each problem.

1. In 1970, the population of a certain city was 70,000, and it has been growing at a steady rate of 9% per year since then. Make a table that shows the population of the city each year from 1970 to 1985. Use your table to find the population (to the nearest thousand) of the city in 1985.

   (a) 165,000   (b) 183,000   (c) 234,000   (d) 255,000

2. Carl placed $900 in a brokerage account that has been increasing its value by 16% per year (i.e., APY = 16%). At the same time, Brad began placing $900 under a mattress at the beginning of each year. Who had more money after 22 years, and by how much?

   (a) Carl, by about $1600
   (c) Brad, by about $1600
            (b) Carl, by about $3800
   (d) Brad, by about $3800

3. The average price of a home in a certain town was $78,000 in 1990, but home prices have been *falling* by 10% per year. Create an exponential function of the form $Q = Q_0 \times (1+r)^t$ to model this situation, where t is the number of years since 1990 and Q is the average home price in thousands.

   (a) $Q = 78(1.1)^t$ (b) $Q = 10(0.78)^t$ (c) $Q = 78(0.1)^t$ (d) $Q = 78(0.9)^t$

4. In 1995, the enrollment at a certain university was 2000 students. If the enrollment increases by 10% per year, what will the enrollment be (to the nearest hundred students) in the year 2010?

   (a) 2200 students   (b) 5000 students   (c) 7600 students   (d) 8400 students

5. Suppose that the average price for a certain product was $14.25 in 1990 and $18.75 in 1998. With an inflation rate of 3% per year, compare the inflation-adjusted prices of this product.

   (a) The price fell by $0.70 (as measured in 1998 dollars).
   (b) The price fell by $4.50 (as measured in 1998 dollars).
   (c) The price increased by $0.70 (as measured in 1998 dollars).
   (d) The price increased by $4.50 (as measured in 1998 dollars).

6. If prices increase at a monthly rate of 2.1 %, how much do they increase in a year?

   (a) 25.2%   (b) 28.3%   (c) 35.6%   (d) 41.5%

7. Suppose that poaching reduces the population of an endangered animal by 10% per year. Further, suppose that when the population of this animal falls below 27, its extinction is inevitable (owing to the lack of reproductive options without severe in-breeding). If the current population of this animal is 2000, in how many years will it face extinction?

   (a) 35 years   (b) 41 years   (c) 48 years   (d) 62 years

8. A toxic radioactive substance with a density of 7 milligrams per square centimeter is detected in the ventilating ducts of an old nuclear processing building. If the half-life of the substance is 17 years, what was the density of the substance when it was deposited 41 years ago?

   (a) 37.2 mg/cm^2 (b) 46.4 mg/cm^2 (c) 83.7 mg/cm^2 (d) 153.2 mg/cm^2

9. A fossilized bone contains about 68% of its original carbon-14. To the nearest hundred years, how old is the bone? (The half-life of carbon-14 is about 5700 years.)

   (a) 2700 years   (b) 3200 years   (c) 3900 years   (d) 4200 years

10. Suppose $400 is invested in a bank account that increases its value annually by 7.2% (i.e., APY = 7.2%), while the inflation rate is 6.1% per year. Find the buying power (in today's dollars) of the account after 95 years.

   (a) $963.45   (b) $1065.62   (c) $1130.89   (d) $295,504.84

Unit 9C Test 4

Choose the correct answer to each problem.

1. In 1970, the population of a certain city was 90,000, and it has been growing at a steady rate of 7% per year since then. Make a table that shows the population of the city each year from 1970 to 1985. Use your table to find the population (to the nearest thousand) of the city in 1985.

   (a) 185,000 (b) 232,000 (c) 248,000 (d) 255,000

2. Celene placed $600 in a brokerage account that has been increasing its value by 12% per year (i.e., APY = 12%). At the same time, Dottie began placing $600 under a mattress at the beginning of each year. Who had more money after 25 years, and by how much?

   (a) Celene, by about $2500
   (c) Dottie, by about $2500
   (b) Celene, by about $4800
   (d) Dottie, by about $4800

3. The average price of a home in a certain town was $92,000 in 1990, but home prices have been *falling* by 6% per year. Create an exponential function of the form $Q = Q_0 \times (1 + r)^t$ to model this situation, where t is the number of years since 1990 and Q is the average home price in thousands.

   (a) $Q = 60(0.92)^t$ (b) $Q = 92(0.06)^t$ (c) $Q = 92(0.94)^t$ (d) $Q = 92(1.06)^t$

4. In 1995, the enrollment at a certain university was 2500 students. If the enrollment increases by 7% per year, what will the enrollment be (to the nearest hundred students) in the year 2014?

   (a) 2900 (b) 5800 (c) 9000 (d) 11,500

5. Suppose that the average price for a certain product was $15.40 in 1990 and $17.25 in 1998. With an inflation rate of 3% per year, compare the inflation-adjusted prices of this product.

   (a) The price fell by $1.85 (as measured in 1998 dollars).
   (b) The price fell by $2.26 (as measured in 1998 dollars).
   (c) The price increased by $1.85 (as measured in 1998 dollars).
   (d) The price increased by $2.26 (as measured in 1998 dollars).

6. If prices increase at a monthly rate of 1.8%, how much do they increase in a year?

   (a) 11.5% (b) 16.9% (c) 21.6% (d) 23.9%

7. Suppose that poaching reduces the population of an endangered animal by 11% per year. Further, suppose that when the population of this animal falls below 44, its extinction is inevitable (owing to the lack of reproductive options without severe in-breeding). If the current population of this animal is 1600, in how many years will it face extinction?

   (a) 14 years (b) 23 years (c) 28 years (d) 31 years

8. A toxic radioactive substance with a density of 9 milligrams per square centimeter is detected in the ventilating ducts of an old nuclear processing building. If the half-life of the substance is 7 years, what was the density of the substance when it was deposited 52 years ago?

   (a) 501.6 mg/cm^2

   (c) 1207.3 mg/cm^2

   (b) 841.2 mg/cm^2

   (d) 1550.5 mg/cm^2

9. A fossilized bone contains about 65% of its original carbon-14. To the nearest hundred years, how old is the bone? (The half-life of carbon-14 is about 5700 years.)

   (a) 2600 years   (b) 2900 years   (c) 3200 years   (d) 3500 years

10. Suppose $200 is invested in a bank account that increases its value annually by 6.5% (i.e., APY = 6.5%), while the inflation rate is 3.8% per year. Find the buying power (in today's dollars) of the account after 75 years.

    (a) $1372.30   (b) $1475.07   (c) $1864.39   (d) $22,503.53

Unit 10A Test 1

Name:_____

Date:_____

1. If the radius of a circle doubles, by how much does the area of the circle increase?

   _____

   _____

   _____

2. Is it possible for two polygons to have the same perimeter but different areas? Explain with an example.

   _____

   _____

   _____

3. Find the length of a side of a regular hexagon with a perimeter of 27 inches.

   _____

   _____

   _____

4. On a clock, one hand is pointing at the 12, the other hand is pointing at the 5. What are the two angles formed by the two hands of the clock?

   _____

   _____

   _____

5. Define a sphere in geometric terms.

   _____

   _____

   _____

6. Explain how the scaling laws affect the surface area and volume of a cube.

   _____

   _____

   _____

Unit 10A Test 1 *(continued)*

7. Draw a triangle with an area of 9 units.

8. A grain silo in the shape of a right circular cylinder holds 275π cubic meters of grain. If the circumference of the silo is 10π meters, find the height of the silo.

   _____

   _____

   _____

9. Use Euclidean geometry to explain why we refer to the expression s^2 as "*s*-squared."

   _____

   _____

   _____

10. Give an example of an everyday object that can be used to represent parallel lines.

    _____

    _____

    _____

Unit 10A Test 2

1. Draw a cube with a surface area of 24 units.

2. Use Euclidean geometry to explain why we refer to the expression s^3 as "*s*-cubed".

   _____

   _____

   _____

3. Define a circle in geometric terms.

   _____

   _____

   _____

4. Suppose you have 2 perpendicular lines. Is it possible to draw a third line which is different from the first two, that does not intersect either line?

   _____

   _____

   _____

5. What are the differences between a circle and a sphere?

   _____

   _____

   _____

6. Determine the radius of a circle with a circumference of 30π inches..

   _____

   _____

   _____

Unit 10A Test 2 *(continued)*

7. Which is a better representation of the planet earth, a flat paper map or a globe? Why?

_____

_____

_____

8. Since there are 12-inches in one foot, how many square inches are there in one square foot?

_____

_____

_____

9. Is it possible for two polygons to have the same area but different perimeters? Explain with an example.

_____

_____

_____

10. Find the volume of a cube with a side of 5 inches..

_____

_____

_____

Unit 10A Test 3

Name:_____

Date:_____

Choose the correct answer to each problem.

1. A point has

    (a) 0 - dimensions.   **(b)** 1 - dimension.   **(c)** 2 - dimensions.

2. Since 1 degree equals 2π/360 radians, 4π radians is

    (a) 2 degrees.   **(b)** 4π/360 degrees.   **(c)** 720 degrees.

3. In Euclidean geometry, two distinct points determine?

    (a) a line
    (b) a plane
    (c) a sphere

4. Which polygon has the greatest area?

    (a) an equilateral triangle with side of length 8.
    (b) a square with a side of length 6.
    (c) a rectangle with sides of length 6 and 7.

5. Which solid has the greatest volume?

    (a) a cube with a side of length 4 inches   **(b)** a sphere with a radius of 4 inches
    (c) a right cylindrical cylinder with a radius of 4 inches and a height of 4 inches

6. The lines B & C in this picture are

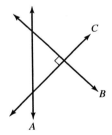

    (a) parallel.   **(b)** perpendicular.   **(c)** neither.

7. A cube has

    (a) 1 - dimension.   **(b)** 2 - dimensions.   **(c)** 3 - dimensions.

8. If an angle subtends $\frac{7}{72}$ of a circle, the angle measure is

    (a) 25 degrees.   **(b)** 35 degrees.   **(c)** 50 degrees.

9. An empty water tank is in the shape of a right cylindrical cylinder with a radius of 12 meters and a height of 10 meters. Water flows into the tank at a rate of 3π cubic meters per second. How long will it take until the tank is full?

    (a) 48 minutes   **(b)** 24 minutes   **(c)** 8 minutes

Unit 10A Test 3 *(continued)*

10. Which of the following is a solid?

   (a) a cube   (b) a triangle   (c) a circle

Unit 10A Test 4

Choose the correct answer to each problem.

1. Which solid has the least surface area?

   (a) A cube with a side of length 4 inches   (b) A sphere with a radius of 4 inches
   (c) A right cylindrical cylinder with a radius of 4 inches and a height of 4 inches

2. A line has

   (a) 0 - dimension.   (b) 1 - dimension.   (c) 2 - dimensions.

3. Which of the following do not determine a plane?

   (a) 2 points   (b) a line and a point not on the line
   (c) 3 non-collinear points

4. Which right cylindrical cylinder has the greatest volume?

   (a) A can with radius 3 centimeters and height 18 centimeters
   (b) A can with radius 9 centimeters and height 3 centimeters
   (c) A can with radius 6 centimeters and height 6 centimeters

5. If an angle subtends $\dfrac{5}{12}$ of a circle, the angle measure is

   (a) 75 degrees.   (b) 150 degrees.   (c) 212 degrees.

6. A plane has

   (a) 1 - dimension.   (b) 2 - dimensions.   (c) 3 - dimensions.

7. Which mathematician was the first to summarize many of the ideas of geometry?

   (a) Euclid   (b) Pythagoras   (c) Newton

8. The lines A & B in this picture are

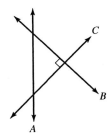

   (a) parallel.   (b) perpendicular.   (c) neither.

9. In a right triangle, the square of the length of the hypotenuse

   (a) Is equal to the area of the triangle.
   (b) Is equal to the sum of the lengths of the other two sides.
   (c) Is equal to the sum of the squares of the other two sides.

Unit 10A Test 4 *(continued)*

10. The word geometry means

(**a**) triangle forming.   (**b**) mountain shape.   (**c**) earth measure.

Unit 10B Test 1

1. Convert $75.12°$ into degrees, minutes, and seconds of arc.

_____

_____

_____

2. Convert $53°12'18"$ into decimal form.

_____

_____

_____

3. Northville, which is directly north of Southtown, is located at latitude $32°N$. Southtown is located at latitude $29°N$. Given that the circumference of the earth is about 25,000 miles, how many miles is it between Northville and Southtown?

_____

_____

_____

4. If Eastville is at longitude $82°W$ and Westville is at longitude $88°W$, is it possible to determine how many miles apart they are located? Explain.

_____

_____

_____

5. A wall clock has a diameter of 1 foot. What is the angular size if viewed from a distance of 15 feet?

_____

_____

_____

6. A sign on an overpass that is rising says it has a grade of 35%. What is the slope of this overpass?

_____

_____

_____

Unit 10B Test 1 *(continued)*

7. What is the slope of an 8 to 15 roof?

_____

_____

_____

8. A jogger running around a park runs 3 miles east, then turns and runs 1 mile north. To return to the starting point, she then cuts diagonally back across the park. What is her total distance?

_____

_____

_____

9. Triangle ABC is similar to triangle A'B'C'. If side a = 8, side b = 12, and side a' = 5, what is the length of side b'?

_____

_____

_____

10. What is the area of a square enclosure that uses 180 meters of fencing?

_____

_____

_____

Unit 10B Test 2

Name:_____

Date:_____

1. Convert $46.24°$ into degrees, minutes, and seconds of arc.

_____

_____

_____

2. Convert $71°\,45'09''$ into decimal form.

_____

_____

_____

3. Greensville, which is directly north of Brownston, is located at latitude $33°\,N$. Brownston is located at latitude $29°\,N$. Given that the circumference of the earth is about 25,000 miles, how many miles is it between Greenville and Brownston?

_____

_____

_____

4. If you travel $3°$ of longitude west, can you determine how far you have traveled?

_____

_____

_____

5. A wall clock in the back of a classroom has a diameter of 1.5 feet. If the professor is standing 25 feet away from the clock, what is the angular size?

_____

_____

_____

6. A sign on a rising mountain road says that it has a grade of 20%. What is the slope of this road?

_____

_____

_____

Unit 10B Test 2 *(continued)*

7. What is the slope of a 9 to 12 roof?

_____

_____

_____

8. A jogger and his dog are running at a park. They run 2 miles west, then turn and run 3 miles north. To return to the starting point, they then cut diagonally back across the park. What is their total distance?

_____

_____

_____

9. Triangle ABC is similar to triangle A'B'C'. If side a = 4, side b = 9, and side a' = 3, what is the length of side b'?

_____

_____

_____

10. What is the area of a circular enclosure that uses 180 meters of fencing?

_____

_____

_____

Unit 10B Test 3

Name:_____

Date:_____

Choose the correct answer to each problem.

1. Convert $123.45°$ into degrees, minutes, and seconds of arc.

   (a) $123°0'75''$
   (b) $123°1'15''$
   (c) $123°16'2''$
   (d) $123°27'0''$

2. Convert $96°30'54''$ into decimal form.

   (a) $96.29°$
   (b) $96.515°$
   (c) $96.59°$
   (d) $97.4°$

3. If you travel from latitude $54°N$ due south to latitude $47°N$, about how many miles have you traveled? Recall: the circumference of the earth is about $25,000$ miles.

   (a) 9.9 miles
   (b) 154.7 miles
   (c) 328.9 miles
   (d) 485.8 miles

4. If you travel due east from a place with longitude $48°W$ to a place with longitude $39°W$, how many miles have you traveled?

   (a) 428.9 miles
   (c) 624.6 miles
   (b) 7.71 miles
   (d) impossible to tell

5. A wall clock has a diameter of 1 foot. What is the angular size if viewed from a distance of 27 feet?

   (a) $2.12°$
   (b) $4.2°$
   (c) $6.7°$
   (d) $9.8°$

6. If a road has a grade of 5%, what is the pitch of the road?

   (a) 1 to 5
   (b) 1 to 20
   (c) 2 to 10
   (d) 5 to 1

7. What is the slope of a roof that has a pitch of 9 to 12?

   (a) 0.25
   (b) 0.5
   (c) 0.75
   (d) 1

8. A right triangle has sides of length 5 and 12. What is the length of the hypotenuse?

   (a) 7
   (b) 10.9
   (c) 13
   (d) 17

9. Triangle ABC is similar to triangle A'B'C'. If side a = 5, side b = 8, and side a' = 2, what is the length of side b'?

   (a) 1.25
   (b) 3.2
   (c) 16
   (d) 20

10. What is the area of a square enclosure that uses 320 meters of fencing?

   (a) $1280\ m^2$
   (b) $6400\ m^2$
   (c) $9400\ m^2$
   (d) $25,600\ m^2$

Unit 10B Test 4

Name:_____

Date:_____

Choose the correct answer to each problem.

1. Convert $41.9°$ into degrees, minutes, and seconds of arc.

   (a) $41°9'0"$
   (b) $41°15'0"$
   (c) $41°54'0"$
   (d) $42°30'0"$

2. Convert $108°15'36"$ into decimal form.

   (a) $108.26°$
   (b) $108.51°$
   (c) $109.05°$
   (d) $109.45°$

3. If you travel from latitude $52°N$ due north to latitude $57°N$, about how many miles have you traveled? Recall: the circumference of the earth is about 25,000 miles.

   (a) 13.88 miles
   (b) 347 miles
   (c) 452.8 miles
   (d) 1388.9 miles

4. If you travel due east from a place with longitude $64°W$ to a place with longitude $60°W$, how many miles have you traveled?

   (a) 277.8 miles
   (c) 624.6 miles
   (b) 359.2 miles
   (d) impossible to tell

5. A wall clock has a diameter of 1 foot. What is the angular size if viewed from a distance of 36 feet?

   (a) $1.59°$
   (b) $2.5°$
   (c) $5.0°$
   (d) $3.18°$

6. If a road has a grade of 8%, what is the pitch of the road?

   (a) 1 to 8
   (b) 1 to 125
   (c) 8 to 1
   (d) 2 to 25

7. What is the slope of a roof that has a pitch of 8 to 12?

   (a) 0.25
   (b) 0.4
   (c) 0.67
   (d) 0.8

8. A right triangle has sides of length 7 and 24. What is the length of the hypotenuse?

   (a) 17
   (b) 25
   (c) 31
   (d) 41

9. Triangle ABC is similar to triangle A'B'C'. If side a = 4, side b = 15, and side a' = 3, what is the length of side b'?

   (a) 8
   (b) 12
   (c) 11.25
   (d) 14

10. What is the area of a square enclosure that uses 312 meters of fencing?

    (a) $6084\ m^2$
    (b) $9140\ m^2$
    (c) $12,168\ m^2$
    (d) $24,336\ m^2$

Unit 10C Test 1

Name:_____

Date:_____

1. Give an example of fractals found in nature.

   _____

   _____

   _____

2. Explain how a boundary between two countries can have different lengths, yet both still be valid.

   _____

   _____

   _____

3. Explain what happens to the number of area elements in a square if we reduce the length of a ruler by a factor?

   _____

   _____

4. Explain why there is an upper limit to the amount of area of an island, but there is not an upper limit to the length of coastline of an island.

   _____

   _____

5. Explain what happens to the number of elements in a line segment if we reduce the length of a ruler by a factor?

   _____

   _____

   _____

6. Explain what fractal dimension is.

   _____

   _____

   _____

Name:_____

7. Create your own snowflake curve, advancing as far as L_2.

8. Explain what makes a fractal self-similar.

_____

_____

_____

9. What does iteration mean?

_____

_____

_____

Unit 10C Test 2

Name:_____

Date:_____

1. Why are computers often necessary to create fractal images?

   _____

   _____

   _____

2. Describe what it means for an object to have a fractal dimension between 2 and 3.

   _____

   _____

   _____

3. What is a fractal object?

   _____

   _____

   _____

4. Draw your own snowflake island, proceeding as far as L_2.

5. Why is dimension important in fractals?

   _____

   _____

   _____

6. Show how to use logarithms to solve $N = R^D$ for the fractal dimension?

   _____

   _____

   _____

Unit 10C Test 2 *(continued)*

7. Explain what happens to the number of volume elements in a cube if we reduce the length of a ruler by a factor.

_____

_____

_____

8. How is it possible to have an object with a finite area, but an infinitely long boundary?

_____

_____

_____

9. Briefly describe a self-similar fractal and give an example.

_____

_____

_____

Unit 10C Test 3

Name:_____

Date:_____

Choose the correct answer to each problem.

1. What mathematical tool is helpful in finding the fractal dimension?

   (a) logarithm   (b) integration   (c) tangent

2. How long is the perimeter of a snowflake island?

   (a) $\frac{1}{2}$ base times height   (b) area ÷ 3
   (c) it is infinite

3. In fractal geometry, the shorter the ruler . . .

   (a) the shorter the perimeter.   (b) the less accurate the measurement.
   (c) the longer the perimeter.

4. Fractal geometry has applications in . . .

   (a) imitating nature.   (b) creating music.   (c) finding parallel lines.

5. For the area of a square, reducing the ruler length by a factor of 6

   (a) reduces the number of elements by a factor of 6.
   (b) increases the number of elements by a factor of 12.
   (c) increases the number of elements by a factor of 36.

6. Suppose that you are measuring an object such that when you increase the ruler length by a factor of 6, the number of elements increases by a factor of 7. What is the fractal dimension of the object?

   (a) 1.16666   (b) 0.85714   (c) 1.08603

7. To create a Sierpinski triangle, start with a solid black triangle and iterate which of the following rules?

   (a) Draw an isosceles triangle extending from each side.
   (b) Connect the midpoints of the sides and remove the resulting inner triangle.
   (c) Delete the middle third of each line segment of the triangle.

8. The fractal dimension of the Cantor set . . .

   (a) is less than 1.   (b) is between 1 and 2.   (c) is greater than 2.

9. In fractal geometry, . . .

   (a) the perimeter of a region is limited, but the area is unlimited.
   (b) the perimeter of a region is unlimited, but the area is limited.
   (c) the perimeter and the area of a region are limited.

10. A fractal object . . .

   (a) is an object with many jagged edges.   (b) is an object that can be magnified.
   (c) is an object that reveals new features at smaller scales.

Unit 10C Test 4

Name:_____

Date:_____

Choose the correct answer to each problem.

1. The fractal dimension of a snowflake curve . . .

   (a) is between 0 and 1.   (b) is between 1 and 2.   (c) is greater than 2.

2. Solving for fractal dimension, we use the rule that

   (a) $\log ab = \log a + \log b$ (b) $\log \dfrac{a}{b} = \log a - \log b$ (c) $\log a^x = x \log a$

3. To create the Snowflake curve, the first step is to . . .

   (a) divide the line segment into three equal pieces.
   (b) find the fractal dimension.
   (c) use a smaller ruler.

4. A self-similar fractal . . .

   (a) looks similar to itself when examined at different scales.
   (b) can be created by finding the fractal dimension.
   (c) has a fractal dimension between 0 and 1.

5. Spain and Portugal disagree upon the length of the border between the two countries . . .

   (a) because they are using different sized rulers.
   (b) because they aren't both using the metric system.
   (c) because their border is on a coastline.

6. Suppose that you are measuring an object such that when you decrease the ruler length by a factor of 2, the number of elements increases by a factor of 5. What is the fractal dimension of the object?

   (a) 0.69897   (b) 0.30103   (c) 2.32193

7. A random iteration . . .

   (a) is an iteration with slight variations in every iteration.
   (b) is an iteration that doesn't produce a fractal.
   (c) is an iteration that is self-similar.

8. The Sierpinski sponge has a fractal dimension . . .

   (a) between 0 and 1.   (b) between 1 and 2.   (c) between 2 and 3.

9. The process of repeating a rule over and over to generate a self-similar fractal is called . . .

   (a) repetition.   (b) iteration.   (c) fractalization.

10. Fractal geometry is not used in . . .

    (a) music.   (b) art.   (c) film.

Unit 11A Test 1

Name:_____

Date:_____

1. Explain how sound is produced.

   _____

   _____

   _____

2. Explain what the frequency of a string is.

   _____

   _____

   _____

3. Explain what consonant tones are.

   _____

   _____

   _____

4. For a 3-tone scale, find the ratio of the frequency of a note to the frequency of the preceding note.

   _____

   _____

   _____

5. If you have a tone with a frequency of 300 cps, find the frequency of the tone two octaves higher.

   _____

   _____

   _____

6. Explain what it means to store music in the analog mode.

   _____

   _____

   _____

Unit 11A Test 1 *(continued)*

Name:_____

7. List three instruments that make sounds with vibrating strings.

_____

_____

_____

8. How can digital signal processing affect the quality of sound?

_____

_____

_____

9. For a 12-tone scale, starting at a tone with a frequency of 618 cps, find the frequency of the note 8 half-steps higher.

_____

_____

_____

10. Explain the dilemma of temperament.

_____

_____

_____

Unit 11A Test 2

Name:_____

Date:_____

1. List three instruments that make sounds with vibrating reeds.

   _____

   _____

   _____

2. For a 12-tone scale, starting at the C with a frequency of 420 cps, find the frequency of the note 3 half-steps higher.

   _____

   _____

   _____

3. Explain the concept of fundamental frequency for a stringed instrument?

   _____

   _____

4. If you have a tone with a frequency of 500 cps, find the frequency of the tone 2 octaves higher.

   _____

   _____

   _____

5. If a 1-foot string has a fundamental frequency of 100 cps, how long would the string have to be to so it would have a frequency of 400 cps?

   _____

   _____

   _____

6. Explain the relationship between wavelength and frequency.

   _____

   _____

   _____

Unit 11A Test 2 *(continued)*

Name:_____

7. Explain what it means to store music in the digital mode.

_____

_____

_____

8. Name an advantage to digital technology in music.

_____

_____

_____

9. List three instruments that make sounds with vibrating columns of air.

_____

_____

_____

10. Explain what happens to the frequency when you pluck one-eighth the length of a string.

_____

_____

_____

Unit 11A Test 3

Choose the correct answer to each problem.

1. Which subject was not a part of the quadrivium - the standard curriculum in medieval universities?

   (a) geometry   **(b)** history   **(c)** music   **(d)** astronomy

2. For a 12-tone scale, starting at a tone with a frequency of 820 cps, find the frequency of the note that is 9 half-steps higher?

   (a) 1379 cps   **(b)** 7380 cps   **(c)** 42 cps

3. The frequency of middle F# is

   (a) 368 cps.   **(b)** 413 cps.   **(c)** 347 cps.

4. If you start at middle A at 440 cps and raise a by a fourth to D, what is the resulting frequency?

   (a) 554 cps   **(b)** 587 cps   **(c)** 659 cps

5. What are the most pleasing combinations of notes?

   (a) fifths   **(b)** first harmonics   **(c)** consonant tones

6. One of the most basic qualities of sound is

   (a) pitch.   **(b)** string.   **(c)** analog.

7. Which of the following frequencies can be made by the human voice?

   (a) 10 cps   **(b)** 50 cps   **(c)** 300 cps

8. Which of the following is a method for storing digital music?

   (a) sheet music   **(b)** vinyl records   **(c)** compact disk

9. The frequency of C one octave below middle C is

   (a) Twice the frequency of middle C.
   (b) One-half the frequency of middle C.
   (c) One-eighth the frequency of middle C.

10. It takes seven half-steps to raise a note by

    (a) a third   **(b)** a fifth   **(c)** a fourth

Unit 11A Test 4

Choose the correct answer to each problem.

1. How many half-steps does it take to raise a tone by a fourth?

   (a) four　　　　　　(b) five　　　　　　(c) eight

2. For a 12-tone scale, starting at a tone with frequency 315 cps, find the frequency of the note that is 7 half-steps higher.

   (a) 472 cps　　　　(b) 2205 cps　　　　(c) 24 cps

3. What types of instruments create music digitally?

   (a) pianos　　　　(b) synthesizers　　　　(c) guitars

4. In a 19-tone scale, how many tones are in one octave?

   (a) one　　　　　　(b) eight　　　　　　(c) nineteen

5. If a strings fundamental frequency is 50 cps, when you pluck only half the string the resulting frequency is

   (a) 25 cps.　　　　(b) 50 cps.　　　　(c) 100 cps.

6. Which of the following frequencies is audible by the human ear?

   (a) 10 cps　　　　(b) 10,000 cps　　　　(c) 1,000,000 cps

7. Which music principle did the Greeks discover?

   (a) The shorter the string, the lower the pitch.
   (b) The shorter the string, the higher the pitch.
   (c) The longer the string, the higher the pitch.

8. Which of these is not a type of picture of music?

   (a) analog　　　　(b) color　　　　(c) digital

9. Which of the following frequencies can be made by a piano?

   (a) 10 cps　　　　(b) 1,000 cps　　　　(c) 10,000 cps

10. The frequency of D (second) is

    (a) 292 cps.　　　　(b) 300 cps.　　　　(c) 309 cps.

Unit 11B Test 1

Name:_____

Date:_____

1. Name a development that made Renaissance artists look to math as an essential tool.

   _____

   _____

   _____

2. Why is the principal vanishing point important.

   _____

   _____

   _____

3. What three aspects of the visual arts relate directly to mathematics?

   _____

   _____

   _____

4. Draw two cubes, one with perspective and one without.

5. Give an example of symmetry in the everyday world.

   _____

   _____

   _____

6. Explain what aperiodic tiling is.

   _____

   _____

   _____

Unit 11B Test 1 *(continued)*

7. Draw an object with rotation symmetry.

8. Explain why tilings of regular polygons can only be done with triangles, squares, and hexagons.

_____

_____

_____

9. Draw an object with reflection symmetry.

10. In *projective geometry* parallel lines intersect. Explain.

_____

_____

_____

Unit 11B Test 2

Name:_____

Date:_____

1. Explain why Renaissance artists viewed mathematics as an essential tool.

   _____

   _____

   _____

2. Draw an object with translation symmetry.

3. Explain what the horizon line is.

   _____

   _____

   _____

4. What would happen if a picture had three horizon lines?

   _____

   _____

   _____

5. Explain how tilings work.

   _____

   _____

   _____

6. Which artist greatly contributed to the science of perspective?

   _____

   _____

   _____

Unit 11B Test 2 *(continued)*

7. Explain what happens to parallel lines in a picture using perspective.

_____

_____

_____

8. Explain what periodic tiling is.

_____

_____

_____

9. Explain the mathematical definition of translating.

_____

_____

_____

10. Define what symmetry is in mathematics.

_____

_____

_____

Unit 11B Test 3

Name:_____

Date:_____

Choose the correct answer to each problem.

1. The first principle of perspective is

   (a) All lines that are parallel in the real scene and perpendicular to the canvas must intersect at the principal vanishing point of the painting.
   (b) All shapes and sizes must remain equal, regardless of their distance from the viewer.
   (c) All parallel lines never intersect, they remain the same distance apart.

2. Which letter is not an example of reflective symmetry?

   (a) I   (b) O   (c) G

3. Which of these arts does not use perspective?

   (a) music   (b) sculpture   (c) architecture

4. Which of the following is a reason why Renaissance artists used mathematics?

   (a) The introduction of color in paintings.
   (b) Cameras were helpful to take realistic pictures.
   (c) There was a renewed interest in natural scenes.

5. When an object can be shifted, say to the left or right, and still remains the same, this is an example of

   (a) reflection symmetry.   (b) rotation symmetry.   (c) translation symmetry.

6. Which regular polygon cannot be used to make a tiling?

   (a) hexagon   (b) octagon   (c) triangle

7. The number of different tilings with irregular polygons is

   (a) Unlimited; you can make many different tilings using irregular polygons.
   (b) Limited; you can only make 3 different tilings using irregular polygons.
   (c) Zero; you cannot make a tiling using irregular polygons.

8. On a painting using perspective there is a row of 6-story buildings extending from the foreground, all the way to the vanishing point. The buildings in the background

   (a) Appear smaller than the ones in the foreground.
   (b) Appear larger than the ones in the foreground.
   (c) Appear to be the same size as the ones in the foreground.

9. A mathematician not known for his work on tilings is

   (a) Pythagoras.   (b) Penrose.   (c) Escher.

10. An aspect of the visual arts that does not relate directly to mathematics is

    (a) symmetry.   (b) pitch.   (c) perspective.

Unit 11B Test 4

Name:_____

Date:_____

Choose the correct answer to each problem.

1. An artist credited with developing a system of perspective that involves geometric thinking in 1430 is

   (a) Escher.   (b) DaVinci.   (c) Alberti.

2. Which letter is not an example of rotation symmetry?

   (a) Q   (b) I   (c) S

3. Which regular polygon can be used to make a tiling with a single polygon?

   (a) hexagon   (b) dodecahedron   (c) pentagon

4. Which of the following is a type of symmetry?

   (a) repetition   (b) rotation   (c) transmittance

5. Which of the following is a reason why Renaissance artists used mathematics?

   (a) Many artists were also engineers and architects.
   (b) Mathematics was considered taboo and mysterious at the time.
   (c) Most of their pictures included regular polygons.

6. In mathematics and physics, translating an object means

   (a) Rewriting it as a mathematical expression.   (b) Finding the vanishing point for the object.
   (c) Moving it in a straight line, without rotating it.

7. The vanishing point of a picture with perspective is

   (a) The point where you cannot see anything on the picture.
   (b) The point where parallel lines meet.
   (c) The point where two perpendicular lines intersect.

8. The word symmetry is not defined as

   (a) a way to solve an equation
   (b) a kind of balance
   (c) a repetition of patterns

9. When making a tiling using only regular hexagons

   (a) The tiles do not fill all of the space, there are gaps between the hexagons.
   (b) The tiles fill all of the space, but there is some overlap of the tiles.
   (c) The tiles fill all of the space, with no overlaps and no gaps.

10. Which of the following is an example of how projective geometry differs from Euclidean geometry?

   (a) Triangles have more than 4 sides.   (b) Perpendicular lines never intersect.
   (c) Parallel lines intersect.

Unit 11C Test 1

1. What is another name for the golden ratio.

   _____

   _____

   _____

2. If you knew the length of the short side of a golden rectangle, how would you find the length of the other side?

   _____

   _____

   _____

3. How could you check to see if a rectangle was a golden rectangle?

   _____

   _____

   _____

4. If the ratios of the larger to smaller sides of two rectangles are different, then is it possible that each rectangle is a golden rectangle? Explain.

   _____

   _____

   _____

5. Suppose a line segment is divided according to the golden ratio. If the length of the longer piece is 7 in, how long is the entire line segment?.

   _____

   _____

   _____

6. Name an everyday object that satisfies the golden ratio.

   _____

   _____

   _____

7. Describe how you would construct a logarithmic spiral.

_____

_____

_____

8. Create your own version of a Fibonnaci sequence, starting with a number other than 1. Does it appear to satisfy the golden ratio? Explain.

_____

_____

_____

9. Name an everyday object that displays the Fibonacci sequence.

_____

_____

_____

10. Use a ruler to find the ratio of the height and width of this page. Is it a golden ratio?

_____

_____

_____

Unit 11C Test 2

1. What question does the golden ratio claim to solve?

   _____

   _____

   _____

2. What is a solution to $x^2 - 6x - 8 = 0$?

   _____

   _____

   _____

3. Generate the first seven numbers of the Fibonacci Sequence.

   _____

   _____

   _____

4. Is it possible to have two different size rectangles, and yet each one is a golden rectangle? Explain

   _____

   _____

   _____

5. Is the rectangle below a golden rectangle? Why?

   _____

   _____

   _____

6. Mark a spot on the line below that separates the line into the golden ratio.

_____

7. How many different ways does the golden ratio occur in the pentagram?

_____

_____

_____

8. What aspect of the golden ratio was troubling to the Greeks?

_____

_____

_____

9. Give an example of an object that uses the golden rectangle.

_____

_____

_____

10. Name a branch of science where Fibonacci numbers are encountered. Explain.

_____

_____

_____

Unit 11C Test 3

Name:_____

Date:_____

Choose the correct answer to each problem.

1. Which of the following is not a major mathematical idea involved with art?

    (a) proportion
    (b) velocity
    (c) symmetry

2. The golden ratio is a(n)

    (a) irrational number.
    (b) whole number.
    (c) rational number.

3. In how many ways does the golden ratio occur in a pentagram?

    (a) five
    (b) at least ten
    (c) none

4. The golden ratio appears in

    (a) posters.
    (b) photographs.
    (c) both (a) and (b).

5. What is the eleventh number in the Fibonacci Sequence?

    (a) 55
    (b) 89
    (c) 144

6. What fraction is approximately equal to the golden ratio?

    (a) 1/5
    (b) 8/5
    (c) 3/5

7. The golden ratio is an example of the use of

    (a) proportion.
    (b) perspective.
    (c) symmetry.

8. What is one way to decide if two numbers follow a Fibonacci sequence?

    (a) If their ratio is approximately the same as the golden ratio.
    (b) If their sum is the same as their difference.
    (c) If each number is prime.

9. What is a golden spiral?

    (a) A circle with radius 5
    (b) A circle drawn inside a golden rectangle
    (c) A curve connecting corners of divided golden rectangles

10. One side of a golden rectangle is approximately 3 cm. Which of the following is not a possible length for the adjacent side?

    (a) 1.618 cm
    (b) 1.854 cm
    (c) 4.854 cm

Unit 11C Test 4

Choose the correct answer to each problem.

1. Which item is claimed to be an application of the golden rectangle?

   (a) The Eiffel Tower   **(b)** The Parthenon   **(c)** The White House

2. In the Fibonacci sequence, what number follows 89?

   (a) 233   **(b)** 56   **(c)** 144

3. Which animal can be referred to when talking about the Fibonacci sequence?

   (a) squirrels   **(b)** Donkeys   **(c)** rabbits

4. In which of the following items does the Golden Ratio not appear?

   (a) cereal boxes.
   (b) basketball.
   (c) windows.

5. Which of the following is a mathematical idea involved with visual arts?

   (a) symmetry   **(b)** pitch   **(c)** harmonics

6. The golden ratio divides a line into how many pieces?

   (a) one   **(b)** two   **(c)** three

7. What question led Greek scholars to formulating the golden ratio?

   (a) What is the square root of 2?
   (b) How are pitch and vibration related?
   (c) What is the best way to divide a line?

8. Which symbol do we use to denote the golden ratio?

   (a) π **(b)** ϕ **(c)** τ

9. What is the Greek philosophy of aesthetics?

   (a) The study of music.
   (b) The study of art and mathematics.
   (c) The study of beauty.

10. How did Fechner determine that the golden rectangle is more pleasing?

    (a) He took a survey.
    (b) He proved it mathematically.
    (c) He found an example of it in nature.

Unit 12A Test 1

1. Suppose there are two candidates in a hypothetical U.S. Presidential election. Smith wins 53,847,684 popular votes and 283 electoral votes, while Furuya wins 52,684,510 popular votes and 252 electoral votes. Contrast the outcomes of the popular and electoral votes in terms of percentages for this election. Who becomes President? (Assume that all votes were cast for either Smith or Furuya.)

_____

_____

_____

2. Of the 100 senators in the U.S. Senate, all but 43 support a new bill on environmental protection. The opposing senators start a filibuster. Is the bill likely to pass?

_____

_____

_____

3. A criminal conviction in a particular state requires a vote by 2/3 of the jury members. On a 17-member jury, 12 jurors vote to convict. Will the defendant be convicted?

_____

_____

_____

4. Consider an election in which the votes were cast as follows.

Candidate	Number of Votes
Abbott	319
Burnaby	126
Costello	194

a. Who wins a plurality? Does any candidate have a majority?
b. How many of Burnaby's votes would Costello need to win the runoff election?

_____

_____

_____

Unit 12A Test 1 *(continued)*

Name:_____

For questions 5–10, refer to the following preference schedule.

First	B	C	A	D	D
Second	A	A	C	A	C
Third	D	B	D	B	A
Fourth	C	D	B	C	B
	16	12	10	9	8

5. How many voters participated in the survey?

_____

_____

_____

6. Find the plurality winner. Did the plurality winner also receive a majority? Explain.

_____

_____

_____

7. Find the winner by a runoff of the top two candidates.

_____

_____

_____

8. Find the winner of a sequential runoff.

_____

_____

_____

9. Find the winner by a Borda count.

_____

_____

_____

Unit 12A Test 1 *(continued)*

Name:_____

10. Find the winner, if any, by the method of pairwise comparisons.

_____

_____

_____

Unit 12A Test 2

1. Suppose there are two candidates in a hypothetical U.S. Presidential election. Jones wins 45,256,981 popular votes and 240 electoral votes, while Smith wins 44,998,273 popular votes and 298 electoral votes. Contrast the outcomes of the popular and electoral votes in terms of percentages for this election. Who becomes President? (Assume that all votes were cast for either Jones or Smith.)

_____

_____

_____

2. A proposed amendment to the U.S. Constitution has passed both the House and the Senate with the required 2/3 super majority. Each state holds a vote on the amendment and it receives a majority vote in 38 of the 50 states. Is the Constitution amended?

_____

_____

_____

3. A criminal conviction in a particular state requires a vote by 3/4 of the jury members. On an 11-member jury, 8 jurors vote to convict. Will the defendant be convicted?

_____

_____

_____

4. Consider an election in which the votes were cast as follows.

Candidate	Number of Votes
Stewart	237
Tilley	403
Umprey	181

a. Who wins a plurality? Does any candidate have a majority?
b. How many of Umprey's votes would Stewart need to win the runoff election?

_____

_____

_____

Unit 12A Test 2 *(continued)*

Name:_____

For questions 5–10, refer to the following preference schedule.

First	D	B	C	A	A
Second	A	C	D	C	C
Third	C	D	A	B	D
Fourth	B	A	B	D	B
	12	9	8	7	6

5. How many voters participated in the survey?

_____

_____

_____

6. Find the plurality winner. Did the plurality winner also receive a majority? Explain.

_____

_____

_____

7. Find the winner by a runoff of the top two candidates.

_____

_____

_____

8. Find the winner of a sequential runoff.

_____

_____

_____

9. Find the winner by a Borda count.

_____

_____

_____

10. Find the winner, if any, by the method of pairwise comparisons.

_____

_____

_____

Unit 12A Test 3

Name:_____

Date:_____

Choose the correct answer to each problem.

1. Suppose there are two candidates in a hypothetical U.S. Presidential election. Atwood wins 53,720,827 popular votes and 262 electoral votes, while Jones wins 53,926,903 popular votes and 276 electoral votes. State who wins the popular vote and who becomes President. (Assume that all votes were cast for either Atwood or Jones.)

   (a) Atwood wins the popular vote and becomes President.
   (b) Jones wins the popular vote and becomes President.
   (c) Jones wins the popular vote, but Atwood becomes President.
   (d) Atwood wins the popular vote, but Jones becomes President.

2. Of the 100 senators in the U.S. Senate, 54 support a new bill on environmental protection. The opposing senators start a filibuster. Is the bill likely to pass?

   (a) Yes   (b) No

3. A criminal conviction in a particular state requires a vote by 5/6 of the jury members. On a 27-member jury, 23 jurors vote to convict. Will the defendant be convicted?

   (a) Yes   (b) No

4. Consider an election in which the votes were cast as follows. How many of Plaxton's votes would Quincy need to win the runoff election?

Candidate	Number of Votes
Plaxton	243
Quincy	389
Rasputin	487

   (a) 99   (b) 170   (c) 171
   (d) Quincy cannot win the runoff election.

For questions 5–10, refer to the following preference schedule.

First	A	B	D	C	C
Second	C	C	C	B	B
Third	B	D	A	A	D
Fourth	D	A	B	D	A
	14	12	10	7	6

5. How many voters participated in the survey?

   (a) 5   (b) 46   (c) 49   (d) 52

6. Find the plurality winner.

   (a) A   (b) B   (c) C   (d) D

355

Name:_____

7. Find the winner by a runoff of the top two candidates.

   (a) A   **(b)** B   **(c)** C   **(d)** D

8. Find the winner of a sequential runoff.

   (a) A   **(b)** B   **(c)** C   **(d)** D

9. Find the winner by a Borda count.

   (a) A   **(b)** B   **(c)** C   **(d)** D

10. Find the winner by the method of pairwise comparisons.

   (a) A   **(b)** B   **(c)** C   **(d)** D

Unit 12A Test 4

Name:_____

Date:_____

Choose the correct answer to each problem.

1. Suppose there are two candidates in a hypothetical U.S. Presidential election. Gonzales wins 47,825,238 popular votes and 230 electoral votes, while Kemper wins 47,721,962 popular votes and 308 electoral votes. State who wins the popular vote and who becomes President. (Assume that all votes were cast for either Gonzales or Kemper.)

    (a) Gonzales wins the popular vote and becomes President.
    (b) Kemper wins the popular vote and becomes President.
    (c) Kemper wins the popular vote, but Gonzales becomes President.
    (d) Gonzales wins the popular vote, but Kemper becomes President.

2. A proposed amendment to the U.S. Constitution has passed both the House and the Senate with the required 2/3 super majority. Each state holds a vote on the amendment and it receives a majority vote in all but 17 of the 50 states. Is the Constitution amended?

    (a) Yes   (b) No

3. A criminal conviction in a particular state requires a vote by 5/7 of the jury members. On a 19-member jury, 14 jurors vote to convict. Will the defendant be convicted?

    (a) Yes   (b) No

4. Consider an election in which the votes were cast as follows. How many of Grafton's votes would Howard need to win the runoff election?

Candidate	Number of Votes
Fuston	374
Grafton	118
Howard	245

    (a) 104   (b) 124   (c) 129
    (d) Howard cannot win the runoff election.

For questions 5–10, refer to the following preference schedule.

First	C	A	B	B	D
Second	D	B	D	C	A
Third	B	C	A	D	B
Fourth	A	D	C	A	C
	18	12	9	5	3

5. How many voters participated in the survey?

    (a) 5   (b) 43   (c) 45   (d) 47

6. Find the plurality winner.

   (a) A   (b) B   (c) C   (d) D

7. Find the winner by a runoff of the top two candidates.

   (a) A   (b) B   (c) C   (d) D

8. Find the winner of a sequential runoff.

   (a) A   (b) B   (c) C   (d) D

9. Find the winner by a Borda count.

   (a) A   (b) B   (c) C   (d) D

10. Find the winner by the method of pairwise comparisons.

    (a) A   (b) B   (c) C   (d) D

Unit 12B Test 1

Name:_____

Date:_____

1. Explain briefly what the majority criterion (fairness criterion 1) means and give a voting method that may violate this criterion.

   _____

   _____

   _____

2. What two groups came up with the four basic fairness criteria that must be met for a fair voting system?.

   _____

   _____

   _____

3. Briefly summarize Arrow's Impossibility Theorem.

   _____

   _____

   _____

4. In a 50-member parliament, a minority party has only two members. The remaining members of the parliament are divided evenly among three parties. Assume that no one ever misses a vote and that the members of any one party always vote the same way. Explain why the votes of the minority party *cannot* control the outcome of a vote.

   _____

   _____

   _____

5. Devise a preference schedule with three candidates in which the top-two runoff system violates the monotonicity criterion (fairness criterion 3). Explain.

   _____

   _____

   _____

6. Describe approval voting.

   _____

   _____

7. Suppose that candidates A and C have moderate political positions, while candidate B is quite liberal. Voter opinions about the candidates are as follows:
   28% want A as their first choice, but would also approve of C.
   40% want B as their first choice, and approve of neither A nor C.
   27% want C as their first choice, but would also approve of A.
   5% want C as their first choice, and approve of neither A nor B.
   a.   If all voters could vote only for their first choice, which candidate would win by plurality?
   b.   Which candidate wins by an approval vote?

_____

_____

_____

For questions 8–10, consider the following preference schedule.

First	B	A	C	D
Second	D	B	A	C
Third	A	D	B	B
Fourth	C	C	D	A
	16	10	7	5

8. Suppose the winner is decided by plurality. Analyze whether this choice satisfies the four fairness criteria.

_____

_____

_____

9. Suppose the winner is decided by pairwise comparisons. Analyze whether this choice satisfies the four fairness criteria.

_____

_____

_____

10. Suppose the winner is decided by the point system (Borda count). Analyze whether this choice satisfies the four fairness criteria.

_____

_____

_____

Unit 12B Test 2

Name:_____

Date:_____

1. Mathematicians and political scientists have decided that for a fair voting system, what has to be met?

_____

_____

_____

2. Explain what Arrow's Impossibility Theorem states.

_____

_____

3. Who wins an approval voting system.

_____

_____

4. In a 91-member parliament, a minority party has only three members. The remaining members of the parliament are divided between two major parties. Assume that no one ever misses a vote and that the members of any one party always vote the same way. Explain how the minority party could control the outcome of a vote.

_____

_____

5. Devise a preference schedule with three candidates in which the point system (Borda count) violates the majority criterion (fairness criterion 1). Explain.

_____

_____

6. Devise a preference schedule with three candidates in which candidate A has a plurality of the votes, but loses according to the sequential runoff method.

_____

_____

Unit 12B Test 2 *(continued)*

Name:_____

7. Suppose that candidates A and B have moderate political positions, while candidate C is quite conservative. Voter opinions about the candidates are as follows:

   27% want A as their first choice, but would also approve of B.

   28% want B as their first choice, but would also approve of A.

   2% want B as their first choice, and approve of neither A nor C.

   43% want C as their first choice, and approve of neither A nor B.

   a.   If all voters could vote only for their first choice, which candidate would win by plurality?

   b.   Which candidate wins by an approval vote?

   _____

   _____

   _____

For questions 8–10, consider the following preference schedule.

First	A	B	C	D
Second	D	D	B	B
Third	B	A	D	C
Fourth	C	C	A	A
	15	10	7	6

8. Suppose the winner is decided by plurality. Analyze whether this choice satisfies the four fairness criteria.

   _____

   _____

   _____

9. Suppose the winner is decided by pairwise comparisons. Analyze whether this choice satisfies the four fairness criteria.

   _____

   _____

   _____

10. Suppose the winner is decided by the point system (Borda count). Analyze whether this choice satisfies the four fairness criteria.

   _____

   _____

   _____

Unit 12B Test 3

Choose the correct answer to each problem.

1. How many criterion must be met in order to have a fair voting system?

   (a) 5   (b) 3   (c) 6   (d) 4

2. Which of the following voting methods does *not* always satisfy the majority criterion (fairness criterion 1)?

   (a) Plurality   (b) Sequential runoff

   (c) Borda count   (d) Pairwise comparison

3. Which of the following statements best summarizes Arrow's Impossibility Theorem?

   (a) It is impossible for one voting system to be better than another.
   (b) No voting system satisfies all four fairness criteria in all cases.
   (c) It is impossible for a voting system to satisfy the independence of irrelevant alternatives criterion (fairness criterion 4).
   (d) The best voting system is approval voting.

4. In a 100-member parliament, suppose that there are 49 members of the White party and 49 members of the Green party, and the rest of the parliament consists of Blue party members. Assume that no one ever misses a vote and that the members of any one party always vote the same way. Are the members of the Blue party able to control the outcome of a vote?

   (a) Yes   (b) No

5. Suppose that candidates A and B have moderate political positions, while candidate C is quite liberal. Voter opinions about the candidates are as follows:
   27% want A as their first choice, but would also approve of B.
   3% want A as their first choice, and approve of neither B nor C.
   25% want B as their first choice, but would also approve of A.
   45% want C as their first choice, and approve of neither A nor B.
   If an election is held using the approval voting method, which candidate wins?

   (a) A   (b) B   (c) C   (d) There is a tie.

For questions 6–7, consider the following preference schedule.

First	C	B	B	A
Second	A	C	A	C
Third	B	A	C	B
	11	**9**	**7**	**6**

6. If the winner is selected by a Borda count, which of the following fairness criteria is violated?

   (a) Condorcet criterion (fairness criterion 2)
   (b) Monotonicity criterion (fairness criterion 3)
   (c) Independence of irrelevant alternatives criterion (fairness criterion 4)
   (d) None of these

7. If the winner is selected by sequential runoffs, which of the fairness criteria is violated?

    (a) Condorcet criterion (fairness criterion 2)
    (b) Monotonicity criterion (fairness criterion 3)
    (c) Independence of irrelevant alternatives criterion (fairness criterion 4)
    (d) None of these

For questions 8–10, consider the following preference schedule.

First	C	B	A	D
Second	A	A	B	B
Third	B	C	D	A
Fourth	D	D	C	C
	11	10	8	5

8. For which of the following voting methods is the Condorcet criterion (fairness criterion 2) satisfied?

    (a) Plurality   (b) Borda count   (c) Sequential runoff   (d) All of these

9. For which of the following voting methods is the monotonicity criterion (fairness criterion 3) satisfied?

    (a) Plurality   (b) Borda count   (c) Top-two runoff   (d) All of these

10. For which of the following voting methods is the independence of irrelevant alternatives criterion (fairness criterion 4) satisfied?

    (a) Plurality   (b) Top-two runoff   (c) Sequential runoff   (d) None of these

Unit 12B Test 4

Name:_____

Date:_____

Choose the correct answer to each problem.

1. In 1952, Kenneth Arrow proved that it is impossible to find a voting system that satisfies all four fairness criteria. His theorem was called

   (a) Kennth's Voting System Proof
   (c) Kenneth's Impossibility Theorem

   (b) Arrow's Impossibility Theorem
   (d) Arrow's Voting System Proof

2. Which of the following voting methods always satisfies the Condorcet criterion (fairness criterion 2)?

   (a) Plurality
   (c) Borda count

   (b) Sequential runoff
   (d) Pairwise comparison

3. In order to have a fair voting system, how many criterion must be met?

   (a) 3   (b) 5   (c) 4   (d) 6

4. In a 33-member parliament, suppose that the Purple party, Burgendy party, and Orange party all have the same number of members, and the rest of the parliament consists of Blue party members. Assume that no one ever misses a vote and that the members of any one party always vote the same way. If the votes of the Blue party can sometimes control the outcome of a vote, what is the smallest possible number of Blue party members?

   (a) 1   (b) 6   (c) 9   (d) 12

5. Suppose that candidate A is quite conservative, while candidates B and C have moderate political positions. Voter opinions about the candidates are as follows:
   35% want A as their first choice, and approve of neither B nor C.
   29% want B as their first choice, but would also approve of C.
   25% want C as their first choice, but would also approve of B.
   11% want C as their first choice, and approve of neither A nor B.
   Which candidate wins by an approval vote?

   (a) A   (b) B   (c) C   (d) There is a tie.

For questions 6–7, consider the following preference schedule.

First	B	C	A	A
Second	A	B	C	B
Third	C	A	B	C
	9	8	7	4

6. If the winner is selected by a Borda count, which of the following fairness criteria is violated?

   (a) Condorcet criterion (fairness criterion 2)
   (b) Monotonicity criterion (fairness criterion 3)
   (c) Independence of irrelevant alternatives criterion (fairness criterion 4)
   (d) None of these

7. If the winner is selected by sequential runoffs, which of the fairness criteria is violated?

   (a) Majority criterion (fairness criterion 1)
   (b) Condorcet criterion (fairness criterion 2)
   (c) Monotonicity criterion (fairness criterion 3)
   (d) Both choices (a) and (c)

For questions 8–10, consider the following preference schedule.

First	B	C	A	D
Second	D	A	B	A
Third	C	B	C	B
Fourth	A	D	D	C
	11	8	7	5

8. For which of the following voting methods is the Condorcet criterion (fairness criterion 2) violated?

   (a) Plurality   (b) Borda count   (c) Top-two runoff   (d) None of these

9. For which of the following voting methods is the monotonicity criterion (fairness criterion 3) satisfied?

   (a) Plurality   (b) Borda count   (c) Top-two runoff   (d) All of these

10. For which of the following voting methods is the independence of irrelevant alternatives criterion (fairness criterion 4) satisfied?

    (a) Plurality   (b) Top-two runoff   (c) Sequential runoff   (d) None of these

Unit 12C Test 1

Name:_____

Date:_____

1. According to the Constitution, the legislative branch of the government consists of two bodies. Name the two bodies.

   _____

   _____

   _____

2. Briefly define apportionment.

   _____

   _____

   _____

3. Explain what is meant by the fractional remainder.

   _____

   _____

   _____

4. What has happened if the population paradox has occurred?

   _____

   _____

   _____

5. State the Quota Criterion.

   _____

   _____

   _____

6. What does the Balinsky and Young theorem tell us?

   _____

   _____

   _____

Unit 12C Test 1 *(continued)*

Name:_____

7. The table below gives the population of four states A, B, C, and D, among which a total of 80 seats are to be apportioned. Find the standard divisor and complete the table using Hamilton's method (Round the standard quotas to two places after the decimal.) How many seats does each state receive?

State	A	B	C	D	Total
Population	8403	13,777	14,579	25,241	62,000
Standard quota					
Minimum quota					
Fractional remainder					
Final apportionment					

8. The table below gives the population of four states A, B, C, and D, among which a total of 80 seats are to be apportioned. Complete the table using Jefferson's method. (Round the standard and modified quotas to two places after the decimal.) How many seats does each state receive?

State	A	B	C	D	Total
Population	8403	13,777	14,579	25,241	62,000
Standard quota					
Minimum quota					
Modified quota (with divisor 764.5)					
Minimum quota (with divisor 764.5)					

9. The table below gives the population of four states A, B, C, and D, among which a total of 80 seats are to be apportioned. Complete the table using Webster's method. (Round the standard and modified quotas to two places after the decimal.) How many seats does each state receive?

State	A	B	C	D	Total
Population	8403	13,777	14,579	25,241	62,000
Standard quota					
Minimum quota					
Modified quota (with divisor 777)					
Rounded quota					

Name:_____

10. The table below gives the population of four states A, B, C, and D, among which a total of 80 seats are to be apportioned. Complete the table using the Hill-Huntington method. (Round the standard and modified quotas to two places after the decimal. Round the geometric means to three places after the decimal.) How many seats does each state receive?

State	A	B	C	D	Total
Population	8403	13,777	14,579	25,241	62,000
Standard quota	10.84	17.78	18.81	32.57	80.00
Minimum quota	10	17	18	32	77
Modified quota (with divisor 780)	10.77	17.66	18.69	32.36	
Geometric mean	10.488	17.493	18.493	32.496	
Rounded quota	11	18	19	32	80

Unit 12C Test 2

1. Explain what apportionment has to do with the U.S. House of Representatives.

_____

_____

_____

2. Explain what the standard divisor is.

_____

_____

_____

3. Explain the Alabama paradox.

_____

_____

_____

4. What has happened if the new states paradox has occurred?

_____

_____

_____

5. Explain why the Hill-Huntington method was adopted by Congress in 1941.

_____

_____

_____

Unit 12C Test 2 *(continued)*

6. A school district has four elementary schools and 15 kindergarten teachers. The following table contains the kindergarten enrollment at each school for the next school year. Complete the following table using Hamilton's method.

School	Greenbreier	Wilcox	Glen Cove	Timor	Total
Kindergarten enrollment	204	143	82	51	480
Standard quota					
Minimum quota					
Fractional remainder					
Final apportionment					

Funding may be available to hire one more kindergarten teacher. Now complete the table using Hamilton's method, assuming there will be 16 kindergarten teachers.

School	Greenbreier	Wilcox	Glen Cove	Timor	Total
Kindergarten enrollment	204	143	82	51	480
Standard quota					
Minimum quota					
Fractional remainder					
Final apportionment					

If you were the administrator of Timor Elementary, would you want the 16th teacher to be hired? Explain.

7. The table below gives the population of four states A, B, C, and D, among which a total of 50 seats are to be apportioned. Find the standard divisor and complete the table using Hamilton's method. (Round the standard quotas to two places after the decimal.) How many seats does each state receive?

State	A	B	C	D	Total
Population	8399	12,537	15,819	25,245	62,000
Standard quota					
Minimum quota					
Fractional remainder					
Final apportionment					

8. The table below gives the population of four states A, B, C, and D, among which a total of 50 seats are to be apportioned. Complete the table using Jefferson's method. (Round the standard and modified quotas to two places after the decimal.) How many seats does each state receive?

State	A	B	C	D	Total
Population	8399	12,537	15,819	25,245	62,000
Standard quota					
Minimum quota					
Modified quota (with divisor 1202)					
Minimum quota (with divisor 1202)					

Name:_____

9. The table below gives the population of four states A, B, C, and D, among which a total of 50 seats are to be apportioned. Complete the table using Webster's method. (Round the standard and modified quotas to two places after the decimal.) How many seats does each state receive?

State	A	B	C	D	Total
Population	8399	12,537	15,819	25,245	62,000
Standard quota					
Minimum quota					
Modified quota (with divisor 1242)					
Rounded quota					

10. The table below gives the population of four states A, B, C, and D, among which a total of 50 seats are to be apportioned. Complete the table using the Hill-Huntington method. (Round the standard and modified quotas to two places after the decimal. Round the geometric means to three places after the decimal.) How many seats does each state receive?

State	A	B	C	D	Total
Population	8399	12,537	15,819	25,245	62,000
Standard quota					
Minimum quota					
Modified quota (with divisor 1238)					
Geometric mean					
Rounded quota					

Unit 12C Test 3

Name:_____

Date:_____

1. Which of the following quantities varies from state to state?

   (a) Number of Senators
   (c) Standard divisor
   (b) Modified divisor
   (d) Standard quota

2. Which method of apportionment **never** leads to a violation of the Quota Criterion?

   (a) Hamilton's method   (b) Jefferson's method   (c) Webster's method
   (d) Hill-Huntington method

3. Which method of apportionment compares a modified quota to a geometric mean?

   (a) Hamilton's method   (b) Jefferson's method   (c) Webster's method
   (d) Hill-Huntington method

4. Which method of apportionment was approved by a Democratic majority in Congress and signed into law by a Democratic president because it gave the Democrats one more seat in the House at that time?

   (a) Hamilton's method   (b) Jefferson's method   (c) Webster's method
   (d) Hill-Huntington method

5. Which of the following best describes how the modified divisor is found?

   (a) Divide the state's population by the standard divisor
   (b) Divide the state's population by the standard quota
   (c) Divide the state's population by the modified quota
   (d) Trial and error

6. The table below gives the population of four states A, B, C, and D, among which a total of 70 seats are to be apportioned. Find the standard divisor for the problem.

State	A	B	C	D	Total
Population	257,500	143,000	105,000	165,240	670,740

   (a) 70   (b) 51,595   (c) 9582   (d) 335,370

7. The table below gives the population of four states A, B, C, and D, among which a total of 70 seats are to be apportioned. Find the standard quota for State A.

State	A	B	C	D	Total
Population	257,500	143,000	105,000	165,240	670,740

   (a) 4.48   (b) 26.87   (c) 3678.57   (d) 9582

Unit 12C Test 3 (continued)

8. The table below gives the population of four states A, B, C, and D, among which a total of 60 seats are to be apportioned. Complete the table using Hamilton's method. (Round the standard quotas to two places after the decimal.) How many seats does State A receive using Hamilton's method?

State	A	B	C	D	Total
Population	256,500	143,000	89,000	51,500	540,000
Standard quota					
Minimum quota					
Fractional remainder					
Final apportionment					

(a) 26   **(b)** 27   **(c)** 28   **(d)** 29

9. The table below gives the population of four states A, B, C, and D, among which a total of 60 seats are to be apportioned. Complete the table using Jefferson's method. (Round the standard and modified quotas to two places after the decimal.) How many seats does State A receive using Jefferson's method?

State	A	B	C	D	Total
Population	256,500	143,000	89,000	51,500	540,000
Standard quota					
Minimum quota					
Modified quota (with divisor 8800)					
Minimum quota (with divisor 8800)					

(a) 26   **(b)** 27   **(c)** 28   **(d)** 29

10. The table below gives the population of four states A, B, C, and D, among which a total of 60 seats are to be apportioned. Complete the table using Webster's method. (Round the standard and modified quotas to two places after the decimal.) How many seats does State D receive using Webster's method?

State	A	B	C	D	Total
Population	256,500	143,000	89,000	51,500	540,000
Standard quota					
Minimum quota					
Modified quota (with divisor 9100)					
Rounded quota					

(a) 5   **(b)** 6   **(c)** 10   **(d)** 28

Unit 12C Test 4

Name:_____

Date:_____

1. Which of the following quantities does **not** vary from state to state?

   (a) Number of Representatives   (b) Minimum quota
   (c) Standard divisor   (d) Standard quota

2. Which of the following varies from state to state?

   (a) The number of representatives.   (b) The number of congressmen.
   (c) The number of senators.   (d) Both choices (a) and (b)

3. What is the name of the process used to divide the number of seats in the House of Representatives among states?

   (a) Apportionment   (b) Jefferson's method   (c) Webster's method
   (d) Hill-Huntington method

4. Which method of apportionment is used today?

   (a) Hamilton's method   (b) Jefferson's method   (c) Webster's method
   (d) Hill-Huntington method

5. Which method of apportionment did George Washington veto?

   (a) Hamilton's method   (b) Jefferson's method   (c) Webster's method
   (d) Hill-Huntington method

6. Which of the following best describes how the modified quota is found?

   (a) Divide the state's population by the standard quota
   (b) Divide the state's population by the standard divisor
   (c) Divide the state's population by the modified divisor
   (d) Trial and error

7. Which of the following is the algebraic mean of x and y?

   (a) $\sqrt{xy}$ (b) $\sqrt{x^2 + y^2}$ (c) $\dfrac{x+y}{2}$ (d) $\dfrac{xy}{2}$

8. The table below gives the population of four states A, B, C, and D, among which a total of 20 seats are to be apportioned. Complete the table using Hamilton's method. (Round the standard quotas to two places after the decimal.) How many seats does State A receive using Hamilton's method?

State	A	B	C	D	Total
Population	544,000	183,000	229,000	98,000	1,054,000
Standard quota					
Minimum quota					
Fractional remainder					
Final apportionment					

   (a) 9   (b) 10   (c) 11   (d) 12

Unit 12C Test 4 *(continued)*

Name:_____

9. The table below gives the population of four states A, B, C, and D, among which a total of 20 seats are to be apportioned. Complete the table using Jefferson's method. (Round the standard and modified quotas to two places after the decimal. How many seats does State A receive using Jefferson's method?

State	A	B	C	D	Total
Population	544,000	183,000	229,000	98,000	1,054,000
Standard quota					
Minimum quota					
Modified quota (with divisor 49,000)					
Minimum quota (with divisor 49,000)					

(a) 9   (b) 10   (c) 11   (d) 12

10. The table below gives the population of four states A, B, C, and D, among which a total of 20 seats are to be apportioned. Complete the table using Webster's method. (Round the standard and modified quotas to two places after the decimal.) How many seats does State B receive using Webster's method?

State	A	B	C	D	Total
Population	544,000	183,000	229,000	98,000	1,054,000
Standard quota					
Minimum quota					
Modified quota (with divisor 52,000)					
Rounded quota					

(a) 2   (b) 3   (c) 4   (d) 5

Unit 13A Test 1

1. Explain what is meant by a network.

   _____

   _____

   _____

2. In Euler's solution of the Königsberg bridge problem, what did each vertex represent?

   _____

   _____

   _____

3. Consider the map of streets and intersections shown. Let edges represent the streets and let vertices represent the intersections. Draw the network that results.

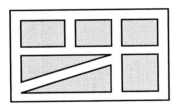

4. Consider the map below, which represents six imaginary countries. Letting vertices represent countries and edges represent the relationship "is a neighbor of," draw a network showing all connections among these countries. What is the order of the network? What is the degree of the vertex corresponding to Ono?

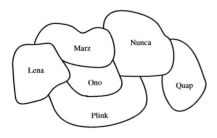

   _____

   _____

   _____

5. Sketch a network that has all three of the following properties:
The order of the network is 8.
The network is not a tree.
Each vertex in the network has odd degree.

6. Sketch a tree of order 5 in which one vertex has degree 3.

7. Sketch a complete network with 5 vertices.

8. Does the network shown have an Euler circuit? Explain.

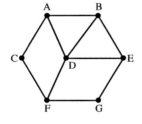

_____

_____

_____

Name:_____

9. Use Kruskal's algorithm to find the minimum cost spanning network of the network shown.

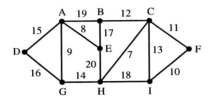

10. In the remaining weeks of the season, the six teams of a baseball league (A, B, C, D, E, and F) must play the games indicated in the following table. (An X means the two teams play, and a blank means they do not play.) Draw a network that shows the teams as vertices and the relationship "plays against" as edges. What is the order of the network you have drawn? What is the degree of each vertex of the network? Is the network complete? Explain.

	A	B	C	D	E	F
A		X		X		X
B	X		X		X	
C		X		X		X
D	X		X		X	X
E		X		X		
F	X		X	X		

_____

_____

_____

Unit 13A Test 2

1. What does it mean for a network to be complete?

    _____

    _____

    _____

2. In Euler's solution of the Königsberg bridge problem, what did each edge represent?

    _____

    _____

    _____

3. Consider the map of streets and intersections shown. Let edges represent the streets and let vertices represent the intersections. Draw the network that results.

    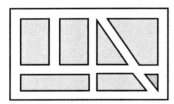

Unit 13A Test 2 *(continued)*

Name:_____

4. Consider the map below, which represents six imaginary countries. Letting vertices represent countries and edges represent the relationship "is a neighbor of," draw a network showing all connections among these countries. What is the order of the network? What is the degree of the vertex corresponding to Grish?

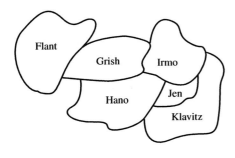

_____

_____

_____

5. Sketch a network that has all three of the following properties:
   The order of the network is 6.
   The network is not a tree.
   Each vertex in the network has odd degree.

6. Sketch a tree of order 7 in which one vertex has degree 4.

7. Sketch a complete network with 5 vertices.

Unit 13A Test 2 *(continued)*

Name:_____

8. Does the network shown have an Euler circuit? Explain.

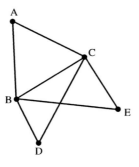

_____

_____

_____

9. Use Kruskal's algorithm to find the minimum cost spanning network of the network shown.

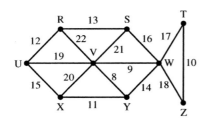

10. In the remaining weeks of the season, the six teams of a baseball league (A, B, C, D, E, and F) must play the games indicated in the following table. (An x means the two teams play, and a blank means they do not play.) Draw a network that shows the teams as vertices and the relationship "plays against" as edges. What is the order of the network you have drawn? What is the degree of each vertex of the network? Is the network complete? Explain.

	A	B	C	D	E	F
A		x	x		x	
B	x			x		x
C	x			x		x
D		x	x			
E	x					x
F		x	x		x	

_____

_____

_____

Unit 13A Test 3

Choose the correct answer to each problem.

1. Which of the following is the term for a network in which all the vertices are connected and there is no path that begins and ends at the same vertex without using any edges more than once?

   (a) Circuit   **(b)** Complete network   **(c)** Tree   **(d)** Euler circuit

2. In Euler's solution of the Königsberg bridge problem, which of the following was used to represent each bridge?

   (a) Network   **(b)** Tree   **(c)** Edge   **(d)** Vertex

3. Consider the map of streets and intersections shown. If a network's edges represent the streets and its vertices represent the intersections, what is the order of the network?

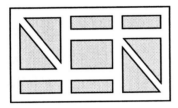

   (a) 9   **(b)** 14   **(c)** 17   **(d)** 22

4. The network below represents six imaginary countries. The vertices represent countries, and edges represent the relationship "is a neighbor of." Which of the following countries is *not* a neighbor of Rontan?

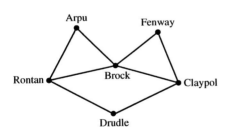

   (a) Arpu   **(b)** Brock   **(c)** Claypol   **(d)** Drudle

Unit 13A Test 3 *(continued)*

Name:_____

For Questions 5–8, refer to the networks shown below. Any network may be chosen once, more than once, or not at all.

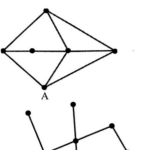

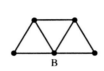

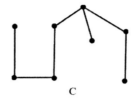

C

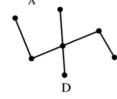

D

5. Which network is a tree?

   (a) A   **(b)** B   **(c)** C   **(d)** Both C and D

6. Which network has order 7?

   (a) A   **(b)** B   **(c)** C   **(d)** D

7. Which network has order 6?

   (a) A   **(b)** B   **(c)** C   **(d)** D

8. Which network has an Euler circuit?

   (a) A   **(b)** B   **(c)** D   **(d)** None of them

9. Use Kruskal's algorithm to find the minimum cost spanning network of the network shown. What is the cost of the minimum cost spanning network?

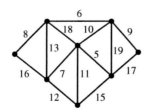

   (a) 56   **(b)** 60   **(c)** 64   **(d)** 68

10. In the remaining weeks of the season, the six teams of a baseball league (A, B, C, D, E, and F) must play the games indicated in the following table. (An X means the two teams play, and a blank means they do not play.) If a network is drawn showing the teams as vertices and the relationship "plays against" as edges, what is the degree of the vertex representing team C?

	A	B	C	D	E	F
A			X	X	X	X
B			X	X	X	
C	X	X		X		X
D	X	X	X			
E	X	X				X
F	X		X		X	

(a) 3   **(b)** 4   **(c)** 5   **(d)** 6

Unit 13A Test 4

Choose the correct answer to each problem.

1. Which of the following is the term for a network where every vertex is directly connected to every other vertex?

    (a) Complete network   **(b)** Euler circuit
    (c) Tree   **(d)** Hamiltonian circuit

2. In Euler's solution of the Königsberg bridge problem, which of the following was used to represent each island?

    (a) Network   **(b)** Tree   **(c)** Edge   **(d)** Vertex

3. Consider the map of streets and intersections shown. If a network's edges represent the streets and its vertices represent the intersections, what is the order of the network?

    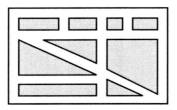

    (a) 9   **(b)** 12   **(c)** 15   **(d)** 23

4. The network below represents six imaginary countries. The vertices represent countries, and edges represent the relationship "is a neighbor of." Which of the following countries is *not* a neighbor of Krupo?

    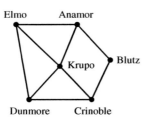

    (a) Anamor   **(b)** Blutz   **(c)** Crinoble   **(d)** Dunmore

    For Questions 5–8, refer to the networks shown below. Any network may be chosen once, more than once, or not at all.

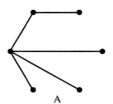

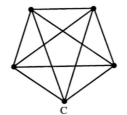
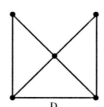

5. Which network has order 7?

    (a) A   **(b)** B   **(c)** C   **(d)** D

6. Which network is a tree?

    (a) A   **(b)** B   **(c)** C   **(d)** D

7. Which network is a complete network?

    (a) A   **(b)** B   **(c)** C   **(d)** D

8. Which network has an Euler circuit?

    (a) A   **(b)** B   **(c)** C   **(d)** D

9. Use Kruskal's algorithm to find the minimum cost spanning network of the network shown. What is the cost of the minimum cost spanning network?

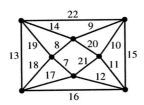

    (a) 68   **(b)** 72   **(c)** 76   **(d)** 80

10. In the remaining weeks of the season, the six teams of a baseball league (A, B, C, D, E, and F) must play the games indicated in the following table. (An X means the two teams play, and a blank means they do not play.) If a network is drawn showing the teams as vertices and the relationship "plays against" as edges, what is the degree of the vertex representing team C?

	A	B	C	D	E	F
A		X		X		X
B	X		X			X
C		X		X	X	
D	X		X		X	
E			X	X		X
F	X	X			X	

    (a) 3   **(b)** 4   **(c)** 5   **(d)** 6

Unit 13B Test 1

1. How many different Hamiltonian circuits are there in a complete network of order $n = 13$?

_____

_____

_____

2. Suppose that a computer could check Hamiltonian circuits at a rate of one per second. How long would it take to check all the circuits in a complete network of order $n = 11$? Express your answer in days.

_____

_____

_____

In Questions 3–5, consider the network shown. Follow the edges according to the arrows, and determine whether that path forms a Hamiltonian circuit. If the path does not form a Hamiltonian circuit, can you find a different path that does? If so, name or sketch such a path.

3.

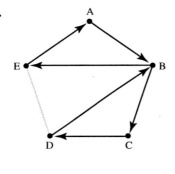

_____

_____

_____

Unit 13B Test 1 *(continued)*

4.

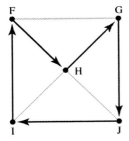

_____
_____
_____

5.

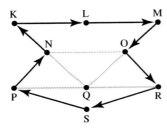

_____
_____
_____

6. Suppose you need to go from your home to the post office, the library, and your school (not necessarily in that order), and then return home. The location of each and the travel times (in minutes) between them are shown. What path should you use to minimize the total travel time?

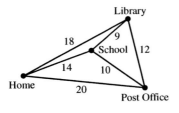

_____
_____
_____

Unit 13B Test 1 *(continued)*

7. The following table shows the distances between pairs of towns in a rural county.
   As a newspaper delivery person, you must visit each town once every Sunday. Use the nearest neighbor method to find a circuit that visits each city exactly once, starting from Durney.

	Durney	**Emago**	**Flipsy**	**Grund**	**Hallo**
Durney	—	11	21	28	20
Emago	11	—	12	18	19
Flipsy	21	12	—	22	14
Grund	28	18	22	—	35
Hallo	20	19	14	35	—

_____

_____

_____

For Questions 8–10, refer to the following figure showing the travel times (in hours) between cities that a salesperson must visit.

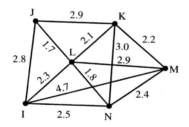

8. Apply the nearest neighbor method to find a circuit that visits each city exactly once, starting from K.

_____

_____

_____

9. Apply the nearest neighbor method to find a circuit that visits each city exactly once, starting from L.

_____

_____

_____

Unit 13B Test 1 *(continued)*

10. Apply the nearest neighbor method to find a circuit that visits each city exactly once, starting from I.

_____

_____

_____

Unit 13B Test 2

1. How many different Hamiltonian circuits are there in a complete network of order $n = 9$?

_____

_____

_____

2. Suppose that a computer could check Hamiltonian circuits at a rate of one per second. How long would it take to check all the circuits in a complete network of order $n = 14$? Express your answer in days.

_____

_____

_____

In Questions 3–5, consider the network shown. Follow the edges according to the arrows, and determine whether that path forms a Hamiltonian circuit. If the path does not form a Hamiltonian circuit, can you find a different path that does? If so, name or sketch such a path.

3.

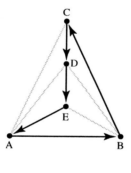

_____

_____

_____

Unit 13B Test 2 *(continued)*

4.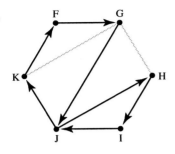

_____
_____
_____
_____

5.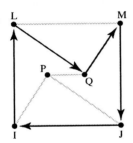

_____
_____
_____

6. Suppose you need to go from your home to the post office, the library, and your school (not necessarily in that order), and then return home. The location of each and the travel times (in minutes) between them are shown. What path should you use to minimize the total travel time?

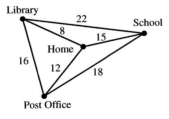

_____
_____
_____

Unit 13B Test 2 *(continued)*

Name:_____

7. The following table shows the distances between pairs of towns in a rural county.
As a newspaper delivery person, you must visit each town once every Sunday. Use the nearest neighbor method to find a circuit that visits each city exactly once, starting from Drury.

	Clinger	Drury	Elbow	Funky	Gridly
Clinger	—	21	20	29	13
Drury	21	—	12	11	15
Elbow	20	12	—	22	23
Funky	29	11	22	—	19
Gridly	13	15	23	19	—

_____

_____

_____

For Questions 8–10, refer to the following figure showing the travel times (in hours) between cities that a salesperson must visit.

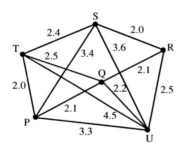

8. Apply the nearest neighbor method to find a circuit that visits each city exactly once, starting from P.

_____

_____

_____

9. Apply the nearest neighbor method to find a circuit that visits each city exactly once, starting from R.

_____

_____

_____

10. Apply the nearest neighbor method to find a circuit that visits each city exactly once, starting from T.

_____

_____

_____

Unit 13B Test 3

Choose the correct answer to each problem.

1. How many different Hamiltonian circuits are there in a complete network of order $n = 10$?

    (a) 181,440   **(b)** 3,628,800   **(c)** 1,814,400   **(d)** 368,880

2. Suppose that a computer could check Hamiltonian circuits at a rate of one per second. How long would it take to check all the circuits in a complete network of order $n = 12$?

    (a) 256 days   **(b)** 300 days   **(c)** 462 days   **(d)** 231 days

In Questions 3–5, consider the network shown. Follow the edges according to the arrows, and determine whether that path forms a Hamiltonian circuit. Also determine whether or not there is another path that forms a Hamiltonian circuit. Choose one of the following four answers.

A   The path forms a Hamiltonian circuit, and it is the only one.
B   The path forms a Hamiltonian circuit, and there is at least one other path that forms a Hamiltonian circuit.
C   The path does not form a Hamiltonian circuit, but another path does.
D   The path does not form a Hamiltonian circuit, and the network has no Hamiltonian circuits.

3.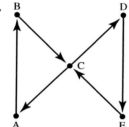

    (a) *A*   **(b)** *B*   **(c)** *C*   **(d)** *D*

4.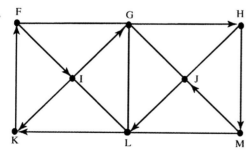

    (a) *A*   **(b)** *B*   **(c)** *C*   **(d)** *D*

Name:_____

5.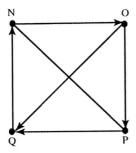

(a) *A*   (b) *B*   (c) *C*   (d) *D*

6. Suppose you need to go from your home to the grocery store, the post office, the library, and your school (not necessarily in that order), and then return home. The location of each and the travel times (in minutes) between them are shown. What path should you use to minimize the total travel time?

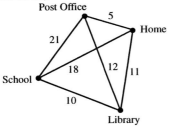

(a) Home to school to post office to library to home

(b) Home to school to library to post office to home

(c) Home to library to school to post office to home

(d) Home to library to post office to school to home

7. The following table shows the distances between pairs of towns in a rural county.
As a newspaper delivery person, you must visit each town once every Sunday. Use the nearest neighbor method to find a circuit that visits each city exactly once, starting from Quodu.

	Peterson	Quodu	Rincon	Salina	Thorton
Peterson	—	21	13	22	14
Quodu	21	—	11	8	16
Rincon	13	11	—	12	12
Salina	22	8	12	—	23
Thorton	14	16	12	23	—

(a) Quodu to Rincon to Peterson to Thorton to Salina to Quodu
(b) Quodu to Salina to Rincon to Thorton to Peterson to Quodu
(c) Quodu to Salina to Rincon to Peterson to Thorton to Quodu
(d) Quodu to Salina to Peterson to Rincon to Thorton to Quodu

Unit 13B Test 3 *(continued)*

For Questions 8–10, refer to the following figure showing the travel times (in hours) between cities that a salesperson must visit.

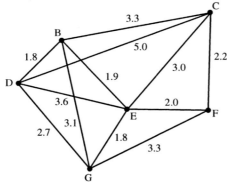

8. Apply the nearest neighbor method to find a circuit that visits each city exactly once, starting from B.

   (a) B to D to G to E to F to C to B
   (c) B to D to E to G to F to C to B

   (b) B to E to G to D to C to F to E to B
   (d) B to E to F to C to D to G to B

9. Apply the nearest neighbor method to find a circuit that visits each city exactly once, starting from C.

   (a) C to E to F to G to D to B to C
   (c) C to F to G to E to D to B to C

   (b) C to F to E to G to D to B to C
   (d) C to D to E to B to G to F to C

10. Apply the nearest neighbor method to find a circuit that visits each city exactly once, starting from F.

    (a) F to E to B to G to D to C to F
    (c) F to E to G to D to B to C to F

    (b) F to C to B to D to G to E to F
    (d) F to G to D to E to B to C to F

Unit 13B Test 4

Choose the correct answer to each problem.

1. How many different Hamiltonian circuits are there in a complete network of order $n = 7$?

   (a) 20,160   (b) 2520   (c) 5040   (d) 360

2. Suppose that a computer could check Hamiltonian circuits at a rate of one per second. How long would it take to check all the circuits in a complete network of order $n = 12$?

   (a) 36,036 days   (b) 18,018 days   (c) 504,504 days   (d) 231 days

In Questions 3–5, consider the network shown. Follow the edges according to the arrows, and determine whether that path forms a Hamiltonian circuit. Also determine whether or not there is another path that forms a Hamiltonian circuit. Choose one of the following four answers.

A   The path forms a Hamiltonian circuit, and it is the only one.
B   The path forms a Hamiltonian circuit, and there is at least one other path that forms a Hamiltonian circuit.
C   The path does not form a Hamiltonian circuit, but another path does.
D   The path does not form a Hamiltonian circuit, and the network has no Hamiltonian circuits.

3.

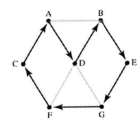

   (a) *A*   (b) *B*   (c) *C*   (d) *D*

4.

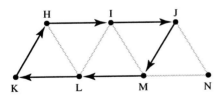

   (a) *A*   (b) *B*   (c) *C*   (d) *D*

5.

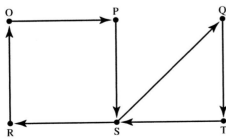

   (a) *A*   (b) *B*   (c) *C*   (d) *D*

Unit 13B Test 4 *(continued)*

6. Suppose you need to go from your home to the post office, the library, and your school (not necessarily in that order), and then return home. The location of each and the travel times (in minutes) between them are shown. What path should you use to minimize the total travel time?

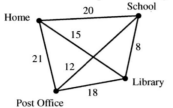

    (a) Home to school to library to post office to home
    (b) Home to school to post office to library to home
    (c) Home to library to school to post office to home
    (d) Home to library to post office to school to home

7. The following table shows the distances between pairs of towns in a rural county.
    As a newspaper delivery person, you must visit each town once every Sunday. Use the nearest neighbor method to find a circuit that visits each city exactly once, starting from Jasmine.

	Inner	Jasmine	Kredly	Minnow	Norton
Inner	—	25	21	27	13
Jasmine	25	—	18	16	12
Kredly	21	18	—	32	20
Minnow	27	16	32	—	14
Norton	13	12	20	14	—

    (a) Jasmine to Minnow to Norton to Inner to Kredly to Jasmine
    (b) Jasmine to Norton to Minnow to Inner to Kredly to Jasmine
    (c) Jasmine to Norton to Inner to Kredly to Minnow to Jasmine
    (d) Jasmine to Kredly to Inner to Norton to Minnow to Jasmine

For Questions 8–10, refer to the following figure showing the travel times (in hours) between cities that a salesperson must visit.

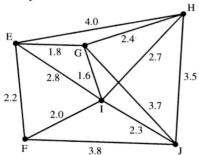

Name:_____

8. Apply the nearest neighbor method to find a circuit that visits each city exactly once, starting from F.

   (a) F to E to G to H to I to J to F
   (c) F to J to H to E to G to I to F

   (b) F to I to G to E to H to J to F
   (d) F to I to E to G to H to J to F

9. Apply the nearest neighbor method to find a circuit that visits each city exactly once, starting from G.

   (a) G to E to F to I to J to H to G
   (c) G to J to F to I to E to H to G

   (b) G to I to J to H to E to F to I to G
   (d) G to I to F to E to H to J to G

10. Apply the nearest neighbor method to find a circuit that visits each city exactly once, starting from I.

   (a) I to G to E to F to J to H to I
   (c) I to F to E to G to H to J to I

   (b) I to G to H to J to F to E to I
   (d) I to F to J to G to H to E to I

Unit 13C Test 1

1. What does EST and EFT stand for?

_____

_____

_____

2. Define critical path?

_____

_____

_____

For questions 3–6, refer to the figure below showing a scheduling network for making cinnamon buns. Completion times, in minutes, are shown on the edges.

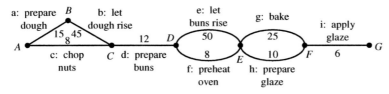

3. Which tasks are on the critical path between *A* and *E*?

_____

_____

_____

4. What is the length of the critical path for the entire project?

_____

_____

_____

5. What is the EST for the task f: *preheat oven*?

_____

_____

_____

Unit 11C Test 1 *(continued)*

Name:_____

6. What is the LFT for the task b: *let dough rise*?

_____

_____

_____

The following table gives the critical times (in days) for the job of buying a house. Refer to this table for questions 7–10.

Task	EST	LST	EFT	LFT	Slack Time
a. *View available homes*	0	0	22	22	
b. *Research schools, etc.*	0	17	5	22	
c. *Sign contract*	22	22	27	27	
d. *Arrange financing*	27	27	87	87	
e. *Inspect house*	27	81	29	83	
f. *Request repairs*	29	83	32	86	
g. *Final inspection*	32	86	33	87	
h. *Sign papers*	87	87	88	88	

7. Fill in the slack time column in the table.

_____

_____

_____

8. Which tasks are on the critical path?

_____

_____

_____

9. How much time is needed for the entire project?

_____

_____

_____

10. Use the table to make the network for the project.

Unit 13C Test 2

Name:_____

Date:_____

1. Define limiting task.

   _____

   _____

   _____

2. What does PERT stand for?

   _____

   _____

   _____

For questions 3–6, refer to the figure below showing a scheduling network for making cinnamon buns. Completion times, in minutes, are shown on the edges.

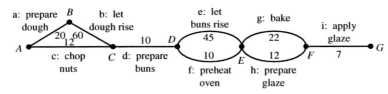

3. Which tasks are on the critical path between *D* and F?

   _____

   _____

   _____

4. What is the length of the critical path for the entire project?

   _____

   _____

   _____

5. What is the EST for the task e: *let buns rise*?

   _____

   _____

   _____

Unit 11C Test 2 *(continued)*

Name:_____

6. What is the LFT for the task c: *chop nuts*?

_____

_____

_____

The following table gives the critical times (in days) for the job of buying a house. Refer to this table for questions 7–10.

Task	EST	LST	EFT	LFT	Slack Time
a. *View available homes*	0	0	14	14	
b. *Research schools, etc.*	0	11	3	14	
c. *Sign contract*	14	14	22	22	
d. *Arrange financing*	22	22	67	67	
e. *Inspect house*	22	58	25	61	
f. *Request repairs*	25	61	30	66	
g. *Final inspection*	30	66	31	67	
h. *Sign papers*	67	67	68	68	

7. Fill in the slack time column in the table.

_____

_____

_____

8. Which tasks are on the critical path?

_____

_____

_____

9. How much time is needed for the entire project?

_____

_____

_____

10. Use the table to make the network for the project.

Unit 13C Test 3

Choose the correct answer to each problem.

1. If there are simultaneous tasks between stages in a project, which of the following refers to the task that requires the most time?

   (a) Slack time   **(b)** Critical path   **(c)** Latest start time   **(d)** Limiting task

2. Which of the following is a technique that can be used to solve scheduling problems when task times are uncertain?

   (a) Slack time   **(b)** PERT   **(c)** EST   **(d)** CPM

For questions 3–6, refer to the figure below showing a scheduling network for making cinnamon buns. Completion times, in minutes, are shown on the edges.

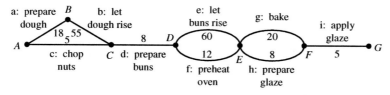

3. Which of the following tasks is *not* on the critical path between *A* and *G*?

   (a) b: *let dough rise*   **(b)** c: *chop nuts*   **(c)** d: *prepare buns*   **(d)** g: *bake*

4. What is the length of the critical path for the entire project?

   (a) 38 minutes   **(b)** 148 minutes   **(c)** 166 minutes   **(d)** 191 minutes

5. What is the LST for the task c: *chop nuts*?

   (a) 0 minutes   **(b)** 18 minutes   **(c)** 68 minutes   **(d)** 73 minutes

6. What is the EST for the task e: *let buns rise*?

   (a) 86 minutes   **(b)** 141 minutes   **(c)** 158 minutes   **(d)** 81 minutes

Unit 13C Test 3 *(continued)*

Name:_____

The following table gives the critical times (in days) for the job of buying a house. Refer to this table for questions 7–10.

Task	EST	LST	EFT	LFT	Slack Time
a. *View available homes*	0	0	45	45	
b. *Research schools, etc.*	0	30	15	45	
c. *Sign contract*	45	45	51	51	
d. *Arrange financing*	51	51	101	101	
e. *Inspect house*	51	93	56	98	
f. *Request repairs*	56	98	58	100	
g. *Final inspection*	58	100	59	101	
h. *Sign papers*	101	101	102	102	

7. Find the slack time for f: *request repairs*.

   (a) 42 days   **(b)** 2 days   **(c)** 40 days   **(d)** 14 days

8. Which of the following tasks is *not* on the critical path?

   (a) a: *view available homes*   **(b)** c: *sign contract*
   (c) d: *arrange financing*   **(d)** f: *request repairs*

9. How much time is needed for the entire project?

   (a) 100 days   **(b)** 101 days   **(c)** 102 days   **(d)** 103 days

10. Which of the following tasks takes place at the same time as a: *arrange financing*?

    (a) b: *inspect house*   **(b)** c: *sign contract*
    (c) d: *arrange financing*   **(d)** g: *final inspection*

Unit 13C Test 4

Choose the correct answer to each problem.

1. The length of which of the following is the minimum completion time for a project?

   (a) Slack time   (b) Critical path   (c) Earliest finish time   (d) Limiting task

2. Which of the following is a technique that can be used to solve scheduling problems when the amount of time needed to complete each task is known?

   (a) Slack time   (b) PERT   (c) EST   (d) CPM

   For questions 3–6, refer to the figure below showing a scheduling network for making cinnamon buns. Completion times, in minutes, are shown on the edges.

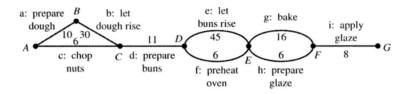

3. Which of the following tasks is *not* on the critical path between *A* and *G*?

   (a) a: *prepare dough*   (b) d: *prepare buns*   (c) f: *preheat oven*   (d) g: *bake*

4. What is the length of the critical path for the entire project?

   (a) 139 minutes   (b) 120 minutes   (c) 110 minutes   (d) 56 minutes

5. What is the EST for the task d: *prepare buns*?

   (a) 51 minutes   (b) 80 minutes   (c) 47 minutes   (d) 40 minutes

6. What is the EFT for the task c: *chop nuts*?

   (a) 6 minutes   (b) 10 minutes   (c) 30 minutes   (d) 41 minutes

Unit 13C Test 4 *(continued)*

The following table gives the critical times (in days) for the job of buying a house. Refer to this table for questions
7–10.

Task	EST	LST	EFT	LFT	Slack Time
a. *View available homes*	0	0	40	40	
b. *Research schools, etc.*	0	30	10	40	
c. *Sign contract*	40	40	49	49	
d. *Arrange financing*	49	49	104	104	
e. *Inspect house*	49	95	53	99	
f. *Request repairs*	53	99	57	103	
g. *Final inspection*	57	103	58	104	
h. *Sign papers*	104	104	105	105	

7. Find the slack time for b: *research schools, etc.*

   (a) 0 days   **(b)** 10 days   **(c)** 30 days   **(d)** 40 days

8. Which of the following tasks is *not* on the critical path?

   (a) b: *research schools, etc.*   **(b)** c: *sign contract*
   (c) d: *arrange financing*   **(d)** h: *sign papers*

9. How much time is needed for the entire project?

   (a) 102 days   **(b)** 103 days   **(c)** 104 days   **(d)** 105 days

10. Which of the following tasks takes place at the same time as f: *request repairs*?

   (a) a: *view available homes*   **(b)** c: *sign contract*
   (c) d: *arrange financing*   **(d)** e: *inspect house*

ANSWERS
TO
UNIT EXAMS

Chapter 1 Answers

Unit 1A Test 1

1. Possible answer: An argument based on the idea that since something has not been proven to be false, it must be true.

2. Possible answer: An argument based on the idea that since a person may not be ethical or reliable, all of that person's beliefs must be untrue.

3. Possible answer: An argument that is based on a distortion of someone else's ideas or beliefs.

4. Possible answer: Isabelle had vegetarian food for lunch every day last week. She must be a vegetarian.

5. Possible answer: A television commercial shows a happy, attractive family dining in Mom and Dad's Restaurant.

6. Possible answer: We've just remodeled the restaurant, so our food is delicious!

7. Possible answer: Appeal to popularity

8. Possible answer: Circular reasoning

9. Possible answer: False cause

10. Possible answer: Hasty generalization

Unit 1A Test 2

1. Possible answer: An argument based on the idea that since something is known to be true sometimes, it must always be true.

2. Possible answer: An argument in which the premise and conclusion say essentially the same thing.

3. Possible answer: An argument in which the premise is not related to the conclusion.

4. Possible answer: Since I brought my umbrella, it didn't rain.

5. Possible answer: A television commercial shows some happy, attractive people listening to Hit Radio 98.

6. Possible answer: Mayor Brown opposes a tax increase to build new schools. A critic states, "Mayor Brown is not concerned with improving the quality of education for our children."

7. Possible answer: Appeal to ignorance

8. Possible answer: Limited choice

9. Possible answer: Personal attack

10. Possible answer: Appeal to popularity

Unit 1A Test 3

1. (c)
2. (d)
3. (b)
4. (a)
5. (b)
6. (a)
7. (d)
8. (b)
9. (d)
10. (c)

Unit 1A Test 4

1. (d)
2. (a)
3. (b)
4. (c)
5. (a)
6. (c)
7. (d)
8. (d)
9. (b)
10. (b)

Unit 1B Test 1

1. Possible answer: A complete sentence that makes a distinct assertion or denial.

2. Possible answer: Statements that share the same truth values.

3. Possible answer: A compound statement made with 'or.'

4. Possible answer: For the proposition "The sky is blue," the negation is "The sky is not blue."

5. Possible answer: For the proposition "If it is a sunny day, it is warm," the inverse is "If it is not a sunny day, it is not warm."

Chapter 1 Answers *(continued)*

6. Possible answer: I have a test tomorrow and my favorite color is green.

7. Answer: *If not p, then q.*

8. Answer:

p	q	not q	if p, then not q
T	T	F	F
T	F	T	T
F	T	F	T
F	F	T	T

9. Answer: False

10.

p	q	not p	(not p) and q
T	T	F	F
T	F	F	F
F	T	T	T
F	F	T	F

Unit 1B Test 2

1. Possible answer: The opposite of a proposition.

2. Possible answer: A statement obtained by switching the order of the propositions in a conditional.

3. Possible answer: A compound statement made with 'and.'

4. Possible answer: I brought my books to school.

5. Possible answer: Any conditional proposition and its contrapositive.

6. Possible answer: The sky is blue or the grass is green.

7. Answer: *If q, then not p.*

8. Answer:

p	q	not q	if p, then not q
T	T	F	F
T	F	T	T
F	T	F	T
F	F	T	T

9. Answer: True

10.

p	not p	q	(not p) and q
T	F	T	F
T	F	F	F
F	T	T	T
F	T	F	F

Unit 1B Test 3

1. (b)
2. (c)
3. (d)
4. (a)
5. (a)
6. (b)
7. (c)
8. (b)
9. (c)
10. (d)

Unit 1B Test 4

1. (b)
2. (c)
3. (c)
4. (c)
5. (b)
6. (a)
7. (d)
8. (d)
9. (b)
10. (b)

Unit 1C Test 1

1. Possible answer: A is a subset of B if all members of A are also members of B.

2. Possible answer: A proposition that expresses the relationship between two categories or sets.

3. Possible answer: They share some of the same members.

4. Possible answer: All lizards are green.

5. Possible answer: Democrats and Republicans.

6. Possible answer: Negative integers.

7. 5

8. 32

Chapter 1 Answers (*continued*)

9. Possible answer:

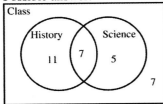

10. Possible answer:

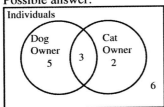

Unit 1C Test 2

1. Possible answer: A collection of objects.

2. Possible answer: A diagram that uses circles to represent sets.

3. Possible answer: Two sets are disjoint when they have no members in common.

4. Possible answer: Any two sets that share some members.

5. Possible answer: Any set consisting of counting numbers.

6. Subject: roses; Predicate: fragrant flowers

7. 10

8. 34

9. Possible answer:

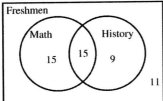

10. Possible answer:

Unit 1C Test 3

1. (c)
2. (a)
3. (d)
4. (c)
5. (c)
6. (a)
7. (d)
8. (a)
9. (b)
10. (c)

Unit 1C Test 4

1. (b)
2. (c)
3. (a)
4. (a)
5. (d)
6. (b)
7. (c)
8. (a)
9. (d)
10. (b)

Unit 1D Test 1

1. Possible answer: An argument whose conclusion follows directly from its premises.

2. Possible answer: A valid argument that has true premises.

3. Possible answer: A subjective judgment about how well the premises support the generalization in the conclusion.

4. Possible answer:
   If it is raining then the picnic is canceled.
   <u>The picnic is canceled.</u>
   It is raining.
   Fallacy of affirming the conclusion.

Chapter 1 Answers *(continued)*

5. Possible answer:
If it is raining then the picnic is canceled.
<u>It is raining.</u>
The picnic is canceled.
Affirming the hypothesis.

6. Possible answer:
If I can borrow your car, then I will go to the market. If I go to the market, then I will do your shopping. So, if I can borrow your car, then I will do your shopping.

7. Possible answer: This argument is not sound even though it is valid because the premises are not true.

8. Possible answer:
Let $a = 3$ and $b = 5$, then $a - b = -2$.
Since a and b are positive, and $a - b$ is negative, the rule is invalid.

9. Answer: If I work hard, then I can buy a new house.

10.

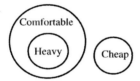

Answer: The argument is valid.

Unit 1D Test 2

1. Possible answer: When you have a conditional proposition 'if p then q' and affirm the truth of the antecedent, p, then you can logically deduce that the consequent, q, is also true.

2. Possible answer: An argument that makes a case for a specific conclusion from more general premises.

3. Possible answer: A proof is a deductive argument that demonstrates the truth of a certain claim or theorem.

4. Possible answer:
All roses are red.
<u>Some roses have thorns   .</u>
Some red flowers have thorns.
This argument is not sound because its first premise is false.

5. Possible answer:
If I go to sleep now, then I will not be tired
        tomorrow.
<u>I am not going to sleep now   </u>.
I am going to be tired tomorrow.
This argument is not valid because it is denying the hypothesis.

6. Possible answer:
Oak trees have leaves.
Maple trees have leaves.
Apple trees have leaves.
<u>Lemon trees have leaves.</u>
All trees have leaves.

7. Possible answer: This argument is sound because it is valid and the premises are true

8. Possible answer:
Let $a = 1$, $b = 2$, and $c = 3$.
Then $(a+b) \times c = (1+2) \times 3 = 9$ and
$a + (b \times c) = 1 + (2 \times 3) = 7$.
Since $9 \neq 7$, $(a+b) \times c \neq a + (b \times c)$ and the rule is invalid.

9. Possible answer: If the gas prices go up, then I will have better health.

10.

Answer: The argument is valid.

Unit 1D Test 3

1. (a)

2. (b)

3. (d)

4. (c)

5. (d)

6. (b)

7. (a)

8. (b)

9. (d)

10. (a)

Chapter 1 Answers (continued)

Unit 1D Test 4

1. (c)
2. (d)
3. (c)
4. (b)
5. (d)
6. (d)
7. (b)
8. (b)
9. (d)
10. (b)

Unit 1E Test 1

1. Possible answer: A product is advertised as "94% fat free", which may mean it is as much as 6% fat.

2. Possible answer: A premise that is not stated, possibly because it is considered obvious.

3. Possible answer: I want to find the best airfare to Phoenix.

4. Possible answer: "The school needs exactly $5,000 to continue its music program. We can sell 500 lottery tickets for $10 each, so the lottery can fund the music program." The intermediate conclusion is that selling 500 lottery tickets for $10 will raise $5,000. This argument is not sound because it does not take into account the costs of putting on the lottery.

5. Possible answer: $20 + $10 per month × 11 months = $130. What is advertised as costing just $20 actually costs $130.

6. Possible answer:
Premise: Bad credit will make it difficult to get a loan.
Hidden assumption: Late bills will result in bad credit.
Intermediate conclusion: Late bills will make it difficult to get a loan.
Conclusion: Bills should be paid on time

7. Possible answer:
Premise: Getting the flu shot every year will keep you from getting the flu.
Hidden assumption: Avoiding getting the flu is important.
Conclusion: Getting a flu shot every year is important.

8. Answer: Driving costs $19 per day, and taking the train costs $18.50 per day.

9. Answer: You will save $5 if you rent the car for one week.

10. Possible answer:
Premise 1: Interest rates are low.
Premise 2: I just received a 3% raise.
Premise 3: My car is old.
Premise 4: My car will need expensive repairs soon.
Intermediate conclusion: I can afford a new car.
Hidden assumption: I want to get rid of my old car.
Conclusion: I should buy a new car.

The argument is strong.

Unit 1E Test 2

1. Possible answer: A *no* vote means that you believe the state legislature should have the authority to restrict religious expression.

2. Possible answer: The dictator knows that an unarmed populace is easier to keep in submission.

3. Possible answer: The stores at the mall should stay open later this month.

Chapter 1 Answers *(continued)*

4. Possible answer: It is raining and if I go outside I will get wet. I should not go outside. The hidden assumption is that I do not want to get wet.

5. Possible answer: $15 + $10 per month X 11 months = $125. What is advertised as costing just $15 actually costs $125.

6. Possible answer:
   Premise: The ranger can cite us for illegal activities.
   Hidden assumption 1: An unattended campfire is illegal.
   Hidden assumption 2: If we go fishing without extinguishing the campfire it will be unattended.
   Intermediate conclusion: The ranger can cite us for an unattended campfire.
   Conclusion: We should extinguish the campfire before we go fishing.

7. Possible answer:
   Premise: Swimming improves your cardiovascular system.
   Hidden assumption: A good cardiovascular system is important to your health.
   Conclusion: Swimming is important to your health

8. Answer: Driving and parking will cost $42, and taking a taxi will cost $44.

9. Answer: You will save $600 if you buy the car and sell it in two years.

10. Possible answer:
    Premise 1: Jeremy rides his bike to school every day.
    Premise 2: Jeremy's bike is old.
    Premise 3: Jeremy's bike is too small for him.
    Premise 4: The new models are safer.
    Intermediate conclusion: Jeremy's old bike is unacceptable.
    Hidden assumption: Safer bikes are better bikes.
    Conclusion: Jeremy needs a new bike.

    The argument is strong.

Unit 1E Test 3

1. (c)
2. (b)
3. (c)
4. (c)
5. (c)
6. (c)
7. (a)
8. (a)
9. (a)
10. (b)

Unit 1E Test 4

1. (b)
2. (d)
3. (c)
4. (c)
5. (c)
6. (d)
7. (c)
8. (b)
9. (b)
10. (b)

Chapter 2 Answers

Unit 2A Test 1

1. feet per second

2. $1 \text{ yd}^3 = (36 \text{ in.})^3 = 46{,}656 \text{ in}^3$

3. Since $\dfrac{\text{hours}}{\text{gallon}} = \dfrac{\text{miles}}{\text{gallon}} \times \dfrac{\text{hours}}{\text{mile}}$

   $= \dfrac{\text{miles}}{\text{gallon}} \div \dfrac{\text{miles}}{\text{hour}}$, you would divide:

   $\dfrac{36 \text{ miles}}{1 \text{ gallon}} \div \dfrac{50 \text{ miles}}{1 \text{ hour}} = \dfrac{0.72 \text{ hour}}{1 \text{ gallon}}$.

4. About 6.71 kroner

5. 345.6 acres

6. $509.17

7. **9 hours**

8. About 0.011 pounds

9. Bathtub (13.5 ft^3, vs 5.25 ft^3 for a shower)

10. 181,440 breaths

Unit 2A Test 2

1. dollars per ton

2. $1 \text{ ft}^3 = (12 \text{ in.})^3 = 1728 \text{ in}^3$

3. Since $\dfrac{\text{gallons}}{\text{hour}} = \dfrac{\text{miles}}{\text{hour}} \times \dfrac{\text{gallons}}{\text{mile}}$

   $= \dfrac{\text{miles}}{\text{hour}} \div \dfrac{\text{miles}}{\text{gallon}}$, you would divide:

   $\dfrac{60 \text{ miles}}{1 \text{ hour}} \div \dfrac{25 \text{ miles}}{1 \text{ gallon}} = \dfrac{2.4 \text{ gallons}}{1 \text{ hour}}$.

4. About 1.379 New Zealand dollars

5. 460.8 acres

6. $686.00

7. 14 hours

8. About 12.397 pesos

9. Bathtub(16.2 ft^3, vs 5.32 ft^3 for a shower)

10. 604,800 breaths

Unit 2A Test 3

1. (d)

2. (c)

3. (b)

4. (a)

5. (c)

6. (b)

7. (a)

8. (c)

9. (b)

10. (c)

Unit 2A Test 4

1. (b)

2. (c)

3. (b)

4. (d)

5. (b)

6. (a)

7. (d)

8. (a)

9. (a)

10. (c)

Unit 2B Test 1

1. Ridiculous, because nobody can run this fast.

2. 189.0 cm

3. 6.3 m$^{3.}$

4. 361.6 miles

5. 0.0523 hm^2

6. $0.22 per pound

7. $33.3^\circ C$

8. 3 cents

9. 0.25 pound per cubic inch

10. 220 carats

Unit 2B Test 2

1. Ridiculous, because distance cannot be measured in liters.

2. 1.6 m

3. 5,810,616.9 cm^3

Chapter 2 Answers *(continued)*

4. 381.5 miles

5. 4.23 dam^2

6. $0.36 per pound

7. Larger, by a factor of 1,000,000

8. 4.4°C

9. 19.2 cents

10. 315 carats

Unit 2B Test 3

1. (c)
2. (d)
3. (d)
4. (c)
5. (a)
6. (a)
7. (c)
8. (c)
9. (b)
10. (a)

Unit 2B Test 4

1. (b)
2. (c)
3. (c)
4. (d)
5. (b)
6. (d)
7. (c)
8. (a)
9. (d)
10. (b)

Unit 2C Test 1

1. Possible answers are: 1 car and 13 light trucks; 4 cars and 11 light trucks; 7 cars and 9 light trucks; 10 cars and 7 light trucks; 13 cars and 5 light trucks; 16 cars and 3 light trucks; 19 cars and 1 light truck

2. Paul

3. 7 socks

4. 42 mi

5. The number of yellow marbles in the red bucket is greater.

6. 68 in.

7. Possible answer: Separate the coins into three sets of five coins. Weigh two of the sets. The lightweight coin is in the lighter of the two sets, or if the two sets balance, it is in the third set. Now weigh two pairs of coins from the lightweight set of five coins. If they balance, the fifth coin is the lightweight coin; otherwise, weigh the lightweight pair to find the lightweight coin.

8. Half girls and half boys

Unit 2C Test 2

1. Possible answers are: 2 cars and 13 light trucks; 5 cars and 11 light trucks; 8 cars and 9 light trucks; 11 cars and 7 light trucks; 14 cars and 5 light trucks; 17 cars and 3 light trucks; 20 cars and 1 light truck

2. Pat

3. 12 socks

4. 57.6 mi

5. The number of green marbles in the black bucket is greater.

6. 150 in.

7. Possible answer: Separate the coins into three sets of six coins. Weigh two of the sets. The lightweight coin is in the lighter of the two sets, or if the two sets balance, it is in the third set. Now weigh two pairs of coins from the lightweight set of six coins. The lightweight coin is in the lighter of the two pairs, or if the two pairs balance, it is in the third pair. Finally, weigh the lightweight pair to find the lightweight coin.

8. Half girls and half boys

Unit 2C Test 3

1. (a)
2. (a)
3. (c)
4. (b)
5. (a)

Chapter 2 Answers *(continued)*

   6. (c)

   7. (b)

   8. (a)

Unit 2C Test 4

   1. (c)

   2. (b)

   3. (d)

   4. (d)

   5. (b)

   6. (d)

   7. (c)

   8. (b)

Chapter 3 Answers

Unit 3A Test 1

1. Express a fraction.

2. Absolute change: $0.14;
   Relative change: 5.2%

3. 42%

4. No, because $(1.01)(1.02) \neq 1.03$.

5. Yes, because 20% of the 50% who are men are men with blond hair, and 20% of 50% is 10%.

6. No, because it is possible that all of the union members are also Democrats, in which case she can only count on 45% of the vote.

7. 840 people

8. $176.30

9. 91%

10. 291%

Unit 3A Test 2

1. Describe a change.

2. Possible answer: absolute difference = compared value – reference value;
   relative difference =
   $$\frac{\text{compared value} - \text{reference value}}{\text{reference value}}$$

3. 110%

4. No, because $(1.04)(1.06) \neq 1.10$.

5. No, because we don't know that 50% of the women have blond hair.

6. Yes, he will receive votes from at least 40% + (25%)(60%) = 55% of the voters.

7. 860 people

8. $78.89

9. 53%

10. 192%

Unit 3A Test 3

1. (c)

2. (d)

3. (a)

4. (b)

5. (d)

6. (c)

7. (c)

8. (b)

9. (c)

10. (c)

Unit 3A Test 4

1. (a)

2. (a)

3. (c)

4. (c)

5. (a)

6. (a)

7. (d)

8. (c)

9. (a)

10. (b)

Unit 3B Test 1

1. 2,000,000,000; two billion

2. 5.9×10^{-4}

3. 10^{67}, because 10^{37} is insignificant in comparison to this large number.

4. 1.8×10^{16}

5. 3.65×10^{7}

6. About 0.25 m

7. About 4.6 days

8. 1 to 3,168,000

9. 3000 km

10. 2.0×10^{9} seconds

Unit 3B Test 2

1. 8,000,000,000; eight billion

2. 3.4×10^{-6}

3. 10^{34}, because 10^{22} is insignificant in comparison to this large number.

4. 2.31×10^{12}

Chapter 3 Answers *(continued)*

5. 2.75×10^7

6. About 1923 years

7. About 54 feet

8. 1 to 7,603,200

9. 1200 km

10. 1.2×10^9 seconds

Unit 3B Test 3

1. (b)
2. (c)
3. (b)
4. (b)
5. (d)
6. (c)
7. (b)
8. (d)
9. (a)
10. (c)

Unit 3B Test 4

1. (d)
2. (b)
3. (d)
4. (c)
5. (b)
6. (c)
7. (c)
8. (c)
9. (b)
10. (d)

Unit 3C Test 1

1. Possible answer: An approximate value is accurate if it is close to the true value; the weight of a puppy is given as 4 pounds when the actual weight is 3.872 pounds.

2. Possible answer: An error that arises because of problems in the system being used to collect data; a telephone survey will not accurately reflect the opinions of people who do not have telephones.

3. Absolute error: –7 years; Relative error: –6.7%

4. Carolyn was more accurate, and Bobby was more precise.

5. 65,152.079; 65,152.1; 65,150; 65,200

6. 5 significant digits; nearest 0.0001 liter

7. 7.800×10^7

8. 424.76

9. 2.8×10^{10}

10. 27.0 m

Unit 3C Test 2

1. Possible answer: An approximate value is precise if it is given to many significant figures; the weight of a puppy is given as 5.1373 pounds when the actual weight is closer to 8 pounds.

2. Possible answer: An error in the collection of data whose impact cannot be predicted; in a written survey, people sometimes make errors in filling out the form.

3. Absolute error: 85 years; Relative error: 16.2%

4. Evelyn was more accurate, and Priscilla was more precise.

5. 32,837.751; 32,837.8; 32,840; 32,800

6. 4 significant digits; nearest 0.01 gallon

7. 3.2000×10^6

8. 2351.8

9. 5.06×10^{11}

10. 2.7 m

Unit 3C Test 3

1. (b)
2. (a)
3. (d)
4. (c)
5. (c)
6. (c)

Chapter 3 Answers *(continued)*

7. (a)

8. (b)

9. (a)

10. (b)

Unit 3C Test 4

1. (a)

2. (c)

3. (a)

4. (d)

5. (d)

6. (c)

7. (d)

8. (c)

9. (b)

10. (c)

Unit 3D Test 1

1. Deflation is a decline in prices and wages over time.

2. The purpose of the CPI is to provide an indication of overall inflation.

3. Monthly

4. $37,514, the median income for Arizona

5. 114.1

6. Alabama: 85.6; Alaska: 120.7; Arizona: 87.7; Arkansas: 67.8

7. 2.83%

8. $4.11

9. $28.93

10. $61,704

Unit 3D Test 2

1. An index number provides a simple way to compare measurements made at different times or in different places.

2. U.S. Bureau of Labor Statistics

3. The CPI represents an average of prices in a sample of more than 60,000 goods, services, and housing costs.

4. The rate of inflation refers to the relative change in the CPI from one year to the next.

5. Gulf Coast Retail Diesel Prices

Date	Price	Price Index
1/29/06	$1.500	100.0
2/02/06	$1.472	98.1
2/12/06	$1.472	98.1
2/19/06	$1.428	95.2

6. 2.29%

7. $2.10

8. $18,874

9. $61.51

10. $46,136

Unit 3D Test 3

1. (a)

2. (d)

3. (c)

4. (c)

5. (b)

6. (a)

7. (a)

8. (c)

9. (b)

10. (b)

Unit 3D Test 4

1. (b)

2. (b)

3. (d)

4. (c)

5. (a)

6. (d)

7. (c)

8. (b)

9. (c)

10. (c)

Chapter 3 Answers *(continued)*

Unit 3E Test 1

1. 62.4%; about 15.9%

2. Possible answer: The data does seem to support the claim since the percentage of coffee drinkers who are violent is more than three times the percentage of non-coffee drinkers who are violent.

3. About 7.3%; about 6.25%

4. 5%; 6%

5. Possible answer: Non-coffee drinkers have the higher rate of violence in both categories. This data certainly does not support the theory that coffee drinkers are more violent. On the other hand, within each category the rates of violence for coffee drinkers and non-coffee drinkers are so close that the data does not support a conclusion that non-coffee drinkers are more violent either.

6. Possible answer: The group of coffee drinkers is comprised of 150 felons and 100 non-felons, while the group of non-coffee drinkers is comprised of 16 felons and 100 non-felons. The greater number of felons, among whom we would expect more violence, virtually guaranteed that the combined rate for the coffee drinkers would be higher.

7. About 1.3%

8. About 2.8%

9. 26%

10. Possible answer: Though the actual number of homicides per year may be increasing, the population of the city is increasing at a higher rate so that the percentage of the population murdered each year is decreasing.

Unit 3E Test 2

1. About 4.8%; 94.5%

2. Possible answer: Though the rate of breast cancer among women who have had an abortion is slightly lower, the difference is hardly enough to conclude that abortion reduces the risk of breast cancer.

3. About 98.9%; 1%

4. 4%; 3%

5. Possible answer: Women who have had abortions have the higher rate of breast cancer in both age groups. However, the differences are so small that it is impossible to make a conclusion about the correlation between abortion and breast cancer.

6. Possible answer: The 225 women who had abortions were unequally divided among the two age groups, 175 in the younger group and 50 in the older group, while the 200 women who did not have abortions were equally divided into the two age groups. The greater number of younger women, among whom we would expect fewer incidence of breast cancer, virtually guaranteed that the combined rate for the group who had abortions would be lower.

7. 9%

8. 6.8%

9. 98.1%

10. Possible answer: Though the actual number of jobs in the city decreased, a large number of the unemployed moved away from the city to find jobs elsewhere so that the percentage of the population that is unemployed decreased.

Unit 3E Test 3

1. (b)

2. (b)

3. (a)

4. (c)

5. (d)

6. (c)

7. (d)

8. (a)

9. (b)

10. (b)

Unit 3E Test 4

1. (a)

2. (c)

3. (c)

4. (b)

Chapter 3 Answers *(continued)*

5. (c)
6. (d)
7. (b)
8. (a)
9. (c)
10. (c)

Chapter 4 Answers

Unit 4A Test 1

1. Possible answer: Keep personal spending under control, stay out of dept, and achieve personal satisfaction.

2. $392

3. $235.20

4. Possible answer: Average an expense that does not occur monthly over the entire year by dividing the total expense for the year by 12.

5. $175.83

6. $46.87

7. 32.1%

8. $1308.33

Unit 4A Test 2

1. List monthly income, list monthly expenses, subtract total expenses from total income, and make adjustments as needed.

2. $548

3. $312

4. Possible answer: Positive cash flow occurs when income exceeds expenses over some fixed period of time.

5. $180

6. $34.67

7. 17.3%

8. $770.83

Unit 4A Test 3

1. (b)
2. (b)
3. (d)
4. (b)
5. (a)
6. (d)
7. (b)
8. (a)

Unit 4A Test 4

1. (c)

2. (a)
3. (c)
4. (c)
5. (b)
6. (c)
7. (c)
8. (d)

Unit 4B Test 1

1. $2367.00
2. $31,592.48
3. $503.41
4. $7184.03
5. 2.83%
6. $1934.75
7. 3.98%
8. 5 years: Ted; 20 years: Bill
9. $7732.21
10. $8596.44

Unit 4B Test 2

1. $3893.90
2. $26,725.37
3. $1175.28
4. $8591.26
5. 4.89%
6. $2526.58
7. 7.14%
8. 5 years: Tweedledum; 20 years: Tweedledum
9. $5054.04
10. $13,019.69

Unit 4B Test 3

1. (b)
2. (a)
3. (c)
4. (a)

Chapter 4 Answers *(continued)*

5. (c)

6. (c)

7. (b)

8. (a)

9. (c)

10. (c)

Unit 4B Test 4

1. (c)

2. (d)

3. (a)

4. (b)

5. (b)

6. (b)

7. (a)

8. (b)

9. (d)

10. (a)

Unit 4C Test 1

1. $11,707.77

2. $62,420.19

3. Brandi

4. $684.86

5. $167.04

6. $2383.67

7. Possible answer: By paying dividends or by increasing in value.

8. −13.58%

9. $505.60

10. 8.70%

Unit 4C Test 2

1. $3792.43

2. $62,286.88

3. $405.38

4. $104.29

5. $1887.25

6. 13.56%

7. −26.67%

8. $144.50

9. Possible answer: Liquidity, rate of return and risk

10. 8.65%

Unit 4C Test 3

1. (c)

2. (a)

3. (c)

4. (a)

5. (a)

6. (a)

7. (b)

8. (b)

9. (a)

10. (c)

Unit 4C Test 4

1. (a)

2. (d)

3. (a)

4. (b)

5. (d)

6. (a)

7. (d)

8. (c)

9. (d)

10. (a)

Unit 4D Test 1

1. Interest

2. Principal of the loan: $15,000; total interest: $3682.80

3. $2352.36

4. $164.81; $11,866.32; $2466.32

5. $507.32; $587.12; $41,726.40

6. $256.93

Chapter 4 Answers *(continued)*

7. $216.75

8. Interest: $11.55; $13.78; $9.36
Balance: $751.55; $510.33; $259.69

Unit 4D Test 2

1. Principal

2. Principal of the loan: $12,000;
total interest: $4876.80

3. $689.78

4. $198.75; $9540.00; $1240.00

5. $1365.27; $1610.44; $104,991.60

6. $353.83

7. $214.67

8. Interest: $6.40; $8.75; $10.80
Balance: $656.40; $810.15; $870.95

Unit 4D Test 3

1. (d)

2. (a)

3. (d)

4. (d)

5. (b)

6. (c)

7. (c)

8. (b)

Unit 4D Test 4

1. (a)

2. (b)

3. (b)

4. (a)

5. (c)

6. (a)

7. (b)

8. (d)

Unit 4E Test 1

1. Gross income: $55,700; adjusted gross
income: $54,200; taxable income: $45,830

2. $660

3. $9710

4. $9535

5. Single: $3140; married: $3140

6. $15,013.44

7. $50,860

8. Decreased by $170

Unit 4E Test 2

1. Gross income: $32,800; adjusted gross
income: $31,600; taxable income: $21,330

2. $650

3. $7760

4. $16,995

5. Single: $2645; married: $2645

6. $10,790.81

7. $52,360

8. Decreased by $648

Unit 4E Test 3

1. (b)

2. (d)

3. (b)

4. (b)

5. (a)

6. (b)

7. (a)

8. (d)

Unit 4E Test 4

1. (c)

2. (c)

3. (b)

4. (d)

5. (a)

6. (d)

7. (a)

8. (b)

Chapter 4 Answers *(continued)*

Unit 4F Test 1

1. Possible answer: Entitlement spending will increase dramatically as retiring "baby boomers" start collecting Social Security and Medicare benefits.

2. Possible answer:
   1. Mandatory expenses, which include interest on the debt and entitlements
   2. Discretionary spending, including spending for national defense and education.

3. The government borrows money from the public by selling Treasury bills, notes, and bonds to investors.

4. Possible answer:
   Controllable outlays: salaries, benefits, insurance, security
   Uncontrollable outlays: rent (or mortgage), power (electricity, gas)

5. $\dfrac{\$232 \text{ billion}}{\$4644 \text{ billion}} = 0.050 = 5.0\%$

6. $277 billion; $164 billion. The government must repay $277 billion.

7. $2219 billion

8. 1417 years

9. $86,957

10. $478 billion in surplus, not deficit

Unit 4F Test 2

1. Possible answer: Net surplus can be increased by cutting entitlement or discretionary spending, or by large tax increases

2. Possible answer: If net income is negative, there is a deficit. Debt is the total amount of money owed to lenders.

3. Possible answer: Discretionary spending includes spending for national defense and scientific research.

4. Possible answers: advertising, security, employee bonuses or incentives.

5. $\dfrac{\$203 \text{ billion}}{\$4351 \text{ billion}} = 0.047 = 4.7\%$

6. $293 billion; $203 billion. The government must repay $293 billion.

7. $1904 billion

8. 1442 years

9. $166,667

10. $581 billion in surplus, not deficit

Unit 4F Test 3

1. (b)
2. (b)
3. (d)
4. (b)
5. (a)
6. (b)
7. (c)
8. (c)
9. (a)
10. (a)

Unit 4F Test 4

1. (a)
2. (d)
3. (c)
4. (b)
5. (d)
6. (a)
7. (b)
8. (b)
9. (c)
10. (d)

Chapter 5 Answers

Unit 5A Test 1

1. Possible answer: When a member of a control group who receives an inactive placebo actually improves.

2. Possible answer: When more than one group of individuals are studied and each group receives a different treatment except for one group which does not receive any treatment.

3. Possible answer: A study draws conclusions about a larger population by studying a smaller sample.

4. Possible answer: In a study of the average weight of all first graders, the weights of every first grader in the sample group.

5. Possible answer: The average weight of all first graders in the sample group.

6. Possible answer: What is the average height of a professional basketball player?

7. Possible answer: Experiment

8. Possible answer: Double-blind experiment

9. Possible answer: Observational study

10. We can be 95% confident that 40% to 50% of Americans spend less than 2 hours a day watching TV.

Unit 5A Test 2

1. Possible answer: All of the data collected in a study.

2. Possible answer: Numbers that summarize the raw data.

3. Possible answer: Members of the study are observed, but not influenced by the researchers.

4. Possible answer: A study subject in a control group was cured of the flu after being given an inactive placebo.

5. Possible answer: When studying the average income of radio disk jockeys, the population is all disk jockeys and the sample is the group of disk jockeys selected to be in the study.

6. Possible answer: Does drinking 3 glasses of milk a day improve your bone density?

7. Possible answer: Single-blind experiment

8. Possible answer: Case-control study

9. Possible answer: Observational study with a survey

10. We can be 95% confident that 60% to 70% of Americans watched the Academy Awards.

Unit 5A Test 3

1. (c)
2. (b)
3. (a)
4. (c)
5. (d)
6. (c)
7. (a)
8. (c)
9. (b)
10. (a)

Unit 5A Test 4

1. (c)
2. (b)
3. (c)
4. (b)
5. (d)
6. (c)
7. (b)
8. (a)
9. (b)
10. (c)

Unit 5B Test 1

1. Possible answer: The process by which scientists examine each others' research.

2. Possible answer: When researchers select a sample that is unlikely to represent the population.

3. Possible answer: Because the study may be biased in favor of those who are carrying it out.

Chapter 5 Answers *(continued)*

4. Possible answer: A survey question that asks whether your favorite cola is Coke or Pepsi has an availability error because someone may have answered Shasta if given an open ended question.

5. Possible answer: A comment box in a grocery store has a participation bias, because people with negative comments tend to participate more than those with positive comments.

6. Possible flaw: The engineers who designed the Vangard tires are an inappropriate source to be testing their own product.

7. Possible flaw: The results of the survey imply that Dentamint is the only gum that will prevent tooth decay, but the dentists may have answered the same way about other brands of sugarless gum.

8. Possible sample: A phone poll of registered voters throughout the state.

9. Possible answer: It can be difficult to define a quantity of interest when it is a part of the population that is difficult to reach. For example, it would be difficult to estimate how many people were *not* counted in the last census.

Unit 5B Test 2

1. Possible answer: Participation bias occurs when participation in a study is voluntary because people who feel strongly are more likely to volunteer.

2. Possible answer: The tendency to make judgments based on what is available in the mind. This can depend on what choices are mentioned or the order that choices are mentioned.

3. Possible answer: A peer review does not guarantee validity. A peer review adds credibility to a study.

4. Possible answer: A magazine calling all of its subscribers to ask if they are satisfied with their articles has a selection bias because subscribers are more likely to be satisfied with the content of the magazine.

5. Possible answer: A political party would be an inappropriate source for an election poll.

6. Possible flaw: The wording of the question is confusing, therefore the results of the study will not reflect the true opinions of the students.

7. Possible flaw: The scientist has misinterpreted the result. The cat is not running forward because it cannot see the treat, not because it is no longer hungry.

8. Possible sample: A telephone survey. Call a sample of county residents from a list of those who filed tax returns last year.

9. Possible answer: A quantity of interest can be difficult to measure if it is not countable. For example, it is easier to measure the average height of a basketball team than it would be to measure which member of the team is the best looking.

Unit 5B Test 3

1. (b)
2. (d)
3. (c)
4. (b)
5. (a)
6. (b)
7. (d)
8. (c)
9. (d)

Unit 5B Test 4

1. (a)
2. (c)
3. (a)
4. (c)
5. (b)
6. (d)
7. (d)
8. (a)
9. (b)

Unit 5C Test 1

1. Possible answer: A bin is a data category in a histogram.

Chapter 5 Answers (*continued*)

2. Possible answer: Brand names of shoes worn by students

3. About 1.1 million Apples, 1.3 million IBMs, 1.6 million Compaqs, and 2.3 million others.

4. Apple's region is 61.2°, IBM's region is 75.6°, Compaq's region is 90°, and the other region is 133.2°.

5.

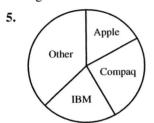

6. There were 430 Representatives. About 3% were at least 70 years old.

7.

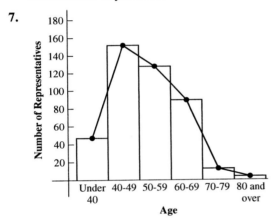

8.

	April 5	April 15	April 25	May 5
Stock Price	$4.50	$5.00	$5.00	$3.50
Invest-ment Value	$225	$250	$250	$175

Unit 5C Test 2

1. Possible answer: Data that represents counts or measurements.

2. The bin labels would be 2004, 2005, and 2006

3. 68 million Americans sleep 6 hours, 78 million Americans sleep 7 hours, and 73 million Americans sleep 8 hours a night.

4. The 'less than 6 hour' region is 43.2°, the '6 hour' region is 93.6°, the '7 hour' region is 108°, the '8 hour' region is 100.8°, and the 'more than 8 hours' region is 14.4°.

5.

6. There were 13.5 million internet users in 2005. About 44% were between the ages of 26 and 35.

7.

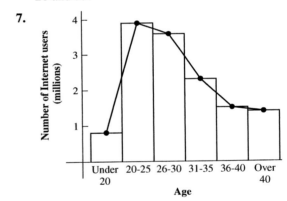

8.

	June 5	June 15	June 25	July 5
Stock Price	$7.50	$8.00	$8.00	$6.50
Invest-ment Value	$300	$320	$320	$260

Unit 5C Test 3

1. (c)

2. (b)

3. (c)

4. (d)

Chapter 5 Answers (*continued*)

5. (a)

6. (c)

7. (c)

8. (b)

Unit 5C Test 4

1. (d)

2. (b)

3. (d)

4. (c)

5. (b)

6. (d)

7. (a)

8. (c)

Unit 5D Test 1

1. Possible answer: On a contour map, quantities are represented by curves. A quantity represented by a curve has the same value along the entire curve.

2. Possible answer: Graphics that require three axes to display three related quantities for each data point.

3. Possible answer: It is sometimes difficult to determine the precise thickness of all but the bottom wedge in a stack plot.

4. Possible answer: An exponential scale is used to display data that is growing or shrinking very rapidly, such as bacteria growth.

5. Possible answer: Tubes of toothpaste could represent the different brands, and toothpaste could be coming out of the tubes in different lengths depending on the popularity of each brand.

6. Possible answer: Inflation is the tendency of prices to rise over time.

7. Possible answer: Nothing can be determined about the real cost of a candy bar from the given graph because the prices in the graph are not adjusted for inflation.

8. Possible answer: The teacher's annual salary is not decreasing, but the percentage by which it is increasing is going down.

9. It is a pie chart and a pictograph.

Unit 5D Test 2

1. Possible answer: A stack plot is a display of data where each category has its own wedge and the wedges are displayed on top of one another. The thickness of a wedge indicates the value at that point.

2. Possible answer: A multiple bar graph is very much like a regular bar graph, except that there are two or more bars in each category.

3. Possible answer: It is sometimes difficult to interpret a three dimensional graph because there is always some visual distortion involved when displaying a three dimensional image on a flat page.

4. Possible answer: Regional data can be clearly displayed on a color coded map. For example the population of each state can be displayed using a different color for each range of numbers.

5. Possible answer: Soda cans could represent the different brands, and straws could be coming out of the cans in different lengths depending on the popularity of each brand.

6. Possible answer: The real cost of an item is the price of an item adjusted for inflation.

7. Possible answer: In order to determine the real cost of greeting cards between 2002 and 2006, you need to know the rate of inflation in those years.

8. Possible answer: On a percent change graph, a decrease in price would be represented by a negative value.

9. It is a multiple bar graph and a pictograph.

Unit 5D Test 3

1. (b)

2. (a)

3. (d)

4. (d)

5. (d)

6. (c)

7. (d)

8. (b)

Chapter 5 Answers (continued)

Unit 5D Test 4

1. (b)
2. (c)
3. (b)
4. (d)
5. (d)
6. (a)
7. (c)
8. (a)

Unit 5E Test 1

1. A correlation exists between two variables when higher values of one variable consistently go with higher values of another, or when higher values of one variable consistently go with lower values of another.

2. Positive correlation; The more hours of exercise, the more calories you will burn; so, higher values of the first variable will go with higher values of the second.

3. No correlation; there is no reason to suspect that heavier people will either consistently score higher or consistently score lower than lighter people on the SAT.

4. Causality

5. Coincidence

6. The tax increase means that tax payers have less money to spend at retailers, causing the retailers' sales to go down.

7. A physical model has been identified that is so successful in explaining how one thing causes another that it seems unreasonable to doubt the causality.

8.

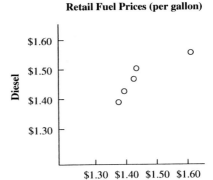

Retail Fuel Prices (per gallon)

9. Yes; positive

10. The result of some common underlying cause; Fuel prices differ by region because states have different air pollution regulations and taxes on fuels, both of which affect the retail price of both gasoline and diesel. Thus a state with high fuel taxes and expensive pollution standards will cause higher gasoline and diesel prices in the region.

Unit 5E Test 2

1. A positive correlation exists between two variables when both variables tend to increase (or decrease) together.

2. No correlation; There is no reason to suspect that people with larger waist size will either have consistently higher IQs or have consistently lower IQs than people with smaller waist size.

3. Positive correlation; As high-school GPAs go up, one would expect college GPAs to do likewise.

4. Common cause

5. Causality

6. Since private ownership of handguns is prohibited, criminals are emboldened by knowing that their potential victims are most likely unarmed and, hence, commit more crimes. Additionally, those who commit a violent crime with a handgun break the added law against private ownership of handguns.

7. A correlation has been discovered but causality has not been established.

Chapter 5 Answers *(continued)*

8.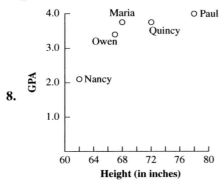

9. Yes; positive

10. A coincidence; There is no apparent explanation for the observed correlation.

Unit 5E Test 3

1. (b)
2. (c)
3. (d)
4. (c)
5. (b)
6. (d)
7. (a)
8. (a)
9. (b)
10. (a)

Unit 5E Test 4

1. (d)
2. (b)
3. (a)
4. (b)
5. (c)
6. (b)
7. (b)
8. (c)
9. (a)
10. (c)

Chapter 6 Answers

Unit 6A Test 1

1. The distribution of a variable describes the values taken on by the variable and the frequency of these values.

2. An outlier is a data value that is much higher or much lower than almost all other values.

3. Since the six possible outcomes are equally likely, we expect the distribution to be uniform with no peak.

4. The distribution would be symmetric, since we would expect that roughly equal numbers of men have shoe sizes smaller and larger than the mean.

5. 3

6. 7

7. 3.5

8. Mean = B, median = B, mode = B

9. The student is finding the mean class size of only two classes, one lecture of 100 students and one lab of 20 students, while the chairperson is finding the mean class size of 18 classes, 3 lectures and 15 labs. The greater number of labs with smaller enrollment in the chairperson's calculation produces a smaller mean.

10. Since the mean price is greater than the median price, the distribution is likely to be right-skewed. There may also be outliers, such as a home price of $1,000,000, that would drastically increase the mean price but have little effect on the median price.

Unit 6A Test 2

1. Possible answer: SAT scores.

2. A uniform distribution has no peaks.

3. We expect two peaks, one corresponding to the mode of the men's weights and the other corresponding to the mode of the women's weights.

4. The distribution would be right-skewed. Most students would be between 18 and 22 years old, but the age of the few older students would pull the mean to the right.

5. 96

6. 22

7. 1.5

8. Mean = C, median = B, mode = A

9. The owner is using the median salary as the average, while the employee is using the mean salary as the average.

10. Since the mean score is less than the median score, the distribution is likely to be left-skewed. There may also be outliers, such as a score of 0, that would drastically reduce the mean score but have little effect on the median score.

Unit 6A Test 3

1. (a)
2. (b)
3. (b)
4. (c)
5. (b)
6. (a)
7. (b)
8. (a)
9. (d)
10. (c)

Unit 6A Test 4

1. (a)
2. (c)
3. (d)
4. (a)
5. (c)
6. (b)
7. (c)
8. (c)
9. (a)
10. (d)

Unit 6B Test 1

1. Possible answer: One quarter of the data lie at or below the lower quartile.

2. standard deviation

3. 3000

Chapter 6 Answers *(continued)*

4. $1.71

5. low = 5.7, lower quartile = 8.9, median = 9.55, upper quartile = 10.6, high = 13.8

6.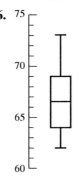

7. 4.8 pounds

8. 11

Unit 6B Test 2

1. Possible answer: One quarter of the data lie at or above the upper quartile.

2. mean

3. 2600

4. $0.39

5. low = 4.3, lower quartile = 5.4, median = 5.9, upper quartile = 7.3, high = 8.2

6.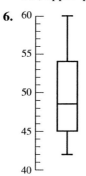

7. 7.98 pounds

8. $0.025

Unit 6B Test 3

1. (c)

2. (b)

3. (c)

4. (a)

5. (d)

6. (c)

7. (b)

8. (a)

Unit 6B Test 4

1. (d)

2. (c)

3. (b)

4. (b)

5. (a)

6. (a)

7. (c)

8. (b)

Unit 6C Test 1

1. 79% of the students who took the test received scores lower than Bob's score.

2. 34% (actually 34.13%)

3. 2.5th percentile (actually 2.28th percentile)

4. 1.75

5. −0.2; 42.07th percentile

6. 0.5 standard deviation above

7. 2177 employees

8. 1.5; 93.32nd percentile

9. 0.2; 57.93rd percentile

10. 34% (actually 34.13%)

Unit 6C Test 2

1. 34% of the students who took the test received scores lower than Carol's score.

2. 47.5% (actually 47.72%)

3. 16th percentile (actually 15.87th percentile)

4. 0.6

5. −0.6; 27.43rd percentile

6. 0.7 standard deviation below

7. 1234 employees

8. −0.6; 27.43rd percentile

9. −0.4; 34.46th percentile

10. 47.5% (actually 47.72%)

Chapter 6 Answers

Unit 6C Test 3

1. (a)
2. (a)
3. (d)
4. (a)
5. (d)
6. (c)
7. (d)
8. (d)
9. (d)
10. (d)

Unit 6C Test 4

1. (c)
2. (b)
3. (c)
4. (b)
5. (c)
6. (a)
7. (a)
8. (b)
9. (a)
10. (d)

Unit 6D Test 1

1. The probability of the difference occurring by chance is 1 in 20 or less.
2. The population proportion
3. 0.025
4. 16% to 26%
5. No, the difference is likely due to chance.
6. The sample indicates that about 18.1% of those whose graduated at least one year ago have never worked in their field of study. If the school's claim is correct, this should be less than 1%. Since the margin of error for 95% confidence for the sample proportion is 2.5%, it is unlikely that the school's claim is true.

7. Alternative hypothesis: The drug was more effective than the placebo at reducing pain. Null hypothesis: The drug was no more effective than the placebo at reducing pain.

8. The percentage of placebo-taking patients who experienced mild or no pain would be greater than or approximately equal to the percentage of drug-taking patients who experienced mild or no pain.

9. The percentage of placebo-taking patients who experienced mild or no pain would be less than the percentage of drug-taking patients who experienced mild or no pain.

10. Since 60% of the placebo-taking patients experienced mild or no pain, and 70% of the drug-taking patients experienced mild or no pain, there is evidence in favor of the alternative hypothesis.

Unit 6D Test 2

1. The probability of the difference occurring by chance is 1 in 100 or less.

2. A sampling distribution is a distribution consisting of proportions from many individual samples.

3. 0.38, or the true population proportion

4. 0.0625

5. You are 95% confident that the true population parameter lies within the interval.

6. 0.001

7. Alternative hypothesis: The drug was more effective than the placebo at reducing the number of pimples.
Null hypothesis: The drug was no more effective than the placebo at reducing number of pimples.

8. The percentage of placebo-taking patients who experienced a reduction in pimples would be greater than or approximately equal to the percentage of drug-taking patients who experienced a reduction in pimples.

9. The percentage of placebo-taking patients who experienced a reduction in pimples would be less than the percentage of drug-taking patients who experienced a reduction in pimples.

Chapter 6 Answers *(continued)*

10. Since 68% of the drug-taking patients experienced a reduction in pimples, and 73% of the placebo-taking patients experienced a reduction in pimples, then the results agree with the null hypothesis.

Unit 6D Test 3

1. (a)
2. (a)
3. (b)
4. (c)
5. (b)
6. (d)
7. (b)
8. (b)
9. (c)
10. (b)

Unit 6D Test 4

1. (d)
2. (b)
3. (c)
4. (b)
5. (b)
6. (a)
7. (a)
8. (c)
9. (a)
10. (a)

Chapter 7 Answers

Unit 7A Test 1

1. An event is a set of one or more outcomes that share a property of interest.

2. 0

3. Subjective method

4. Empirical method

5. Theoretical method

6. 36

7. 5

8.

Sum	Probability
2	$\frac{1}{36}$
3	$\frac{1}{18}$
4	$\frac{1}{12}$
5	$\frac{1}{9}$
6	$\frac{5}{36}$
7	$\frac{1}{6}$
8	$\frac{5}{36}$
9	$\frac{1}{9}$
10	$\frac{1}{12}$
11	$\frac{1}{18}$
12	$\frac{1}{36}$

9. 0.68

10. 1 to 3

Unit 7A Test 2

1. Outcomes

2. 1

3. Empirical method

4. $\frac{1}{7}$

5. 32

6. 6

7.

Number of Heads	Probability
0	0.0625
1	0.25
2	0.375
3	0.25
4	0.0625

8. The probabilities do not add up to 1.

9. 0.73

10. 3 to 2

Unit 7A Test 3

1. (a)

2. (b)

3. (b)

4. (a)

5. (a)

6. (b)

7. (c)

8. (b)

9. (c)

10. (b)

Unit 7A Test 4

1. (b)

2. (d)

3. (a)

4. (d)

5. (b)

6. (a)

7. (d)

8. (c)

9. (b)

10. (c)

Unit 7B Test 1

1. Dependent; doing well on the midterm implies mastery of half the material on the final, which increases the chances of doing well there, also.

2. 0.003

Chapter 7 Answers *(continued)*

3. Independent; the test results for one pool has no relationship to the test result for the other pool.

4. $\dfrac{1}{221}$

5. Yes; one cannot be registered both as a Democrat and as a Republican.

6. 80%

7. No; an engine can be overheating and stalling at the same time.

8. $\dfrac{10}{13}$

9. 0.216

10. 0.021

Unit 7B Test 2

1. Dependent; if one circuit shuts down, the load on the other will increase, and that increases the probability of its shutting down, also.

2. 0.48

3. Independent; the failure of one drive has no effect on the likelihood of failure of the other.

4. $\dfrac{1}{21}$

5. No; a person can have red hair and blue eyes.

6. $\dfrac{77}{81}$

7. Yes; a voter can only vote for a single candidate for President.

8. 85%

9. 0.912

10. 0.251

Unit 7B Test 3

1. (b)
2. (d)
3. (c)
4. (a)
5. (b)

6. (c)
7. (b)
8. (c)
9. (c)
10. (d)

Unit 7B Test 4

1. (a)
2. (d)
3. (a)
4. (b)
5. (b)
6. (c)
7. (d)
8. (b)
9. (a)
10. (c)

Unit 7C Test 1

1. 20,010
2. 18
3. not repay: 5700; with difficulty: 9500; without incident: 22,800
4. ... the gambler's fallacy.
5. $32,100
6. $256,000
7. 21.3 minutes
8. $2,884,000
9. 4 cents per dollar
10. about 7.69 cents per dollar

Unit 7C Test 2

1. 24,839
2. 120
3. innocent: 5175; minor: 180; serious: 45
4. ... the gambler's fallacy.
5. $3640
6. $340,000

Chapter 7 Answers *(continued)*

7. 260 years

8. $105,000

9. 5 cents per dollar

10. about 3.70 cents per dollar

Unit 7C Test 3

1. (a)
2. (b)
3. (b)
4. (c)
5. (a)
6. (d)
7. (d)
8. (b)
9. (d)
10. (c)

Unit 7C Test 4

1. (c)
2. (c)
3. (b)
4. (d)
5. (a)
6. (b)
7. (d)
8. (a)
9. (b)
10. (d)

Unit 7D Test 1

1. 0.76%
2. about 0.54%
3. about 17,000 miles
4. about 118 accidents per 1000; about 11.8%
5. about 69 accidents per 10 million miles
6. about 2.32 per 100,000; about 0.0023%
7. about 0.0021%
8. about 0.0044%

Unit 7D Test 2

1. 1.74%
2. about 0.212%
3. about 9770
4. about 80 accidents per 1000; about 8.0%
5. about 82 accidents per 10 million miles
6. about 12.69 per 100,000; about 0.0127%
7. about 0.0148%
8. about 0.027%

Unit 7D Test 3

1. (d)
2. (d)
3. (a)
4. (c)
5. (b)
6. (c)
7. (d)
8. (b)

Unit 7D Test 4

1. (c)
2. (d)
3. (a)
4. (b)
5. (d)
6. (b)
7. (c)
8. (c)

Unit 7E Test 1

1. 96
2. 30
3. 17,576,000
4. 1,188,137,600
5. 5814
6. 10
7. 6840

Chapter 7 Answers *(continued)*

8. 132,600

9. 36

10. 1,344,904

10. (a)

Unit 7E Test 2

1. 12

2. 12

3. 1,188,137,600

4. 6,760,000,000

5. 7980

6. 420

7. 4896

8. 148,824

9. 20

10. 111,930

Unit 7E Test 3

1. (b)

2. (c)

3. (b)

4. (d)

5. (b)

6. (a)

7. (a)

8. (c)

9. (d)

10. (b)

Unit 7E Test 4

1. (d)

2. (c)

3. (a)

4. (b)

5. (b)

6. (c)

7. (d)

8. (d)

9. (b)

Chapter 8 Answers

Unit 8A Test 1

1. Exponential
2. Linear
3. 2^{11}
4. $2^{18} - 1$
5. $40.96
6. 2^{25}
7. $\dfrac{1}{512}$
8. About 667 m
9. 2,368,000 people

Unit 8A Test 2

1. Linear
2. Exponential
3. 2^{17}
4. $2^{16} - 1$
5. $5.12
6. 2^{27}
7. $\dfrac{1}{64}$
8. About 2669 m
9. 48,000; 96,000; 192,000; 384,000; 768,000

Unit 8A Test 3

1. (d)
2. (c)
3. (c)
4. (d)
5. (b)
6. (b)
7. (c)
8. (b)
9. (d)

Unit 8A Test 4

1. (b)

2. (a)
3. (a)
4. (c)
5. (b)
6. (c)
7. (a)
8. (d)
9. (c)

Unit 8B Test 1

1. 8 days
2. 16
3. $\dfrac{1}{128}$
4. 114 years
5. $3805.46
6. 11.1 years
7. 39.3 milligrams
8. 16.3 years
9. 3.5% per year
10. No; least accurate for large decay rates.

Unit 8B Test 2

1. 9 days
2. 32
3. $\dfrac{1}{256}$
4. 65 years
5. $3527.78
6. 11.3 years
7. 74.3 milligrams
8. 11.5 years
9. 4.375% per year
10. No; most accurate for small decay rates.

Unit 8B Test 3

1. (c)
2. (b)

Chapter 8 Answers *(continued)*

3. (d)

4. (c)

5. (c)

6. (b)

7. (a)

8. (a)

9. (d)

10. (a)

Unit 8B Test 4

1. (b)

2. (c)

3. (b)

4. (b)

5. (d)

6. (c)

7. (b)

8. (c)

9. (a)

10. (d)

Unit 8C Test 1

1. Possible answer: The number of people (or other organisms) that an environment can support for a long period of time.

2. 1.5 % per year

3. 22.6 years

4. 4,776,294

5. 212 million

6. Possible answers:
   a. The birth rate has been decreasing.
   b. The death rate has been increasing.
   c. 0.63% per year, 0.09% per year, 0.00% per year
   d. The population appears to have leveled off so it is likely to begin decreasing. This prediction may not be reliable because unforeseen events may occur and because the effects of immigration have not been taken into account.

7. 0.67% per year

8. 1.76%

Unit 8C Test 2

1. Possible answer: A model of population growth that is based on the assumption that the rate of growth decreases smoothly, and becomes zero when the carrying capacity is reached.

2. 0.4% per year

3. 36.8 years

4. 4,998,269

5. 188 million

6. Possible answers:
   a. The birth rate has been decreasing.
   b. The death rate has been decreasing.
   c. 0.46% per year, 0.42% per year, 0.20% per year
   d. The population is likely to level off and then decrease. This prediction may not be reliable because unforeseen events may occur and because the effects of immigration have not been taken into account.

7. 0.10% per year

8. 3.45%

Unit 8C Test 3

1. (c)

2. (a)

3. (c)

4. (c)

5. (b)

6. (b)

7. (b)

8. (c)

9. (d)

Unit 8C Test 4

1. (b)

2. (b)

3. (b)

4. (b)

5. (c)

6. (a)

Chapter 8 Answers (*continued*)

7. (c)

8. (b)

9. (c)

Unit 8D Test 1

1. Possible answer: Energy released by earthquakes in surface waves tend to cause more damage than energy released in interior waves.

2. Possible answer: After the devastation of 1990 more funds were directed towards construction designed to withstand moderate earthquakes.

3. $\dfrac{E_{1990}}{E_{1997}} = 10^{1.5(7.7-7.5)} = 1.995$, so the 1990 earthquake released almost twice as much energy as the 1997 earthquake.

4. A sound of 0 decibels is the softest sound audible to the human ear.

5. $10\log_{10}(90) = 20$ dB

6. $\dfrac{10^{7.9}}{10^{1.7}} = 1{,}584{,}893$ times more intense

7. 3.16 meters

8. Possible answer: any kind of citrus juice

9. $-\log_{10}10^{-8} = 8$

10. Possible answer: The burning of fossil fuels can cause acid rain.

Unit 8D Test 2

1. Possible answer: the city of San Francisco can afford more expensive construction than the country of Iran.

2. Possible answer: Scientists use a scale of magnitudes, which are logarithmically related to the amount of energy released by earthquakes.

3. $\dfrac{E_{1989}}{E_{1994}} = 10^{1.5(7.1-6.7)} = 3.98$, so the 1989 San Francisco earthquake released almost four times as much energy as the 1994 Los Angeles earthquake.

4. The intensity of the sound decreases by a factor that is the square of the distance you move away from the source.

5. $10\log_{10}(10{,}000) = 40$ decibels

6. $\dfrac{10^{7.0}}{10^{4.0}} = 1000$ times more intense

7. 10 meters closer, i.e. 20 meters away from the siren.

8. Possible answers: baking soda, ammonia, antacid tablets.

9. $-10\log_{10}10^{-3} = 3$

10. Possible answer: Acid rain can kill plants and trees.

Unit 8D Test 3

1. (d)

2. (a)

3. (b)

4. (d)

5. (b)

6. (c)

7. (b)

8. (a)

9. (a)

10. (b)

Unit 8D Test 4

1. (b)

2. (a)

3. (d)

4. (c)

5. (d)

6. (c)

7. (b)

8. (a)

9. (b)

10. (b)

Chapter 9 Answers

Unit 9A Test 1

1. It is a compact representation.

2. Data table, graph, and equation

3. The variable which is not affected by / is independent of the other variable

4. Possible answer: At time = 0, the ball is at initial height = 200 ft; as time goes on, the ball's height decreases to 0 ft at time = x sec.

5. Possible answer: (time in seconds, altitude in feet)

6.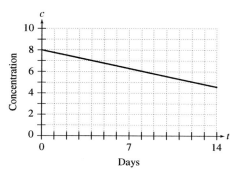

7. Domain: all t such that $4.5 \le t \le 14$; range: all c such that $0 \le c \le 8$

8. The concentration starts at 8 ppm and steadily declines over the course of 14 days.

9. 6.5 ppm

10. Day 11

Unit 9A Test 2

1. A graph is easy to interpret and consolidates a great deal of information.

2. The variable which is effected by / dependent upon the other variable

3. A function which continuously repeats a pattern

4. Possible answer: At time = 0 seconds, the water is a tap temperature. As time goes on, the temperature increases.

5. Possible answer: (time in seconds, temperature in Fahrenheit or centigrade)

6.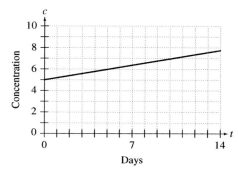

7. Domain: all $t \ge 0$; range: all c such that $5 \le c$

8. The concentration starts at 5 ppm and steadily rises over the course of time.

9. 6.2 ppm

10. Day 8

Unit 9A Test 3

1. (c)
2. (c)
3. (b)
4. (b)
5. (d)
6. (d)
7. (c)
8. (a)
9. (a)
10. (a)

Unit 9A Test 4

1. (a)
2. (b)
3. (c)
4. (c)
5. (b)
6. (d)
7. (a)
8. (d)
9. (b)
10. (c)

Chapter 9 Answers (*continued*)

Unit 9B Test 1

1. 3 ppm

2. $-\dfrac{1}{3}$ ppm per day

3. 2 ppm

4. 6 ppm

5. $c = 6 - \dfrac{1}{3}t$

6. 1 ppm

7. $x = \dfrac{y+3}{-4}$

8. $y = 32x - 18$

9. 94

10. $750

Unit 9B Test 2

1. 4.5 ppm

2. $\dfrac{1}{6}$ ppm per day

3. 1 ppm

4. 3 ppm

5. $c = 3 + \dfrac{1}{6}t$

6. 6 ppm

7. $x = \dfrac{y+7}{6}$

8. $y = -10x + 5$

9. -20

10. $840

Unit 9B Test 3

1. (b)

2. (c)

3. (b)

4. (a)

5. (b)

6. (a)

7. (c)

8. (b)

9. (b)

10. (d)

Unit 9B Test 4

1. (b)

2. (b)

3. (a)

4. (a)

5. (d)

6. (c)

7. (a)

8. (c)

9. (c)

10. (c)

Unit 9C Test 1

1. 80,000; 86,400; 93,312; 100,777; 108,839; 117,546; 126,950; 137,106; 148,074; 159,920; 172,714; 186,531; 201,454; 217,570; 234,975; 253,774

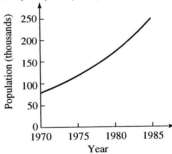

2. John, by $11,937.69

3. Possible answer: $Q = 86(0.96)^t$, where Q is the average home price (in thousands of dollars) and t is the number of years after 1990.

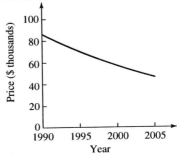

Chapter 9 Answers *(continued)*

4. 18,941 students

5. The price increased by $2.02 (as measured in 1998 dollars).

6. 19.6%

7. 27 years

8. 54.8 mg/cm^2

9. 3931 years

10. $6143.53

Unit 9C Test 2

1. 40,000; 44,800; 50,176; 56,197; 62,941; 70,494; 78,953; 88,427; 99,039; 110,923; 124,234; 139,142; 155,839; 174,540; 195,484; 218,943

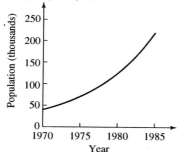

2. Paul, by $3931.03

3. Possible answer: $Q = 74(0.92)^t$, where Q is the average home price (in thousands of dollars) and t is the number of years after 1990.

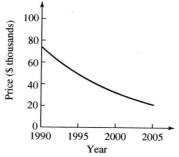

4. 4966 students

5. The price fell by $1.58 (as measured in 1998 dollars).

6. 15.4%

7. 51 years

8. 158.4 mg/cm^2

9. 4768 years

10. $998.31

Unit 9C Test 3

1. (d)

2. (b)

3. (d)

4. (d)

5. (c)

6. (b)

7. (b)

8. (a)

9. (b)

10. (b)

Unit 9C Test 4

1. (c)

2. (d)

3. (c)

4. (c)

5. (b)

6. (d)

7. (d)

8. (d)

9. (d)

10. (a)

Chapter 10 Answers

Unit 10A Test 1

1. Possible answer: the area increases by a factor of 4

2. Possible answer: yes, for example a square with each side of length 3 units has a perimeter of 12 units and an area of 9 square units. A right triangle with legs of length 3 and 4 and a hypotenuse of length 5 also has a perimeter of 12 units, but its area is only 6 square units.

3. 4.5 inches

4. 150° and 210°

5. Possible answer: a sphere is the collection of all of the points in a 3 dimensional space, equidistant from a given point.

6. Possible answer: as you change the length of al sides by a scale factor the surface area changes with the square of the scale factor, and the volume changes with the cube of the scale factor

7. Possible answer:

8. The height is 11 meters

9. Possible answer: if we have a square with a side of length s, then to find the area of the square we multiply s by itself. That is, s^2 gives the area of the square.

10. Possible answer: train tracks.

Unit 10A Test 2

1.

2. Possible answer: if we have a cube with a side of length s, then to find the volume of the cube we multiply $s \times s \times s$. That is, s^3 gives the volume of the cube.

3. Possible answer: a circle is the collection of all of the points in a plane equidistant from a given point

4. Possible answer: no, because if it did not intersect one of the lines, then it would be parallel to that line, and that would make it perpendicular to the second line.

5. Possible answer: a circle is the set of points equidistant from a fixed point in a plane; whereas a sphere is a set of all points in space which are equidistant from a fixed point.

6. 15 inches

7. Possible answer: A globe is a better representation because it is spherical, like the earth.

8. 144 square inches.

9. Possible answer: Yes. A right triangle with legs 6 and 8 inches and hypotenuse 10 inches has an area of 24 square inches, and a perimeter of 24 inches. A rectangle with two sides 8 inches long and two sides 3 inches long has an area of 24 square inches, but a perimeter of 22 inches.

10. 125 inches^3

Unit 10A Test 3

1. (a)
2. (c)
3. (a)
4. (c)
5. (b)
6. (b)
7. (c)
8. (b)
9. (c)
10. (a)

Unit 10A Test 4

1. (a)
2. (b)
3. (a)
4. (b)
5. (b)
6. (b)
7. (a)

Chapter 10 Answers (*continued*)

8. (c)

9. (c)

10. (c)

Unit 10B Test 1

1. 75°07'12"

2. 53.205°

3. about 208.3 miles

4. Possible answer: Lines of longitude are not parallel to each other. You would also have to know their latitude.

5. 3.82°

6. 7 / 20

7. 8 / 15 = 0.53

8. 7.2 miles

9. 7.5

10. 2025 m^2

Unit 10B Test 2

1. 46°14'24"

2. 71.7525°

3. about 277.8 miles

4. No, because the lines of longitude are not parallel to each other. You would have to know what latitude you are at.

5. 3.44°

6. 1 / 5

7. 3 / 4 = 0.75

8. 8.6 miles

9. 6.75

10. 2578.3 m^2

Unit 10B Test 3

1. (d)

2. (b)

3. (d)

4. (d)

5. (a)

6. (b)

7. (c)

8. (c)

9. (b)

10. (b)

Unit 10B Test 4

1. (c)

2. (a)

3. (b)

4. (d)

5. (a)

6. (d)

7. (c)

8. (b)

9. (c)

10. (a)

Unit 10C Test 1

1. Possible answer: Coastline.

2. Possible answer: The countries used two different ruler lengths to measure.

3. Possible answer: Reducing ruler length by a factor increases the number of elements by a square of that factor.

4. Possible answer: An island can be surrounded by an imaginary rectangle, and the area of the rectangle is larger than the area of the island. So this can be an upper limit to the area of the island. But as we use smaller units to measure the island's coastline, we will continue to find a larger coastline.

5. Possible answer: Each factor reduction of a ruler increases the number of elements in a line segment by the same factor.

6. Possible answer: Fractal dimension is a number describing the relationship between the factor by which the number of elements increases as the ruler is shortened by a reduction factor.

Chapter 10 Answers (*continued*)

7. Possible answer:

8. Possible answer: A fractal is self-similar if it looks similar to itself when examined at different scales.

9. Possible answer: Iteration is repeating a rule over and over.

Unit 10C Test 2

1. Possible answer: Many fractal images require repeating a process many times. Often this process would take hundreds of years if done by hand.

2. Possible answer: The object has more than 2-dimensional space, but less than 3-dimensional space.

3. Possible answer: An object that continually reveals new features at smaller scales.

4. Possible answer:

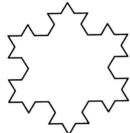

5. Possible answer: The dimension gives us an idea of how similar the object is to standard 1, 2, and 3 dimensional objects.

6. Possible answer: $\log_b N = \log_b R^D$

$$\log_b N = D \log_b R$$

$$D = \frac{\log_b N}{\log_b R}$$

7. Possible answer: Reducing ruler length by a factor increases the number of elements by a cube of that factor.

8. Possible answer: If the boundary is fractal, then the length of the boundary will continue to increase as R is reduced. But the area of the object will still remain within a certain limit.

9. Possible answer: It looks similar to itself when examined at different scales, e.g., snowflake curve.

Unit 10C Test 3

1. (a)

2. (c)

3. (c)

4. (a)

5. (c)

6. (c)

7. (b)

8. (a)

9. (b)

10. (c)

Unit 10C Test 4

1. (b)

2. (c)

3. (a)

4. (a)

5. (a)

6. (c)

7. (a)

8. (c)

9. (b)

10. (a)

Chapter 11 Answers

Unit 11A Test 1

1. Possible answer: Sound is produced by any vibrating object. The vibrations produce a wave that is perceived as sound.

2. Possible answer: The rate at which the string moves up and down.

3. Possible answer: Consonant tones are those whose frequencies have a simple ratio.

4. $2^{1/3} = 1.25992$

5. 1200 cps

6. Possible answer: It means to store the sound as sound waves.

7. Possible answer: guitar, bass, violin

8. Possible answer: Digital signal processing improves the quality of sound by using a computer to modify the sounds of a musical recording.

9. 981 cps

10. Possible answer: the ratios of frequencies in a 12-tone scale are not exactly ratios of whole numbers.

Unit 11A Test 2

1. Possible answer: saxophone, clarinet, oboe

2. 499 cps

3. It is the lowest possible frequency for a particular string.

4. 2000 cps

5. 3 inches, or $\frac{1}{4}$ foot

6. Possible answer: The shorter the wavelength, the higher the frequency.

7. Possible answer: Sound waves are represented by lists of numbers.

8. Possible answer: digital storage of music has fewer undesirable changes due to wear

9. Possible answer: trumpet, flute, organ

10. Possible answer: the frequency is multiplied by eight.

Unit 11A Test 3

1. (b)

2. (a)

3. (a)

4. (b)

5. (c)

6. (a)

7. (c)

8. (c)

9. (b)

10. (b)

Unit 11A Test 4

1. (b)

2. (a)

3. (b)

4. (c)

5. (c)

6. (b)

7. (b)

8. (b)

9. (b)

10. (a)

Unit 11B Test 1

1. Possible answer: a renewed interest in natural scenes, many artists were also engineers and architects

2. Possible answers: Because all lines parallel in the scene and perpendicular to the canvas will intersect at the principal vanishing point.

3. Possible answer: Perspective, symmetry, and proportion.

4. Possible answer:

5. Possible answer: the human body has reflective symmetry w/eyes, ears, arms, etc.

Chapter 11 Answers (*continued*)

6. Possible answer: Aperiodic tiling does not have a pattern that is repeated throughout the tiling.

7. Possible answer:

8. Possible answer: Tiling with other regular polygons leave gaps between the polygons

9. Possible answer:

10. Possible answer: The lines intersect at the vanishing point.

Unit 11B Test 2

1. Possible answer: They wanted to paint natural scenes with realism, and many of them also worked as engineers and architects.

2. Possible answer:

3. Possible answer: The horizon line is the line where all of the vanishing points lie.

4. Possible answer: The parallel lines might not meet at the same point.

5. Possible answer: Copies of the same shape are placed on a surface, so they cover the surface with no gaps or overlaps.

6. Possible answer: Leonardo da Vinci

7. Possible answer: The parallel lines meet at the vanishing point.

8. Possible answer: Periodic tiling is a tiling that has a pattern repeated throughout.

9. Possible answer: To translate an object means to move it in one direction, without rotating it.

10. Possible answer: A property of an object that remains unchanged under certain operations.

Unit 11B Test 3

1. (a)
2. (c)
3. (a)
4. (c)
5. (c)
6. (b)
7. (a)
8. (a)
9. (a)
10. (b)

Unit 11B Test 4

1. (c)
2. (a)
3. (a)
4. (b)
5. (a)
6. (c)
7. (b)
8. (a)
9. (c)
10. (c)

Unit 11C Test 1

1. Possible answer: Divine Proportion

2. Possible answer: Multiply the length of the short side by $\left(\dfrac{1+\sqrt{5}}{2} \right)$

3. Possible answer: Measure the sides and see if they satisfy the golden ratio.

4. Possible answer: No. The only way a rectangle can be a golden rectangle is if its ratio of the sides is the golden ratio.

Chapter 11 Answers (*continued*)

5. Approximately 11.3

6. Possible answer: A 35 mm slide

7. Possible answer: Start with a golden rectangle and divide it to make one side a square. Repeat this process many time then connect opposite corners of all of the squares with a smooth curve.

8. Possible answer: 3, 3, 6, 9, 15, 24, 39, 63, 102, 165. This appears to satisfy the golden ratio. Notice that $165/102 = 1.6176$.

9. Possible answer: Sunflowers

10. Answers may vary

Unit 11C Test 2

1. Possible answer: How can a line segment be divided into two pieces that have the most visual appeal and balance?

2. $x = 3 + \sqrt{17}$ or $3 - \sqrt{7}$

3. 1, 1, 2, 3, 5, 8, 13

4. Possible answer: Yes. The size of the rectangle does not affect the golden ratio. Only the ratio of the sides matters when determining if a rectangle is a golden rectangle.

5. Possible answer: No, because the ratio of the sides does not satisfy the golden ratio.

6. Possible answer:

———————————+———————————

7. Possible answer: At least 10

8. Possible answer: They weren't comfortable with irrational numbers.

9. Possible answer: the Pyramids in Egypt

10. Possible answer: Botany, where pine cones and leaves on a stem exhibit the Fibonacci numbers.

Unit 11C Test 3

1. (b)

2. (a)

3. (b)

4. (c)

5. (b)

6. (b)

7. (a)

8. (a)

9. (c)

10. (a)

Unit 11C Test 4

1. (b)

2. (c)

3. (c)

4. (b)

5. (a)

6. (b)

7. (c)

8. (b)

9. (c)

10. (a)

Chapter 12 Answers

Unit 12A Test 1

1. Smith wins 50.55% of the popular vote and 52.90% of the electoral votes. Smith becomes President.

2. No

3. Yes

4. (a) Abbott; no

   (b) 126

5. 55

6. D; No, because 17 is not greater than $\frac{1}{2} \times 55$.

7. B

8. D

9. A

10. A

Unit 12A Test 2

1. Jones wins with 50.1% of popular vote and Smith wins with 55.4% of the electoral vote.

2. No

3. Yes

4. (a) Tilley; no

   (b) 174

5. 42

6. A; No, because 13 is not greater than $\frac{1}{2} \times 42$.

7. D

8. D

9. C

10. None

Unit 12A Test 3

1. (b)

2. (b)

3. (a)

4. (c)

5. (c)

6. (a)

7. (c)

8. (c)

9. (c)

10. (c)·

Unit 12A Test 4

1. (d)

2. (b)

3. (a)

4. (d)

5. (d)

6. (c)

7. (b)

8. (a)

9. (b)

10. (b)

Unit 12B Test 1

1. If a candidate receives a majority of the first-place votes, that candidate should be the winner; point system (Borda count)

2. Mathematicians and political scientists.

3. It is impossible to create a voting system that always satisfies all four fairness criteria.

4. Possible answer: The minority party cannot be part of a majority unless two other parties vote the same way. But, in that case, the two other parties already determine the outcome by themselves.

Chapter 12 Answers (continued)

5. Possible answer: In the preference schedule below, A wins the election. However, if the two voters in the final column were to change their vote to ACB, A would lose and B would win.

First	A	B	C	C
Second	C	A	B	A
Third	B	C	A	B
	6	5	4	2

6. Voters decide whether they approve of or disapprove of each candidate. The candidate with the most appeal wins.

7. (a) B

   (b) C

8. Majority criterion (fairness criterion 1) does not apply.
   Condorcet criterion (fairness criterion 2) is satisfied.
   Monotonicity criterion (fairness criterion 3) is satisfied.
   Independence of irrelevant alternatives criterion (fairness criterion 4) is not satisfied.

9. Majority criterion (fairness criterion 1) does not apply.
   Condorcet criterion (fairness criterion 2) is satisfied.
   Monotonicity criterion (fairness criterion 3) is satisfied.
   Independence of irrelevant alternatives criterion (fairness criterion 4) is satisfied.

10. Majority criterion (fairness criterion 1) does not apply.
    Condorcet criterion (fairness criterion 2) is satisfied.
    Monotonicity criterion (fairness criterion 3) is satisfied.
    Independence of irrelevant alternatives criterion (fairness criterion 4) is satisfied.

Unit 12B Test 2

1. The four basic fairness criteria.

2. An economist named Kenneth Arrow mathematically proved that it is impossible to find a voting system that always satisfies all four of the fairness criteria.

3. The candidate who has the most approval votes.

4. Possible answer: Since the minority party plus either major party forms a majority, the votes of the minor party will determine the outcome of a vote whenever the major parties disagree.

5. Possible answer: In the preference schedule below, B wins according to the Borda count, but A has the majority of first-place votes.

First	A	B	C
Second	B	C	B
Third	C	A	A
	10	5	4

Chapter 12 Answers (*continued*)

6. Possible answer:

First	A	B	C
Second	B	C	B
Third	C	A	A
	5	4	3

7. (a) C

(b) B

8. Majority criterion (fairness criterion 1) does not apply.
Condorcet criterion (fairness criterion 2) is not satisfied.
Monotonicity criterion (fairness criterion 3) is satisfied.
Independence of irrelevant alternatives criterion (fairness criterion 4) is not satisfied.

9. Majority criterion (fairness criterion 1) does not apply.
Condorcet criterion (fairness criterion 2) is satisfied.
Monotonicity criterion (fairness criterion 3) is satisfied.
Independence of irrelevant alternatives criterion (fairness criterion 4) is satisfied.

10. Majority criterion (fairness criterion 1) does not apply.
Condorcet criterion (fairness criterion 2) is satisfied.
Monotonicity criterion (fairness criterion 3) is satisfied.
Independence of irrelevant alternatives criterion (fairness criterion 4) is satisfied.

Unit 12B Test 3

1. (d)

2. (c)

3. (b)

4. (a)

5. (a)

6. (d)

7. (d)

8. (b)

9. (d)

10. (d)

Unit 12B Test 4

1. (b)

2. (d)

3. (c)

4. (c)

5. (c)

6. (c)

7. (d)

8. (d)

9. (d)

10. (d)

Unit 12C Test 1

1. Senate and House of Representatives

2. Process used to divide the available seats in the House of Representatives among the 50 states.

3. The fractional remainder is the fraction that remains in the standard quota after subtracting the minimum quota.

4. A slow-growing state gained a seat at the expense of a faster-growing state.

5. In a fair apportionment, the number of seats assigned to each state should be its standard quota rounded either up or down to the nearest integer.

Chapter 12 Answers (*continued*)

6. The Balinsky and Young theorem tells us that we cannot choose between apportionment procedures on the basis of fairness alone.

7. The standard divisor is 775.

State	A	B	C	D	Total
Population	8403	13,777	14,579	25,241	62,000
Standard quota	10.84	17.78	18.81	32.57	80
Minimum quota	10	17	18	32	77
Fractional remainder	0.84	0.78	0.81	0.57	3
Final apportionment	11	18	19	32	80

A receives 11 seats, B 18 seats, C 19 seats, and D 32 seats.

8.

State	A	B	C	D	Total
Population	8403	13,777	14,579	25,241	62,000
Standard quota	10.84	17.78	18.81	32.57	80
Minimum quota	10	17	18	32	77
Modified quota (with divisor 764.5)	10.99	18.02	19.07	33.02	81.10
Minimum quota (with divisor 764.5)	10	18	19	33	80

A receives 10 seats, B 18 seats, C 19 seats, and D 33 seats.

9.

State	A	B	C	D	Total
Population	8403	13,777	14,579	25,241	62,000
Standard quota	10.84	17.78	18.81	32.57	80
Minimum quota	10	17	18	32	77
Modified quota (with divisor 777)	10.81	17.73	18.76	32.49	79.79
Rounded quota	11	18	19	32	80

A receives 11 seats, B 18 seats, C 19 seats, and D 32 seats.

10.

State	A	B	C	D	Total
Population	8403	13,777	14,579	25,241	62,000
Standard quota	10.84	17.78	18.81	32.57	80
Minimum quota	10	17	18	32	77
Modified quota (with divisor 780)	10.77	17.66	18.69	32.36	79.48
Geometric mean	10.488	17.493	18.493	32.496	
Rounded quota	11	18	19	32	80

A receives 11 seats, B 18 seats, C 19 seats, and D 32 seats.

Chapter 12 Answers *(continued)*

Unit 12C Test 2

1. It is the process used to divide the available seats in the House of Representatives among the 50 states.

2. The standard divisor is the average number of people per seat in the House of Representatives for the entire U.S. population.

3. This occurs when the total number of available seats in the House of Representatives increases, yet one or more states lose a seat as a result.

4. The addition of seats for a new state changed the apportionment for existing states.

5. Adopting the Hill-Huntington method was a purely political move on the part of the Democratic majority in Congress because it gave the Democrats one more seat in the House at the time.

6. For 15 teachers:

School	Greenbreier	Wilcox	Glen Cove	Timor	Total
Kindergarten enrollment	204	143	82	51	480
Standard quota	6.38	4.47	2.56	1.59	15
Minimum quota	6	4	2	1	13
Fractional remainder	0.38	0.47	0.56	0.59	2
Final apportionment	6	4	3	2	15

For 16 teachers:

School	Greenbreier	Wilcox	Glen Cove	Timor	Total
Kindergarten enrollment	204	143	82	51	480
Standard quota	6.80	4.77	2.73	1.70	16
Minimum quota	6	4	2	1	13
Fractional remainder	0.80	0.77	0.73	0.70	3
Final apportionment	7	5	3	1	16

If I were the administrator at Timor, I would not want the teacher to be hired since I would lose a teacher. This is known as the Alabama paradox, which can occur when Hamilton's method is used.

7. The standard divisor is 1240.

State	A	B	C	D	Total
Population	8399	12,537	15,819	25,245	62,000
Standard quota	6.77	10.11	12.76	20.36	50
Minimum quota	6	10	12	20	48
Fractional remainder	0.77	0.11	0.76	0.36	2
Final apportionment	7	10	13	20	50

A receives 7 seats, B 10 seats, C 13 seats, and D 20 seats.

Chapter 12 Answers *(continued)*

8.

State	A	B	C	D	Total
Population	8399	12,537	15,819	25,245	62,000
Standard quota	6.77	10.11	12.76	20.36	50
Minimum quota	6	10	12	20	48
Modified quota (with divisor 1202)	6.99	10.43	13.16	21.00	51.58
Minimum quota (with divisor 1202)	6	10	13	21	50

A receives 6 seats, B 10 seats, C 13 seats, and D 21 seats.

9.

State	A	B	C	D	Total
Population	8399	12,537	15,819	25,245	62,000
Standard quota	6.77	10.11	12.76	20.36	50
Minimum quota	6	10	12	20	48
Modified quota (with divisor 1242)	6.76	10.09	12.74	20.33	49.92
Rounded quota	7	10	13	20	50

A receives 7 seats, B 10 seats, C 13 seats, and D 20 seats.

10.

State	A	B	C	D	Total
Population	8399	12,537	15,819	25,245	62,000
Standard quota	6.77	10.11	12.76	20.36	50
Minimum quota	6	10	12	20	48
Modified quota (with divisor 1238)	6.78	10.13	12.78	20.39	50.08
Geometric mean	6.481	10.488	12.490	20.494	
Rounded quota	7	10	13	20	50

A receives 7 seats, B 10 seats, C 13 seats, and D 20 seats.

Unit 12C Test 3

1. (d)
2. (a)
3. (d)
4. (d)
5. (d)
6. (c)
7. (b)
8. (c)
9. (d)
10. (b)

Unit 12C Test 4

1. (c)
2. (d)
3. (a)
4. (d)

Chapter 11 Answers *(continued)*

5. (a)
6. (c)
7. (c)
8. (b)
9. (c)
10. (c)

Chapter 13 Answers

Unit 13A Test 1

1. It is a collection of points or objects that are interconnected in some way.

2. A land mass (island, north shore, or south shore)

3.

4. Order is 6; degree of Ono is 4.

5. Possible answer:

6. Possible answer:

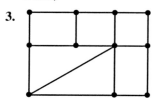

7. Possible answer:

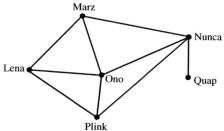

8. No, because vertices A and E as well as B and F each have odd degree.

9.

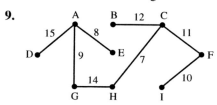

10. Order is 6; degree of A, B, C, and F is 3; degree of D is 4; degree of E is 2; not complete; every team does not play every other team.

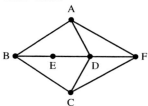

Unit 13A Test 2

1. Every vertex is connected to each other vertex.

2. A bridge

3.

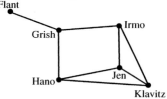

4. Order is 6; degree of Grish is 3.

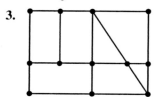

5. Possible answer:

6. Possible answer:

7. Possible answer:

8. Yes, because each vertex has even degree.

464

Chapter 13 Answers (*continued*)

9.

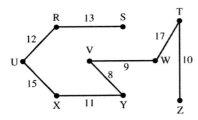

10. Order is 6; degree of A, B, C, and F is 3; degree of D and E is 2; not complete; every team does not play every other team.

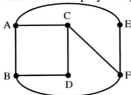

Unit 13A Test 3

1. (c)
2. (c)
3. (b)
4. (c)
5. (d)
6. (d)
7. (a)
8. (d)
9. (a)
10. (b)

Unit 13A Test 4

1. (a)
2. (d)
3. (c)
4. (b)
5. (b)
6. (a)
7. (c)
8. (c)
9. (b)
10. (a)

Unit 13B Test 1

1. 239,500,800
2. 21 days
3. Not a Hamiltonian circuit; one Hamiltonian circuit is ABCDEA.
4. The path shown is a Hamiltonian circuit.
5. Not a Hamiltonian circuit; one Hamiltonian circuit is NKLMOQRSPN.
6. Home to school to post office to library to home, or home to library to post office to school to home
7. Durney to Emago to Flipsy to Hallo to Grund to Durney
8. K to L to J to I to N to M to K
9. L to J to I to N to M to K to L
10. I to L to J to K to M to N to I

Unit 13B Test 2

1. 20,160
2. 36,036 days
3. The path shown is a Hamiltonian circuit.
4. Not a Hamiltonian circuit; one Hamiltonian circuit is FGHIJKF.
5. Not a Hamiltonian circuit; one Hamiltonian circuit is LQMNPOL.
6. Home to school to post office to library to home, or home to library to post office to school to home
7. Drury to Funky to Gridly to Clinger to Elbow to Drury
8. P to T to S to R to Q to U to P
9. R to S to T to P to Q to U to R
10. T to P to Q to R to S to U to T

Unit 13B Test 3

1. (a)
2. (d)
3. (d)
4. (b)
5. (c)
6. (b)

Chapter 13 Answers *(continued)*

7. (b)

8. (a)

9. (b)

10. (c)

Unit 13B Test 4

1. (d)

2. (d)

3. (b)

4. (c)

5. (d)

6. (c)

7. (c)

8. (b)

9. (d)

10. (a)

Unit 13C Test 1

1. Earliest start time, Earliest finish time

2. It is the path that includes all the limiting tasks through a network.

3. a: *prepare dough*, b: *let dough rise*, d: *prepare buns*, e: *let buns rise*

4. 153 minutes

5. 72 minutes

6. 60 minutes

7. 0, 17, 0, 0, 54, 54, 54, 0

8. a: *view available homes*, c: *sign contract*, d: *arrange financing*, h: *sign papers*

9. 88 days

10.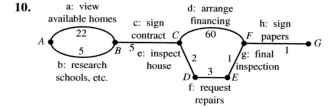

Unit 13C Test 2

1. It is the task that requires the most time when two (or more) tasks can occur at the same time between two stages of the project.

2. Project evaluation and review technique

3. e: *let buns rise*, g: *bake*

4. 164 minutes

5. 90 minutes

6. 80 minutes

7. 0, 11, 0, 0, 36, 36, 36, 0

8. a: *view available homes*, c: *sign contract*, d: *arrange financing*, h: *sign papers*

9. 68 days

Chapter 12 Answers *(continued)*

10.

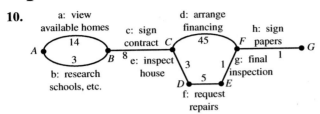

Unit 13C Test 3

1. (d)
2. (b)
3. (b)
4. (c)
5. (c)
6. (d)
7. (a)
8. (d)
9. (c)
10. (a)

Unit 13C Test 4

1. (b)
2. (d)
3. (c)
4. (b)
5. (d)
6. (a)
7. (c)
8. (a)
9. (d)
10. (c)